Strategy in Politics

Strategy in Politics

Plotting Victory in a Democracy

F. CHRISTOPHER ARTERTON

OXFORD
UNIVERSITY PRESS

Oxford University Press is a department of the University of Oxford. It furthers the University's objective of excellence in research, scholarship, and education by publishing worldwide. Oxford is a registered trade mark of Oxford University Press in the UK and certain other countries.

Published in the United States of America by Oxford University Press
198 Madison Avenue, New York, NY 10016, United States of America.

© Oxford University Press 2023

All rights reserved. No part of this publication may be reproduced, stored in a retrieval system, or transmitted, in any form or by any means, without the prior permission in writing of Oxford University Press, or as expressly permitted by law, by license, or under terms agreed with the appropriate reproduction rights organization. Inquiries concerning reproduction outside the scope of the above should be sent to the Rights Department, Oxford University Press, at the address above.

You must not circulate this work in any other form
and you must impose this same condition on any acquirer.

Library of Congress Cataloging-in-Publication Data
Names: Arterton, F. Christopher, author.
Title: Strategy in politics : plotting victory in a democracy / F. Christopher Arterton.
Description: New York : Oxford University Press, [2023] |
Includes bibliographical references and index.
Identifiers: LCCN 2022036110 (print) | LCCN 2022036111 (ebook) |
ISBN 9780197644836 (hardback) | ISBN 9780197644843 (paperback) |
ISBN 9780197644874 (ebook) | ISBN 9780197644867 (epub)
Subjects: LCSH: Political planning. | Power (Social sciences) | Strategic planning.
Classification: LCC JF1525 .P6 A78 2023 (print) | LCC JF1525 .P6 (ebook) |
DDC 320.6—dc23/eng/20220923
LC record available at https://lccn.loc.gov/2022036110
LC ebook record available at https://lccn.loc.gov/2022036111

DOI: 10.1093/oso/9780197644836.001.0001

1 3 5 7 9 8 6 4 2
Paperback printed by Integrated Books International, United States of America
Hardback printed by Bridgeport National Bindery, Inc., United States of America

For Janet

Contents

Preface: To Create the Future: Strategic Thinking in Politics   ix
Acknowledgments   xv

PART I: INTRODUCTION TO STRATEGY

1. Politics: The Quest for Power   3
2. A First Look at Strategic Thinking   28

PART II: ARENAS OF STRATEGY

3. War and Democratic Conflict   41
4. Strategic Planning   61
5. Strategic Political Communications   91
6. Managing Strategic Interaction   117
7. Guidelines to Effective Strategy   145

PART III: PLACING STRATEGY IN PERSPECTIVE

8. Strategy and Negotiations in Politics   173
9. Political Leadership   197

Notes   219
Index   239

Preface
To Create the Future: Strategic Thinking in Politics

"Strategy" is an overused word. When such terms are used in a vast variety of contexts to cover a broad range of behaviors, they acquire vagueness. Overused words take on a universality that defies the precision needed to guide effective action. Thus, "strategy" has diminished as a useful concept that can steer those engaged in political combat toward effective action.

Over the past three decades, I have been engaged with the students at George Washington University's Graduate School of Political Management in a collective effort to retrieve the concept of strategy from its overemployment and supply it with sufficient precision to be useful for those who seek to create the future through politics. While the reader may conclude that this will be primarily an exercise in definitional argumentation, this author is not, in fact, interested in squabbles over definitions. Instead, this volume will bring together a variety of vantage points through which one can understand the process of strategy making in politics. These perspectives add up to a complex notion that should shepherd political managers toward effective strategic thinking. I see strategy as a way of approaching the world, of dealing with opposition, of creating the future through democratic politics. Understanding the process by which strategy is formulated will allow political managers to plot more victories for their side, for their vision, for their ideals, and for themselves.

We need to start by identifying several parameters of this conversation. First, I have chosen to write a guide that will be useful to practitioners. Having spent all of my professional life as an academic, this is something of a change and a challenge. But I have long believed that political science should be relevant to the work of those attempting to bring about a desired future. I firmly believe, moreover, that institutions of higher education have an obligation, through their research and teaching, to define the boundaries of appropriate conduct in democratic politics. Too often academics regard the push and pull of practical politics as demeaning and dirty. From this viewpoint, the concept of strategy comes off as the core of a manipulative approach to the making of public policy. My motivation for writing this volume comes from the fact that despite a lot of analysis by journalists of the latest campaign strategy, the term is poorly understood and even more poorly practiced. I hope the busy practitioner will find the chapters that follow to be concise enough to fit into his or her hassled, professional life.

A second signpost for the reader is that inevitably strategy is situational, meaning that how one behaves strategically ought to be heavily influenced by the situation in which one finds oneself. This realization implies that providing general guidance without reference to concrete circumstances will only carry us so far. So, while I aspire to give usable advice to the practitioner, the reader should not assume that he or she will discover here how to act in a given fight. My hope instead is to provide a general orientation toward thinking strategically that will allow practitioners to improve their performance across the board in whatever competitive situation they find themselves.

A third overarching bit of guidance as to what follows: the reader can expect to find highly useful advice on how to work successfully in democratic systems and a set of guidelines for thinking and acting strategically. But these directions fall short of an inventory of rules or laws to follow. There are two important reasons for this absence. First, because strategy is situational, strategic thinking must be anchored in the immediate environment one confronts. In political life, one needs to respond to real circumstances in a real fight with a real opponent. How one plots and acts will inevitably be determined by that situation. Second, the strategist must recognize—along with Karl von Clausewitz, the great Prussian military theoretician from the Napoleonic era—that, to the extent one follows a rulebook, one's opponent may read that book and use that knowledge to predict and counter one's action. Even if the opponent has no access to the same rulebook, the point still stands that to the extent that one's actions become predictable, one becomes vulnerable to the countermoves of the opposition.

The readers should keep in mind yet another caveat. For many citizens of contemporary democracies, "politics" is a dirty word. Not so for the author. In fact, politics is the only way to resolve social disputes peacefully. Every polity is a snake pit of competing interests; democratic politics provide the way to achieve agreements on policy. Remember, however, that politics trump policy. You may have the very best vision for the future, but you will need to be engaged in politics to make that vision a reality.

Finally, in discussing strategy in politics, I will frequently resort to drawing examples from competition in an electoral context. But I mean political strategy to refer to broader usage. There is a vast realm of human behavior to which the term "political" justly applies. We cannot confine the meaning to electioneering as do many news organizations when they give the job title "political reporter" to the person who covers election politics. Instead, in the broader sense used here, "political" should apply to advocacy, issues management, public relations, legislating, fundraising, public communications, policymaking, and community organizing as well as campaign management. All of these collective human endeavors are amenable to strategy.

Nevertheless, examples in terms of election campaigning are quite useful to our purposes here as providing a model for our understandings of the essence of strategy. Campaigns take place in an intense environment of direct, overt opposition most often marked by "zero-sum" competition. They are most often fought over a finite period with a definite endpoint. They are intense, all consuming, and demanding, requiring a fluidity of action that often is not true of engagements in, for example, advocacy politics where the fight may be more or less continuous. In developing and implementing strategy, campaigns more closely resemble war and sports than they do the world of commercial business. By contrast, issue advocacy and nonprofit management, even though applied to the "political" arena, may resemble more closely strategy development in a business setting. But election politics offers a compressed version of strategic maneuvering, from which we can abstract understandings that generalize to other forms of politics.

Throughout this study, I will use the term "political manager" to describe those who pursue a career in public life. They may be candidates or public officeholders—which I will often designate as "politicians"—or they may hold jobs and appointed positions that are deeply engaged in the world of politics. Political managers handle the politics of their employers, be that a candidate, officeholder, corporation, association, interest group, university, etc. They work for politicians and organizations engaged in policymaking, providing services such as strategic advice, public relations, digital communications, fundraising expertise, and an abundance of similar areas of technical knowledge. Professionally, as dictated by the fortunes of politics and personal careers, they move in and out of the formal institutions of government and politics: political parties, political action groups, campaign organizations, legislative staff, executive branch agencies.

Whatever their career choices, political managers are united by a common language; a set of shared skills; a strategic mindset; and, hopefully, an appreciation of their professional responsibilities to the institutions of democracy. Their community is more than a craft in that it emphasizes change, innovation, and entrepreneurialism, but less than a profession in that it lacks a hard boundary of licensure or certification. While they are sharply, viciously divided by vision and purpose, they share the twin common traits of commitment to political activity to mold the future and the understanding that power and strategy are critical requirements to that process. The best among them are, thus, simultaneously visionaries and manipulators, and they balance themselves precariously between these values.

We conclude this Preface with explicit attention to this question: Why do we need better strategy formulation in politics? The most obvious answer is because politics is important. Those at work in the field are seeking to mold our world so as to achieve a set of values they hold dear. While those values can certainly be for private gain, the best political managers are laboring to nudge the future toward a vision that will benefit all, even those who oppose them.

To be sure, political management and strategy can allow evil people to succeed. It is an unhappy fact of life that the approach to strategic thinking taught here can be used to achieve wicked goals. This leads us into an enduring debate as to whether the ends justify the means or, more narrowly, whether some ends justify some means. Ultimately, we have to rely upon the good judgment of political managers, just as Machiavelli wished his prince to be virtuous. Democratic institutions provide some protections, steering political managers toward the common good. But democracy cannot guarantee good behavior, for it is not just the political leaders that we have to worry about. Human history provides numerous examples—the Inquisition, the Holocaust, the genocides in Bosnia and Rwanda—in which large numbers of citizens joined willingly in evil deeds. Citizens can be stampeded into malevolence; democratic norms can be brushed aside. In arming readers with strategy, I plead for principled and laudable behavior, especially avoiding actions that weaken democratic institutions in the pursuit of short-term political goals.

Strategy lies at the core of political management. Strategic ability should make political managers more effective in pursuing their dreams. This is not the place to rehearse all of the justifications for democracy. Nevertheless, still democratic politics hold out the promise of—and draw strength from—the peaceful resolution of conflicting values. Those who struggle to fulfill their goals through the institutions of democratic politics should employ strategy to achieve their visions. If political managers are adroit in their strategic thinking, they may enter this battlefield better prepared for the conflict of ideas. They may be better able to understand the dilemmas inherent in democratic politics, between power and purpose, between strategy and leadership, between empowerment and manipulation. To these ends, this writing is dedicated.

Acknowledgments

Numerous colleagues, friends and loved ones have contributed to this volume through conversations and critiques. I count as principal among these the generations of students whom I had the privilege of teaching at the Graduate School of Political Management (GSPM) at George Washington University. Over 30 years, the ideas in this volume gradually took shape through robust discussion, sometimes expressed in heated disagreement and often in enlightenment. Teaching is ever a learning process, hopefully for the students, but in this case, emphatically for the professor. I thank them all heartily.

This book is dedicated to Janet Bond Arterton. Without her strong, and at times aggressive, encouragement, this book would not have reached completion. I wish also to acknowledge and thank my GSPM colleagues, especially Dean Ali Eskandarian; Mark Kennedy; and Lara Brown, my successors at the helm of GSPM. I am indebted to my faculty colleagues at the GSPM including Dennis Johnson, Michael Cornfield, Carol Darr, Steven Billet, Doug Bailey, Luis Raul Matos, and Roberto Izurieta. Among these, William Greener deserves special mention. Bill and I taught a GSPM graduate seminar on media relations for over 15 years. We developed a professional relationship and friendship which nurtured many of the ideas in this volume. Through informal conversations and classroom presentations, my GSPM faculty colleagues contributed many insights as to how democratic politics takes place. Also, my colleagues and graduate students at GSPM's sister school—FOCOM, the Faculty of Communication at the University of Navarra—markedly enriched my thinking through their observations and probing questions. I owe a special debt of gratitude to John "Jack" Pitney who read the entire manuscript and offered innumerable helpful critiques and suggestions.

The original idea for a school of applied politics—instead of public policy—came from Neil Fabricant, a lobbyist for the Civil Liberties

Union in New York. Without him, there would be no school and thus no book like this.

At Oxford University Press, Angela Chnapko guided me through the editorial process with grace and wisdom. Angela put together a great team, including Alexcee Bechthold at OUP and Kavitha Yuvaraj of Newgen Knowledge Works in Chennai, India, who, in turn, brought in Karen Jameson of Sugar Land TX. Alexandra Dauler in New York and Lauren Starling in Washington provided expert editorial assistance. Truly an international network of professional competence and know-how.

PART I
INTRODUCTION TO STRATEGY

1
Politics
The Quest for Power

If you want to succeed in politics, understand that politics is about power. In turn, through politics we collectively shape the future. Those who would guide our posterity must understand that the essence of politics is power. Put another way, influencing the thinking and actions of others constitutes the core of political engagement. This book is intended to assist activists and politicians, amateurs and political professionals, in their efforts to orchestrate our future. But some readers may not be entirely comfortable with the assertion that politics is power employed. Power per se implies forcing one's will upon another. Yet, if politics is the means through which we can shape our collective future, how can we come to terms with the necessity of power? Even discussing the fact that in our quest to shape our tomorrows, the idea of asserting power may be troublesome to some readers. They recognize that the exercise of power may not be pleasant for those being influenced or, for that matter, the individual who is trying to force his or her will upon another. They may derive some reassurance, however, from the fact that in a democracy, power normally derives more from voluntary support than from coercion. We stand with Winston Churchill who famously opined, "Democracy is the worst form of government, except for all the rest."[1] Participation in democratic politics provides the best vehicle available for collectively achieving the ideal society through nonviolent means. Political managers[2] who would operate within a democratic system must become comfortable with the fact that nurturing, managing, and applying political power is, simply put, essential.

Even so, we cannot escape the coercive nature of political influence. Much of political life can be antidemocratic. Our purpose here is to describe the habits of mind necessary for one to be effective within democratic politics short of using unconscionable force. Yet for those who seek to advance their vision of an ideal society through politics, the stark reality begins with the recognition that politics is power exercised. There are, to be sure, softer and harder forms of influence. Even the adroit, but often maligned, Niccolo Machiavelli preferred achieving agreements when possible to the aggressive use of cruel force. And, though Machiavelli has a lot to teach us about power, we have learned a great deal more about managing politics through democratic institutions in the 500 years since he wrote *The Prince* and his *Discourses*. Fortunately, Machiavelli has not had the last word.

Ambitious political managers need to understand that even though their goals may be the most benign, even with the highest hopes for nothing more than to improve the standing of all around, even with a vision of an enlightened future of boundless progress, they cannot be squeamish about the necessity of power. Whatever the purpose, vision, or objective you bring to political life, however noble your aspirations might be, you should realize that there will be those who will disagree, propose alternatives, attempt to delay, work to undermine, complain and criticize, and endeavor to persuade others to the contrary. You will need to be persistent in pursuit of power, not for its own sake, but because power provides the energy to secure desired policies. Countering those who are foolish enough not to see the wholehearted merits in what you are trying to accomplish will require a grasp of strategic insight in the application of power.

The anthropologist Margaret Mead has been quoted many times as follows: "Never doubt that a small group of thoughtful committed individuals can change the world. In fact, it's the only thing that ever has." Here's a prime example of what Mead meant. On December 22, 1971, President Richard Nixon signed into law the National Cancer Act, which created the National Cancer Institute and with it a greatly enhanced commitment to cancer research. On its face, the policy ideas promoted in the act might not seem to be terribly controversial. But the details of the case well illustrate that it can take a great deal of pushing and hauling to energize the policymaking machinery, even though the cause may command wide approval. Nixon and the US Congress only acted to address this growing killer disease after decades of pressure lead by a privately funded interest group, the American Society for Control of Cancer (later named the American Cancer Society). The story is one of leadership by two committed activists, Dr. Sidney Farber of Boston Children's Hospital and Mary Woodward Lasker of the Citizens Committee for the Conquest of Cancer. Lasker decided to give the drive for the federal funding the appearance of a national crusade. She adopted or invented all the techniques of modern grass-roots lobbying. As a matter of adroit strategy, she decided to position the issue as directed against the "dreaded disease" of cancer among children. She bought TV ads in the Washington area; she took out full page ads in the *New York Times* and the *Washington Post*; she organized Washington visits so the members of Congress could be personally lobbied by affected families; and she arranged for high-profile witnesses to testify at congressional hearings. Through these efforts, she became a very influential force advancing medical research. An outspoken Democrat, she eventually brought a Republican president to her vision. Eventually, Lasker won her battle, creating the "war on cancer" and a better future for all of us.

These are the purposes of this volume: (1) to understand the nature of democratic politics and the need to husband and utilize power, (2) to comprehend the concept of strategy as it applies to democratic politics, and (3) to appreciate the reasons that political leadership requires the use of strategy *and* power. Power and strategy are inextricably intertwined: strategy is the means of employing power to your benefit. We will mostly present arguments and understandings at the level of social politics where groups, organizations, institutions, and individual leaders compete to determine collective public policies. For example, we need to learn how a small group of committed activists can exercise power within governing institutions. Through their actions such as lobbying, letter writing, attending town hall meetings, demonstrating and protesting, contributing money, staging events to attract favorable news coverage, proselytizing among the uncommitted, and filing court actions, interest groups composed of ardent citizens can exercise power far above their numbers in a democratic system.[3]

There are, however, two additional political arenas in which power and strategy come into play: individual one-on-one conflict and international affairs. Many lessons learned in social politics also have direct application in interpersonal encounters. Calculations of strategy on an individual basis may also influence the actions of subordinates, peers, and even superiors. We shall also have occasion to consider another level of conflict, namely disputes between nations. We need to keep international conflict within our ken precisely because so much useful theorizing has been undertaken at that level.[4] Nevertheless, our primary focus on domestic, democratic politics lies in interaction that falls between the personal and the international spheres. We propose to address how political managers achieve influence within the organizations and institutions of democratic politics.

The three levels—individual, social, and international—are often interrelated. Strategic insights from one arena may inspire understandings germane to our primary focus, social, democratic, domestic politics. Consider, for the moment, that in large measure, Machiavelli's capacity to bring together understandings from these three levels allowed *The Prince* to remain so enduring. His primary purpose was to assist Lorenzo de' Medici to maintain Florence's dominance within the seething conflict among Italian city states. But Machiavelli argued that the prince had to be simultaneously a strong individual seeking to impose his will on others, a political player of the first order in the internal politics of Florence, and the embodiment of the interests and power of the Florentine city state. Strength on each level magnified the prince's power in the other spheres. Similarly, while our interest here lies in exercising power within democratic politics, we will profit from remaining open to lessons imported from international and interpersonal conflict.

The Ways of Power

What then is power? How is it obtained? How is it exercised?

As a first step, it should be fairly obvious that exercising power will be markedly shaped by the strategic environment within which one is operating. Influencing legislative politics requires a different approach than, say, trying to win an election. Engagements at this level include both policy conflicts among a narrow segment of activists and political officials as well as clashes within the public sphere involving mobilization of mass constituencies composed of supporters, hostiles, and the indifferent. Accordingly, we shall discover several instances in which concepts can be usefully translated from one level to others.

Starting from ground zero, as in relations between two individuals, power is the capacity of one actor to intentionally and successfully influence the behavior of another actor even if the latter resists the resulting behavior. On an individual level, this relationship is tantamount to one person making another do something he or she would not do otherwise and even wholeheartedly wish not to do. On the level of nation-states, power is the demonstrated ability of one country to shape the behavior of others and of international entities. This may be achieved through force of arms, infiltration, economic pressure, subterfuge, subversion, public diplomacy, persuasion, negotiated agreements, or leadership.[5] Regardless of the means, whether as soft power or hard, the result is that one nation-state is able to affect the actions of another collective entity, be that another country or an international organization such as a nongovernmental organization (NGO) or even the United Nations. As we shall see, moreover, when national survival is imperiled as during a state of war, moral dictates on the use of power tend to be loosened. In contrast, in interactions between individuals or within democratic institutions, we hope that scruples of appropriate conduct will limit the use of aggressive force.

For the sake of clarity, let us first turn attention to the interaction between two individuals, and then we can scale up our analysis to observe differences in collective action. According to political scientist Frederick W. Frey,[6] an analysis of power requires us to identify five essential elements: at least two separate individuals—an "influencer" and an "influencee"—an intentional action by the former and the resulting behavior of the latter, and, finally, a setting in which their interaction takes place. An adaptation of Frey's model appears in Figure 1.1.

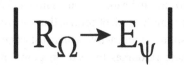

Figure 1.1 The Five Elements of a Power Relationship

In this model, "R" represents the influencer and "E" is the person being influenced. The influential behavior initiated by R is represented by the Greek letter omega [Ω], while E's response is symbolized by the Greek psi [ψ]. The two vertical lines establish the setting or boundaries within which this influential relationship occurs.

To assert that power has been exercised, one must clearly specify each of the five components. The benefit of Frey's model is that it serves to make concrete a rather nebulous concept. We know that some individuals have power over others, but all too often, we cannot pin down that relationship. That difficulty arises from the fact that the very bases upon which power rests are numerous and range from the very tangible down to rather impressionistic. Authority, as we shall argue below, constitutes one of the more tangible sources of power. As specified laws and the Constitution, a public official such as a governor can issue constraints on individual and corporate activity during a declared public health emergency. We can identify each of Frey's components in this interaction. The decision may not be popular and is likely to be opposed by some critics on the grounds that the governor does not have that power. But still, most of the affected individuals will comply with the order until it is effectively challenged in the courts or by electoral defeat. An adroit politician is likely to engage in informal negotiations with other elected officials and organized groups of angry citizens. Such pushback does not fundamentally change our observation of a power relationship.

The initiating action in exercising influence can provide some benefit or instigate some sanction for the influenced party. Whether reward or punishment, the influential action could be based upon a considerable variety of resources that can be brought to bear upon their relationship. Knowledge, information, money and material possessions, and social prestige fall into the category of resources that one party can bring to bear to influence the other. Denial of these positive values, moreover, can be used as punishment in the event that the influencee fails to comply. And, of course, there are many other means of inflicting punishment more actively than just a denial of benefits.

In bringing these resources to bear on power relationships, the acting individual may promise a benefit that will be delivered later as a consequence of compliance. Conversely, a threat of future punishment may be proposed as the certain result of defiance. Thus, a carrot and stick are two ingredients of power, but to be effective, they must be accompanied by a perceived willingness to use them.

Establishing Credibility

The willingness to use power to influence the behavior of others begs us to consider some of the subtle nuances in human interactions. In order for a threat or promise to be successful in inducing the desired behavior, it must be credible. The person being influenced must believe that the acting party has the capacity to actually deliver the sanction or reward and that there is at least some probability that he or she has the will to carry out the promised threat or benefit. But establishing credibility may not be as easy as would first appear, for once the desired behavior has been produced (or not), the power wielder may have little incentive in the short run to actually carry through as promised. Providing a reward entails some cost for the deliverer as does following through on a threatened punishment. In addition, he or she must consider that having to deliver on an ineffective threat may, in fact, either create grievances in the influencee or may itself signal a weakness that could encourage future instances of defiance. Those who seek to exercise power may find themselves facing a trade-off between what is in their best interests in the short run—that is, in the immediate situation—versus their long run need to make their promises in the future credible.

A successful strategist will employ several ways of establishing the credibility of threats or promises. The more common means is to establish a reputation for always delivering upon one's word. Political managers in democratic politics place a high value upon those whose past reveals a pattern of following through on their words. Within the community of political managers, phrases abound like the following two examples: "He's a man of his word," and "Her word is her bond."

There is, of course, ample reason why reputation should be significant in the personal interactions so necessary in politics. Collective action demands predictability. Individuals proceed with the calculated knowledge of how those with whom they must interact—either as allies or opponents—will behave. Those who have established a reputation for following through as they have promised engender trust in their future assurances. Where imposing sanctions may be unpleasant for both parties—undoubtedly more so for the punished party—the willingness to inflict harm or pain defined broadly is also essential to reputation. The effective political manager should remember that when building a reputation of reliability in delivering rewards or sanctions, the target lies in the perceptions of those one would influence. Perceptions can alone be strong motivators of behavior, but there will certainly be times in which it becomes essential to actually deliver on a promise or threat or lose the power of reputation.

Another vehicle for making credible a threat or promise can be called "burning the bridges behind you." This strategy relies on destroying the alternatives to delivering on promises made. In politics this often means issuing a bold, flat, public statement of future actions that makes retreat impossible or so costly to reputation as to be inconceivable. American presidents have frequently resorted to blanket messages threatening to veto legislation that is working its way through Congress. Sometimes, these statements are enough to induce Congress to modify the legislation to the president's liking; sometimes Congress goes right ahead and passes a law in the face of a veto threat, thereby confronting the administration with a decision as to whether to follow through a veto. A president who, for the convenience of immediate considerations, decides not to honor his threats in so doing risks being challenged more readily in the future. Since both sides know this to be true, a public threat carries the implication that the president has burned his bridges, giving himself no options other than exercising the veto.

Of course, we should acknowledge that since we are discussing here acts in the political realm, sometimes this dance between the president and Congress is just for theater. Both sides are playing to the public audience, rather than really interacting with and trying to influence each other. Nonetheless, the lessons should be clear on the individual level: we can create credibility for a promise of future reward or punishment by figuring out how to give ourselves no other options. Another lesson emerges from this understanding as well: presidents and would-be power wielders should not make threats or promises that they would be adverse to carrying out if the other party does not behave as desired. Nothing destroys a reputation faster than failing to deliver as promised. And, since a reputation for power is a central component of actually being able to exercise influence, weakening your own reputation strikes severely at your power. Further, the more public is the breech of a promise, the more costly will be its consequences in diminished influence.

Finally, calculations about the adroit exercise of power should include the trade-offs that occur between what may be in our best interests in the long run rather than in the immediate circumstances. Creating or maintaining a reputation of integrity behind our words may hold much more value in future power relationships than the disagreeable costs incurred at present.

A third means of establishing the credibility of our words depends upon the notion of stakeholder. Gamblers who do not trust each other may resort to depositing their wager with a neutral third person who is pledged to award the prize to the winner. In effect, the two need a third party to establish their bona fides. In many cases that neutral third party is a judge, as contract law acts more or less as a guarantor that both parties will honor their commitments.

In addition to the struggle for power among individuals and between the institutions of governance within a polity, all of these lessons apply as well to the interaction between nation-states. The government of one country ought to be cautious about the kind of threats it makes to its neighbors and, when they do make threats, they should be feasible, credible, and implemented if challenged. Nations need to follow through on their promises of rewards as well. Within the lifetime of the author, there have been numerous breaches of these simple rules. The nation of North Korea, for example, regularly issued dire warnings of future aggression to the point at which other countries in the region treated them less seriously. The United States and many European countries have, to cite another example, developed an unfortunate habit of pledging substantial aid at international gatherings convened for the purpose of alleviating human suffering from some natural disaster, only to deliver far less in actual help. President Barack Obama once threated that the use of chemical weapons during a civil war in the Middle East would constitute "crossing a red line," only to stand impotent when in fact that government so warned went right ahead and gassed its citizens. In each case, these nations have a more difficult time establishing the credibility of their promises or threats made subsequently.

The Sources of Power

The subtleties of power relationships stem from the fact that political managers can employ multiple resources to influence others. They range from concrete and observable to nebulous and debatable. The sources of political power contained in Table 1.1 constitute types of assets that would be power wielders can mobilize to enforce their will.

Authority carries with it the understanding that the person or group being influenced recognizes that the action by the influencer is legitimate, perhaps even justified. If those on the receiving end of a power relationship perceive the influence to be legitimate, compliance is more likely. The presence of legitimate authority may incentivize or coerce action. This is not to say it is more pleasant; being told what you're going to do by an authority is rarely fun, even when you acknowledge his or her right to give orders. In democratic systems, governmental authority is carefully bounded by laws, customs, and political resistance, and by constitutional limits. In fact, the whole

Table 1.1 Sources of Political Power

[From most concrete to most nebulous]

1. **Authority**—power perceived as legitimate by the influence.
2. **Money and Material Resources**—used as rewards; withheld as punishment.
3. **Information**—knowledge that others lack and value.
4. **Political Support**—popularity among a sizable following of citizens/voters.
5. **Charisma**—personal traits and attractiveness that others admire.
6. **Social Prestige**—standing in society or the economy that others admire.
7. **Strength of Conviction**—within limits, confidence is contagious.

thrust of the US Constitution—written in reaction to the perceived abuse of power by the English king—was an effort to narrow the boundaries within which government power could be used legitimately. Even so, citizens may not extend their sense of acceptability to all the powers and resources that are actually available to those wielding governmental power.[7] These are, of course, areas for reasonable political disagreements. Reaching as far back as the 1930s in the United States, politicians of all parties have argued over a perceived drift of presidential power gradually encroaching on the authority of Congress. The fact that these criticisms often depend on partisanship should not obscure the fact that there exists an ongoing, robust, and valid argument over what is or is not legitimate in the use of political power. In other words, within functioning democracies, authority is not always sharply delimited. Authority, moreover, is not restricted to government and politics. Employment settings define a range of legitimate dictates and decisions that superiors can exercise over their employees, and behaviors that are not sanctioned by that authority. Thus, in both organized politics and in power exhibited between individuals, it is important to recognize authority as a critical resource in power relations.

Money and Material Resources provide a second commonly used means of influencing others. Rewards for compliance can be legitimate benefits or bribes outside the laws. Political managers may control any number of funds or material assets that they can bestow or promise to subordinates or others in the political arena. Early in the 21st century, the amount of money flowing into US politics has skyrocketed. Whether one is considering election campaigns or legislative battles, well-positioned political managers have access to abundant resources to incentivize desired behavior from others. In addition, as with every concrete value, withholding that benefit produces a punishment.

Information can be critical to effective participation in political disputes. Among both officeholders and their staff engaged in legislative policymaking, for example, simply understanding what is going on among members of the key committees and the party leadership can be crucial in determining one's influence. Conversely, those who possess accurate information may jealously guard this precious resource. The old saying "information is power" is true in many instances.

Political Support may, at first blush, appear to be a tautology. Political managers are powerful if a number of supporters will follow their wishes. But it is true in politics that success breeds success. The idea that a particular politician has a base of support that she can rely upon to agree with her policies is fundamental to success in a democracy. Political supporters—if sufficiently numerous and loyal—provide both a source of confidence and a protection against challenge.

Charisma comes about as a personal attribute that generates a followership devoted to the person rather than his public policies. The term, as elucidated by the sociologist Max Weber, refers to extraordinary leadership based upon the personal attractiveness of the individual.[8] Scholars of leadership debate whether charisma is inherent in one's makeup or can be learned and developed in the individual.[9]

Social Prestige allows certain individuals to exercise power simply because they represent the social values that a society and culture uphold. Those who are "better off" are all too often given greater latitude in social influence. Education, wealth, and institutional position all combine to advantage some members of society and award them greater influence than their peers.

Strength of Conviction is the most imprecise basis upon which personal power can rest. Nonetheless, we must acknowledge that within limits, confidence is contagious. Individuals who are markedly convinced of the correctness of their vision of the good society often inspire supporters to accept their lead. Because of the swirl of ambition, aggression, and competition found in the actual workings of democratic politics, this arena is not for the faint hearted.

The astute reader will understand innately that the bases of power in the above roster are not mutually exclusive. Political power will accumulate from several of these sources simultaneously. Nor will the power curve be uniformly upward. Democratic politics takes place within webs of interconnected relationships. Political managers function within networks of connections in which they are simultaneously influential and influenced. A given individual may be highly forceful in some policy areas and inconsequential in others. The most effective lobbyists, for example, often specialize in a narrow range of policy matters being debated within a legislature. Theirs is a natural response to the pluralism of democratic politics to be discussed below.

Understanding the Subtleties of Power in Human Interactions

Careful readers are likely to have thought about the fact that in dealings between two actors, one party may anticipate the desires of the other and adapt her or his behavior preemptively. Particularly in exchanges between a stronger party and one considerably weaker, there may be a great deal of appeasement and accommodation in order to avoid harmful consequences in the relationship. Can we say that power has been exercised in this instance? Short of an overt action by the influencer, how can we know his or her intentions and, if we cannot be certain, is it not possible that the actions were in fact not desired? Admittedly, this is a conceptual problem, but it is primarily a problem in the abstract. In given circumstances, the two parties are likely to acknowledge whether or not an action has been induced as intended by the stronger.

Within the conception of political power proposed above, there are nuances aplenty to consider. In exercising power, for example, one individual may influence another's cognitive processes—perceptions, beliefs, values, biases, etc.—in addition to his behavior, though, as noted, actual deeds may be a great deal easier to observe. As we encounter in many aspects of human interaction, this may produce dramatic differences between effects visible in the short term versus those in the long run. The exercise of power may, on the one hand, produce immediate compliance and delayed resentment, resistance, and counterattack. Or on the other hand, with cognitive change in beliefs, the ultimate result may be the kind of supportive following that every political leader aspires to obtain.

As we know, coercive power can be exercised well beyond mere denial of material possessions. Threats of violence, incarceration, pain, torture, even death, can be mobilized behind a dictatorial demand for compliant behavior. High motivated and deeply committed individuals will forever test the limits of their authority. Whether inspired by urges of self-aggrandizement or by a genuine commitment to a vision of a perfect future, leaders seek power through politics. Power energizes their quest for policy. They become restive within the limits of their powers. Accordingly, the coercive relationships in a dictatorial political system tend to expand into an ever-larger range of interactions between leaders and the populous. The inequalities of power across many spheres of life can become so great that the subordinate has no choice but to yield to the dominant dictator. If, however, the subordinate accords no sense of legitimacy to the power forcing his or her compliance, then we cannot call that relationship one involving authority. Dictatorial governments—like dictatorial bosses—may exercise ruthless power that exceeds markedly any sense of legitimate authority.

Our emphasis so far has placed the definition of power largely within interpersonal relationships in which one individual influences another. For simplicity, we have pretended that these connections are a one-way street. In reality, a critical characteristic of influential relations between people is that only rarely are they one way. Usually both parties exercise some degree of reciprocal influence over the other. Mutual influence can exist even when one party in the relationship is substantially dominant. In the Middle Ages, for example, where serfs were clearly exploited on balance, yet there were obligations that the lords of the manor owed to their vassals. And, of course, we all participate in personal relationships that are fairly equal in influence, while each of the two humans may be more potent in different aspects of their joint engagement. For example, he knows a lot about entertainment; she is much better at travel and driving. When they go out together, he shapes what they will do; she determines how they will get there.

How then do democratic institutions seek to contain unequal yet reciprocal power? The norm has been that political managers agree beforehand on a set of rules deemed to be "fair" to the parties involved and then to employ those rules in ways that allow the institutions to function. But this does not mean that coercion is entirely absent. In legislative processes, for example, leadership will inevitably work to narrow the range of alternatives in policy outcomes down to a few options, a process that will involve screening out the preferred policies of some participants. Predictably, those on the losing side of an internal conflict will see the rules as biased against them. And, just as inevitably, political managers on all sides of a fight will employ the rules to their favor. If they can, they may even attempt change the rules in order to predetermine an outcome to their liking. Taking disputes to that level, however, can raise a host of issues about the ethical responsibilities that political managers owe to the institutions of democracy. We will address those problems in the final chapter. Here, suffice it to note that the rules of political combat within democratic institutions are often protected by requirements that mandate a supermajority to alter the rules of the game. Amending a constitution, for example, ought to require more broad-based support than a simple majority to achieve.

Moral Responsibility and Power

In general, as our attention moves upward in matters of scale, we observe a greater degree of coercion on the collective level. The greater the number of humans involved in a political fight, the greater is the need for coordinating action through leadership. Resolution may come about through beneficial transactions or inspirational goal setting, but just as likely will be some degree of coercion.

As noted above, we can gain important insights by projecting lessons from international conflicts onto individual personal influence or domestic political problem-solving. When state sovereignty is involved, however, we should be cautious about justifying too literally applications of power in international politics. Serious concerns exist about the severity and morality of power applied on the level of nation-states. There, the norms managing conflict and the restraints on the unbridled use of coercion are comparatively weak, far weaker than experienced on an individual or group level within an effective polity. In the 21st century, nation-states still interact in a lawless world. Sovereignty can justify unscrupulous behavior.

Consider the fact that both Machiavelli[10] and Sun Tzu[11] were writing about the management of political power in very similar strategic situations. The princes governing the city states of renaissance Italy and the Chinese kings and generals during the period of the warring states were both confronted by anarchic external environments comprised of numerous rivals of more or less equal powers. Survival of any one of these sovereign entities was threatened by external enemies and by internal dissention that could hamper its ability to mobilize for self-defense. In these circumstances, at the extreme upper bound of conflict, these two theorists of conflict developed a hard-edged approach to the exercise of power and the manipulative spirit that lies behind ensuring national survival. The lessons they taught remain relevant to our world on the three levels: mostly as concerns engagements among nation-states, less so in regard to interaction among private individuals or as guides to behavior within democratic politics. Nevertheless, both of these writings have long been standard readings for contemporary political managers.[12]

Of the two, Machiavelli has gotten the worse press. It is not often that one's very name becomes an adjective, much less one that bears connotations of dastardly manipulation. Perhaps this condemnation stems from the fact that he was writing about statecraft as opposed to open warfare. One can accept Sun Tzu's—and for that matter Clausewitz's[13]—advice as necessary because they focused on the overt, violent conflict of war. In contrast, Machiavelli has received some appreciation but near universal criticism, derived from our tendency to take his words of counsel that he directed toward sovereign rulers engaged in statecraft and we apply them to the level of individual, personal behavior. Though we aspire to hold leaders to high standards of moral behavior, the fact is that in times of national crisis, they are responsible for the survival of their nation and the lives of its citizens. This is not to argue that the ends always justify the means, but rather that some ends justify some means. In fact, Machiavelli is not always the brutal character captured by the popular use of his name. He had, for example, a high regard for republics, writing that . . . "[It] is only in republics that the common good is looked to properly . . ."[14] But, he would certainly have been vastly more skeptical of their ultimate success than was Benjamin Franklin when asked what the Constitutional Convention was producing: "A Republic," he replied, "if you can keep it."

Elsewhere in his writings, Machiavelli discusses three means of engaging others: agreement, trickery, and force.[15] He then counsels us that the closer someone is to us, the more we should prefer agreement. Meanwhile, trickery and force—for which he is most frequently castigated—come into play mainly when dealing with rivals and with other sovereign entities. Machiavelli was also writing about what we would call today "pre-conflict" situations among sovereign city states and was perceptive enough to realize that perceived weakness would invite aggression. When national survival is at stake, and in recognition of their responsibilities, perhaps we should give the benefit of doubt to political leaders. In those moments of crisis, perhaps their ethical conduct is not that which we aspire to achieve on the individual level. The best, balanced summary of Machiavelli's argument was first quoted to me by my colleague, Carol Darr: "Be as good as you can; be as bad as you must; know the difference; and don't squirm!"[16]

This does not mean that norms of conduct for heads of government are completely absent. Crimes against humanity are and should be prosecuted by international tribunals. But actions that would seem unconscionable on an individual level are sometimes required of political leadership. A poignant example can be drawn from the actions of a universally admired leader, Winston Churchill. While there is some debate as to the precise facts, numerous works allege that Churchill learned in advance that the German Luftwaffe would stage a massive raid on the city of Coventry on November 14, 1940. Ordering an evacuation might have alerted the Germans to the fact that the allies, having broken the Enigma coding machine, were reading their secret orders. Coventry was left to suffer incredible but avoidable devastation. On an individual level, surely we would condemn a person who could easily stop a mass shooting in a shopping center but did nothing. But, should we condemn Churchill? He bore both personal and leadership responsibilities to the survival of the nation in the long run. What was the trade-off he faced? After Coventry, British intelligence continued to decode messages from the German cipher machine; the entry of the United States shifted the tide of the war; the British and Americans successfully landed in Normandy; and eventually the allies defeated Germany. Whether or not the story of this decision is completely true in all details is rather beside the point. Churchill was confronting a typical dilemma between a short-term benefit—saving Coventry—versus a longer-term greater good—preserving the secrecy of a vital tool that could help win the war. We can understand and even sympathize with Churchill as he faced an excruciating dilemma and chose the longer-term goal. We would probably be deeply disappointed and even angry with an individual who made such a choice in his or her private life.

Exercising Power within Democratic Politics

Between person-to-person engagements and the dynamics of international relations lie the internal politics of nation-states, the major focus of this volume. If the lessons of strategy are to be of assistance to political managers, then it is here where they should direct the most attention. Politics play a central role in the internal dynamics of nation-states, even those that are not democratic. Our focus will, nevertheless, be upon the politics of democracies. We seek to comprehend and surmount the swirl of political jostling that takes place between officeholders and activists, acting through organized groups or channeled through the institutions of government. Our goal is to give counsel to political managers so they can prosper in the ongoing conflict among citizens and leaders who are engaged in political struggles. We believe that to be successful, those working in democratic politics need to understand the nature of strategy and the critical role that power plays in strategic behavior. Here political managers and politicians, by their very behavior, can either strengthen or weaken the political institutions of their democracy. We strongly urge political managers to protect, and indeed nurture, the democratic institutions by which power is acquired, exercised, and contained.

For many in politics, power is assembled by combining the resources of institutional position, by the individual's will to seize and employ power, as well as by the degree to which an individual's sense of vision hits a responsive chord among those politically active or capable of being mobilized to action. Power is therefore the creation of individual strength—in the sense of a willingness to seek and use power—and institutional position. Individuals who commandeer or create institutions that can accumulate resources become more powerful by their ability to deploy those resources. Thus, an elected official has access to the powers of the office that is denied to private citizens, much as a corporate CEO can direct how the assets of the company will be directed into lobbying.

Ideas alone and the ability to symbolize and communicate them can have a catalytic effect on a polity, bringing power to the leader. That is, a formal position is not essential to the creation of power. There are numerous examples of individuals who had a remarkable influence on the future of their nation—indeed of the world—without holding any formal position whatever. The Mahatma (Mohandas Karamchand Gandhi) and the Reverend Martin Luther King, Jr., come readily to mind as individuals who successfully shaped their nations without holding formal political office. The strength and resonance of their ideas drew supporters to their cause, and with them the resources necessary to forge change.

In order to pursue this discussion in the chapters that follow, we need to take a brief detour into the nature of democracy itself. Too often, democracy is only identified as—and confused with—election politics. Certainly, majoritarian rule as determined by candidate appeals and mass voting is a component of modern democracies especially where the citizenry is too large to engage in direct democracy. Modern nations are simply too large and too complex to practice the direct political engagement as benefited the citizens of the city states of ancient Greece or New England town meetings. Moreover, as Bernard Crick has forcefully argued in *In Defense of Politics*,[17] mass participation can be easily manipulated to support authoritarian dictatorship. Recognizing that election politics are the bedrock of democracy, however, we need more than just elections to constitute a democracy.[18]

To start with the basic conduct of elections, democracies require that elections be implemented through provisions regulating the actions of various participants—citizens, candidates, party organizations, voters, administrators, financial backers, the news media, a growing array of new channels of political communications. Laws such as those determining voter registration, access to the ballot by candidates, the institutionalization of political parties, election administration and vote tallying, and the financing of candidates and parties must provide guarantees that the elections are not just a sham for regime support. All of these numerous safeguards ensure that elections are conducted in a manner that allows them to serve as effective barometers of citizen preference.

Even presented with a polity that regularly holds open, fair, and valid elections, we would require it to manifest substantially more in the way of democratic principles before we would consider it a democracy.

Freedom of the assembly and of the press, a system of impartial rule of law, and a plurality of institutions through which citizens can collectively shape public policies are some of the minimum requisites for a thriving, functioning democracy.

In democracies, political power is fragmented, derived from different bases, and shared unequally among citizens. Democracies require that which Robert Dahl and his disciples refer to as "pluralism."[19] They argue that active citizens should have multiple channels through which they can influence the direction of government policy. In practice, this means that the bases upon which effective citizen influence rests should be multiple. The structure of power relationships and institutions engaged in establishing foreign policy, for example, should be distinct from policymaking in education, just as education policy emerges from a different set of institutions and leaders than does infrastructure development. Citizens contending over environmental issues will have at their disposal an array of resources they can bring to the fight: information, volunteerism, petitioning, protesting, financing, electoral mobilization, and the like. But if we turned instead to the politics of housing, we would likely find a distinctive cluster of citizens and organizations using different resources and working through an alternative variety of political institutions. This plurality of institutions, of groups and individuals engaged, of leadership, of structure in power relationships, and of resources that can be effectively brought to bear creates a vibrancy of democratic practice far beyond the occasional participation of citizens in elections.

We need, therefore, to allow ambitious political managers a certain amount of latitude in exercising power to achieve their purposes, as long as their pursuit of power stops short of weakening democratic institutions and principles. This leeway may involve a degree of shaping the institutions themselves, for, as noted above, changing the rules in order to win in politics is a frequent tactic of political managers. Of course, that behavior will be controversial; one leader's idea of political "reform" is likely to be seen as sabotage by her opponents. So inevitably exercising power in a democracy will involve maintaining a balance between personal power and pluralism, a fine line that may be difficult to define in concrete instances. Nevertheless, the obligations that political managers owe to the democratic system require vigilance both in recognizing that choice is at issue and then in upholding the functioning of democratic institutions.

While a fully functioning democracy demands a high degree of pluralism, in order for a polity to move forward, someone has to exercise power. Too fragmented a polity may lead to stagnation and to an inability of organizations or the nation to adapt to changing conditions such as demographic pressures, economic growth or decline, external threats, emerging social issues, or technological advances. The governmental and political institutions must therefore provide a balance between openness to different points of view and different power resources, and yet at the same time endow political leadership with sufficient capacity to force through needed change.

Within democratic institutions and within the groups and organizations contesting for political influence, leadership and power manifest themselves in a capacity to build and maintain a substantial constituency. This realization begs the question: What precisely does one mean by the "constituency" of a political leader? A narrow definition refers to the citizens entitled to vote for a given elected official by virtue of residing in a given territory.[20] In that sense, constituencies have a hard boundary defining who is in the constituency and who is not. We feel this is too narrow a definition. Instead, we mean a constituency to designate a broader and more amorphous concept, referring to the group of individuals that can, at any one point in time, be counted on to approve and support the actions of those engaged in political combat. In short, not just public officeholders but all political managers need to create and nurture constituencies of their own. Supporters like these deliver the seeds of political power. As pluralism teaches us, they may demonstrate their support for a given political leader through a myriad of channels such as making financial contributions; attending meetings; writing letters; lobbying public officials; knocking on doors; and, of course, voting and simply expressing their approval in conversations with their friends. Moreover, given the abundance of public opinion polls, public opinion as mobilized and molded by active constituencies can have a palpable influence on policymaking.

In this broader sense of constituency, even those holding a seat in Congress may claim a national audience of supporters in addition to their formal electorate. Within the community of those who generally support a politician, moreover, the boundaries between those who are infinitely loyal and more marginal supporters will be permeable. Should the leaders call for some action, some expression of support from their constituency, they may not know for certain which of their supporters will actually show up and do what is asked of them. Thus, maintaining a constituency is not an easy process nor one that can be neglected for very long. The engagement strategy employed by political managers needs to be a cycle of continual renewal through constant interaction and networking. Politicians who wish to remain in power should constantly make use of all the tactical vehicles through which constituencies can be contacted and nurtured: projecting vision, setting goals, communicating frequently, providing favors and rewards, soliciting advice, demonstrating personal charisma, and manifesting self-confidence.

In addition to the positive inducements necessary to recruit potential supporters, in some circumstances, political leaders should be prepared to castigate those who disagree with them. Strategy may require carrying out threats and imposing punishments against opponents. This treatment may be unfortunate but necessary. Political leaders have long known that an effective tactic in energizing a supportive constituency is to give them an enemy to abhor. Sanctions against an opponent can generate a rallying cry within a group of supporters. Maintaining and inspiring a political constituency may require both supportive incentives and negative condemnation of an enemy.

Here again, two rules of power relationships are present. First there is usually an element of reciprocity in power interactions; democratic support imposes obligations on leaders as well as on followers. If she or he wants to preserve political support, a public official is not free, for example, to rapidly revise his or her thinking, even if abundant evidence suggests that the initial position was in error. Gradual, calculated, subtle shifts may be necessary to bring a constituency along with a leader. A supportive electorate expects certain behaviors of the leader and can dissipate like smoke if once disappointed.

Second, as noted above, in taking full advantage of the support of a large and seemingly committed constituency, political leaders may draw upon the perception that they are influential. Perception can be as potent as actual mobilization. As long as power perceived is not power challenged, the appearance of power may be just as effective as the reality. In fact, the ability to project an image, to exert influence without actually having to mobilize one's constituency is not only more efficient, it may avoid a downward spiral of impotence if, once mobilized, the supportive constituency fails to materialize. The content of political discourse is, thus, ever full of bluster, as political leaders endeavor to convey to their constituencies images of their own potency.

But all is not mere smoke, for there is a reality to political power. Elected officials, interest group leaders, or corporate CEOs combine institutional position with the attendant resources and powers that command over institutions can bring. To those resources, they add at least the *perception* of a willing and mobilizable political constituency supporting them. This combination can create real, substantial, and effective political power in a democratic system. That power is what allows certain individuals to impose their will in a polity and effectively shape its evolving future. As we shall argue in subsequent chapters, power is not the same thing as political leadership, but leadership does not exist without power.

Limiting the Pursuit of Power

Power is tactical, not strategic. Power is a means to achieving one's goals and, though essential, should remain secondary to those ends. The danger for political managers is that power can become an end unto itself. Paradoxically, this problem can be most severe among those who are most committed to certain policy outcomes. All too frequently, these ardent policy proponents forget that democratic politics requires compromises that should minimally satisfy the desires of the widest possible groups. Those are the leaders who can become so convinced that their views must predominate that they are likely to become riveted upon the pursuit of the power so necessary to affect their will. When Lord Acton coined the observation, "Power tends to corrupt and absolute power corrupts absolutely," he was not referring to corruption in the venal sense of bribery and extortion.

Rather, he—John Emerich Edward Dalberg-Acton—understood that the need for power can corrupt one away from vision, principle, and proportion.

We have hit upon the first of several profound dilemmas confronting those who make their careers in politics and public life. We understand why political managers must acquire power to pursue their vision, and yet we acknowledge that there must be restraints—personal and institutional—that circumscribe that quest. Both are realities of political engagement.

I conclude here by returning to Machiavelli's three means of influencing others: force, trickery, and agreement. So far, we have examined one of these strategies: "force." That is, in our terms here, "power." Machiavelli's "Prince" had to understand that governing would at times demand ruthless, raw state power employed against one's enemies, including imprisonment, corporal punishment, and death.

Yet, in today's democracies, power is exercised in more benign ways through strategies of political management. Still contemporary political contests are often hard fought and bruising. And, recourse to coercive force still exists as a last resort. As the American Congressman Steve Chabot once observed, "Politics is a contact sport."[21] For Machiavelli, the survival of Florence as an independent city state justified a harsher politics than we should accept in the internal politics of a democracy. For him, "ruling"—what we would today refer to as "governing"—could be likened to holding a pack of wolves at bay. At times, a prince had to be both a lion and a fox, exercising both the strength of the lion and the cunning of the fox. Machiavelli associated trickery with the fox; the ability to see traps ahead and to outthink one's opponents.

As it turns out, effective political management requires a blend of all of these talents: power, strategy, negotiation, and leadership. These are not always compatible. Force can become counterproductive to strategic objectives and force can be the antithesis of leadership. The demands of strategy may collide with the principles of leadership. Negotiating may inevitably undercut one's power. Yet recognizing these contradictions and finding an appropriate balance among them leads us to the essence of strategic political management.

The Essence of Power in Democratic Politics

1. Democratic politics constitute a struggle—often brutal and bruising—in which participants articulate and advance competing visions of a desired future. We agree with Winston Churchill[22] who observed that "... democracy is the worst form of government... except for all the rest."[23]
2. Power is essential to achieving purpose in the swirling competition that constitutes civil politics. To be effective, political managers must not be squeamish about accumulating and exercising power. But this pursuit must be balanced by the values inherent in democratic politics.
3. Functioning democratic systems exhibit the characteristic of "pluralism," meaning that power can be mobilized through multiple institutions for shaping public policy. The diffusion of power into different channels of influence offers political managers multiple opportunities to effectively pursue their policy goals.
4. In their quest for winning, political managers should not weaken the institutions of democratic politics through which power is accumulated and exercised.

2
A First Look at Strategic Thinking

Tactics without strategy is the noise before defeat.
—Sun Tzu

Political success is achieved through strategy. In building the effective political support necessary to accomplishing one's objectives, political managers are well served by devising and implementing explicit strategies. In comparison to their counterparts in business and war, those who labor in politics often pay too little attention to the nature of strategy, which is rather surprising given their omnipresent plotting for strategic advantage in pursuit of victory. In other words, too often, political managers use the word "strategy" to describe their actions without precisely comprehending what that word means. This is more than just a definitional problem, for imprecision of concept leads to vagueness in thinking, which in turn creates sloppiness and confusion in performance.

Defining and implementing strategy in the political realm may be more difficult than in other sectors of human behavior. The goals to be achieved in public life can be inordinately complex, frequently ill defined, and inevitably disputed by allies and opponents. Measurements of success are likely to be subject to debate that is rooted in contradictory beliefs and interests. The resources that one can bring to bear to influence outcomes are multiple and often of unknown potency. The assumptions that combatants must make about factors they cannot control are hazardous. Nevertheless, since the human interaction we know as politics literally determines our collective future, we must bring as much precision as possible to this inquiry. Hopefully, improved understanding will allow political managers to accomplish their objectives even while advancing the values of democratic institutions.

Strategy is highly situational. The actions political managers should take toward achieving their goals are unavoidably determined by concrete circumstances in which they must act. This means, among other things, that guidance for those operating in the political world will necessarily be general rather than tangibly concrete. Accordingly, this book endeavors to impart a general orientation toward political strategy. We aspire to sharpen our readers' ability to think strategically. But readers cannot expect specific advice as to how they should act in actual, concrete situations. Following formal guidelines that dictate a specific strategy under given circumstances can prove to be self-defeating. Instead, we intend to convey to readers an awareness of the importance of *strategic thinking* and an alertness of mind that is able to seize onto strategic opportunities. By advancing their understanding of the complexities of strategy, political managers will improve their ability to think strategically. Armed with that knowledge, they will be better able to design more effective strategies.

Our efforts to comprehend the nature of strategy in political disputes are complicated by the indiscriminate use of the term. Any quick read of the writings and quotes of professional political managers would document that "strategy" is almost synonymous with politics itself. Their comments are full of references to fundraising strategy, communications strategy, legislative strategy, advocacy strategy, GOTV strategies, digital strategy, lobbying strategy, persuasion strategy, and the like. Tack the word "strategist" onto any of these references and you have a title to be fought over. A strategist has achieved the heights from where she can direct the overall course of the endeavor, whatever that may be. The above-mentioned functions clearly refer to strategic operations, yet in some cases, they actually describe the tactical elements of an overall political strategy. Such confusion suggests that we need to draw a sharp distinction between strategy and tactics, a conceptual task that can only be achieved with a clear definition of what strategy entails in the political realm.

At this point, the reader may be expecting a succinct, formal definition of the term "strategy." So be it, though succinct will escape us. Strategy is a sequence of thought for ordering tactical action through calculated decisions to achieve specific outcomes in a situation of conflict. A statement of a strategy requires a well-defined goal, the resources that can be mobilized toward that end, the barriers that must be overcome to achieve one's ends, and the assumptions one makes as to the factors that will significantly impact the achievement of the goal. Especially pertinent to a delineated strategy are the competitive interactions likely to occur between the strategist and his or her opponents as each endeavor to implement tactical decisions guided by their strategic thought. Political strategy places this approach to competitive interaction within the institutions of democratic support associated with the determination of social policies. As such, the tactical goals, resources, and assumptions all relate to the securing of power necessary to advance political ideals.

Less formally, suffice it for the reader to consider "strategy" to be a roadmap toward an important goal, a roadmap that specifies in some detail the concrete goal to be achieved and the tactical actions necessary to achieve it. In an important way, however, this entire book is intended to provide readers with a complex, operational definition that will equip them as effective strategists. Our roadmaps will inevitably include a variety of elements and choice points. By considering strategy from four different perspectives, we hope to arm the reader so that he or she can achieve victory in the arena of democratic politics.

Inevitably, we will resort to using the word strategy with multilayered meanings. For example, in military parlance, scholars refer to "grand strategy" as engaging the overriding interests of the nation within which "military strategy" certainly plays a prominent role. In politics, an overarching strategy might be partially fulfilled, for example, by a fundraising strategy or by the digital communications strategy. But, in our overuse of strategy, we are falling victim to the very problem that justifies this book. Constant overuse of the term *strategy* generates imprecision that frustrates careful application of this concept that is so critical to successful political action. Vagueness confounds efforts to think rationally and act deliberately.

The unavoidable distinction between strategy and tactics creates one source of confusion. Misperceptions arise not solely as a matter of analytic concept, but operationally in concrete situations where one is trying to adopt a strategic posture. Tactical actions are often much more likely to pull our attention away from the conceptual level, so there is a constant and inevitable drag from the strategic to the tactical. As the military historian B. H. Liddell Hart[1] has written,

> When the application of the military instrument merges into actual fighting, the dispositions for and control of such direct action are termed 'tactics.' The two categories, although convenient for discussion, can never be truly divided into separate compartments because each not only influence but merges into the other.

Here we shall urge a somewhat brighter line than the convenience advanced by Hart. Even while conceding his argument that the strategic and tactical are enmeshed, we draw a brighter distinction by insisting that strategy is a purely cerebral exercise. Remember that! Whether engaged in war or in politics, the strategic actor should be thinking, not doing. "Tactics" refer to *actions* that implement a strategy. But as the noun in "political manager" implies, we naturally tend to gravitate toward action. In the process, we lose sight of thinking on the level of strategy. An aspiring political manager will be more successful in maintaining her focus on the strategy necessary for victory if she keeps reminding herself that crafting strategy is an analytical exercise. Thinking, not doing.

Next are four different ways of thinking about strategy. These are not meant to be alternative or contrasting definitions, but different and complementary aspects of this singularly complex idea. Each viewpoint conveys important understandings to the overall concept. Each will be dealt with more extensively in a subsequent chapter.

Strategy Derived from Military Conflict

The roots of strategy lie in warfare. In fact, the term itself comes from a Greek word that refers to a general in command of an army. In effect, the Greek word "στρατηγός" or "*strategos*" translates to mean both a military general and a strategist. "*Strategia* is derived from two words in ancient Greek '*stratos*' referring to a multitude or army and '*agos*' for leader."[2]

The fact that warfare and politics are related should not surprise us. Both provide the means of settling social conflicts: one by force of arms, the other by civil engagement. As the Prussian soldier Karl von Clausewitz realized, wars are essentially political in that political objectives lie at the heart of armed conflict.[3]

> The war of a community—of whole nations, particularly civilized nations—always arises from a political condition and is called forth by a political motive. It is therefore a political act.

Where von Clausewitz saw war as an extension of politics into the domain of violence, the reverse formulation is also true: politics is an extension of warfare onto a domain of civil conduct.[4] Political scientists have long recognized that politics involves more or less peaceful *conflict*. Take housing policy for example. The political system must balance conflicting interests such as those of landlords versus tenants, homeowners versus bankers, builders versus urban planners. Whether they are economic or social, whether they are differences of social identity rooted in religion, language, culture, geography, or class, such factors create conflicts that must be managed by politics. Given these social differences, interests and ideals naturally diverge, setting the stage for conflict. Divergences in policy preferences emerge from visions of a better society, visions that are likely to be contrary and even mutually exclusive. Add to this idealism the role that personal ambition can play in securing power, wealth, and satisfaction, and you have volatile competition. With his typical mixture of insight and humor, Sir Winston Churchill once opined, "Politics are almost as exciting as war, and—quite as dangerous . . . [I]n war, you can only be killed once. But in politics many times."[5] In truth, in tasking democratic politics to ameliorate such conflict, we are asking a lot.

If we are to understand the role that strategy plays in political management, we cannot ignore this underlying struggle despite our instinctual preferences for peaceful, democratic resolution of societal disputes. We follow Harold Lasswell, one of the founders of modern political science, who observed that politics is about "who gets what, when, and how."[6] Conflict is very likely to arise over each of these four queries: who, what, when, and how. The struggle to define public policy will produce both winners and losers. The outcome of these battles will also determine who *doesn't* get what. In consequence, losing can trigger resentment and spur action. Unhappy individuals and interest groups are apt to organize and press for redress. Effective political managers must deal with opposition, or it can fester and grow.

Scholars and practitioners of the military arts have been writing about strategy for over 2,000 years. As a result, a great deal can be learned from discussions of strategy in the context of military theorizing. Suffice it to say that war and politics lie at different points on a continuum of violence. Democratic politics—broadly defined— has proven capable of ameliorating social conflict short of violence. Inevitably, however, the primary tool of military strategy resides in the possibility of force. The mindset of the political manager and the warrior must be similar, but for the former the warfare should be civil.

Strategy as an Exercise in Planning

The most widely accepted notion of strategy is of purposeful planning designed to achieve a defined objective. Note that if this definition is all that "strategy" means, the term "strategic planning" becomes redundant. That said, those who write about strategic planning as opposed to simple "planning" believe themselves to be focused on accomplishing larger purposes, broader goals, or longer-run objectives.[7] In doing so, they are signing onto a quest for higher-order thinking. Strategic planning deals with the big picture, the important factors that determine whether the organization thrives or diminishes.

Strategic planning involves several elements: (1) a concise definition of the goals one hopes to achieve, (2) a statement about the strategic circumstances in which one will operate, (3) the assumptions one makes about the evolving situation, (4) a clear delineation of the resources one can bring to bear upon the problem, and (5) linking statements that relate the actions one might take to the outcomes likely to be achieved. In most concrete situations, these are not simple tasks. To make things more difficult, the plan must be written down, even if it is to be secreted away. Without a document to anchor their thinking, political managers can slowly alter their perceptions as the conditions they face evolve. Their priorities can shift unnoticed. In military parlance, this is known as "mission creep." Such gradual evolution is tantamount to not having a plan at all. Instead of proactively implementing a carefully thought-out document, the political manager is essentially reacting to external events. Yet, how can we reasonably argue that plans should not be adapted to changing conditions? This conundrum constitutes a major challenge in implementing a strategic plan, one that will be discussed in Chapter 7. How does one know when to stay with the original strategy versus when it is important and necessary to change the plan?

Thinking of strategy solely in the sense of an exercise in planning is essential but inadequate. Clearly in any situation in which one wishes to exert an influence, one needs to develop an inventory of the resources at hand and devise a carefully thought-out, rational design for how they should be employed. But that exercise inherently forces the political manager to focus on the decisions and actions within her or his control. So doing tends to downplay the importance of considering those factors that cannot be controlled and how opponents might respond. Planning can put blinders on the strategist by creating a static view of situations that are fundamentally fluid. In a political campaign, for example, a strategy team might devise a sequence of television advertising starting with a biographical spot, moving on to the candidate's central policy positions, and ending with attack ads contrasting the opponent on the issues deemed most important by voters. But the opponent's actions might throw this neatly planned progression into disarray by launching a massive attack early in the campaign. Once a substantial effort at drafting a plan has been expended, implementation naturally tends to follow a predetermined—and hopefully accurate—rollout of the effort to achieve one's goals. Too often missing in that exercise is an effort to think through the evolving scenarios that might occur as the planned actions materialize. Planning is an indispensable skill in political management, but one must also be able to react to changing circumstances.

Strategy as an Exercise in Communication

Politics entails the communication and persuasion necessary to build a constituency. Political power—by which we mean the ability to command, persuade, and mobilize both active supporters and a larger, relatively passive constituency—is the fundamental currency of politics. As a general statement—and some would say a lamentable statement—those in public life do not produce a concrete product other than words, policies, programs, and laws. Perhaps not surprisingly, another conception of strategy focuses upon the processes of communication.

The essence of communications boils down to two questions: Whom do I need to reach? What do I need to say to them? They should be answered in that order, for understanding with whom one needs to communicate will largely determine what one needs to say.[8] Consider that we all speak very differently to different audiences. We use different modes, different syntax, and a different vocabulary when speaking to close family members than to workplace associates. We address strangers in different terms than we do friends. A speech to a large audience is conducted entirely differently than conversation in a small group. More to the point, a good deal of research documents that people are prepared to hear only a limited range of content, particularly information relevant to political choice.[9]

Another critical aspect of communications is the content of the messages to be delivered. Most political consultants believe, for example, that an election campaign is not the time to try to educate the electorate about policy issues. Instead, a substantial research effort—both qualitative as in focus groups and quantitative as in polling—should give political managers a sense of what the target groups are prepared to hear. The art of mobilization lies in folding communications into preexisting values, preferences, and knowledge and tying those positive presumptions to a given candidate while attaching the negatives to the opponent. The primary tool that strategic communications use to expand power is its ability to persuade other actors to your way of seeing and modifying the future.

Strategy as an Exercise in Controlling Human Interaction

Politics also involves dynamic interaction between two or more opposing forces. For those who make their careers in politics, opposition is inevitable. As in warfare, politics entails competing forces driven by different values and objectives, each trying to impose their desires upon the other. Conflict inherent in political struggle is inevitably such a strong component of public life that, as a matter of definition, the term "strategy" should be used in politics only in situations involving direct, overt opposition. Whether as ideologues or professionals, those contending in politics are often—some would say too often—engaged in winner-take-all competition. It is the purpose and goal of strategy to allow political practitioners to win within this highly competitive environment.

Competition among political actors sets up an interaction that is difficult to predict and hard to control. Once a dynamic element is introduced to political interaction, reciprocal actions between the combatants can spiral out of the control of either party. Predicting how the other party will react to one's action is a difficult but essential skill in achieving success in politics. Nevertheless, such is the essential task of strategy in this interactive sense. The primary tool of strategic interaction is the ability to control these dynamics.

In 1687, Sir Isaac Newton published *Philosophiae Naturalis Principia Mathematica* in which he proposed his third law of motion: "For every action, there is an equal and opposite reaction." Though we cannot presume that in political interactions every reaction will be exactly equal and opposite in nature, the principle is generally true. The acts of one party stimulate the reactions of others. Accordingly, strategy simply cannot be complete when political managers ignore the possible and likely reactions of their opponents. Incorporating the dynamics of human interactions into the calculations of political strategy is essential.

Strategy in a Business Context

The informed reader may wonder why I have chosen not to delve into the concept of strategy as developed in the voluminous business literature.

Superficially, shouldn't there be some compatibility? Companies seek to market products to consumers just as political parties want to sell their candidates to voters. There are two reasons, however, for the decision to by and large ignore the world of business strategy. First, while it is true that, within certain market dynamics, each side may recognize that they confront zero-sum competition. To cite a prominent example, perhaps Coca Cola and Pepsi are engaged in a vicious rivalry such that we can draw lessons applicable to politics from them. But, in fact, their struggle over "market share" means that one company is not trying to utterly eliminate the competition. Except in rare circumstances, business strategies do not entail a winner-take-all mentality in the same way that warfare and political competition do. As in war, competition in politics involves a core survival largely absent in the conduct of business.

Second, numerous propositions qualify as different business strategies. One compilation, written by Martin Reeves and Knut Haanaes,[10] lists well over 50 distinguishable strategies contained in the literature on conducting business. Most of these approaches to business strategy concentrate on managing growth by supervising those factors that the business can control. Thus, they share some of the same limitations as the planning method discussed earlier in this chapter. To comprehend and engage strategy in public life, we need a conception that focuses squarely upon the dynamics of the interaction between competitors These are, essentially, factors that one cannot control. Too often the strategies employed by businesses to bring their products to market strictly attend to factor they *can* control such as the complex of internal matters of market timing or product development. In short, examining the applicability of business strategies to political competition would become a voluminous and ultimately unrewarding proposition.

Strategy Going Forward

In the next four chapters, we will take up strategy from the perspectives of the military, of planning, of communications, and of human interaction. These four perspectives or arenas in which strategy is advanced should not be understood as suggesting that distinct definitions of strategy exist. Rather, I argue that each viewpoint contributes to our overall understanding of this critically important aspect of political success. The four approaches are intended to give the reader a nuanced conception of political strategy and to provide an idea of how strategy facilitates the achievement of goals and vision.

Following these definitional chapters, the reader will find in Chapter 7 numerous guidelines for operating strategically in politics, advice to political managers as to how they should behave when they find themselves in competition with other actors.

In Chapter 8, I take up the importance of negotiations for achieving success in politics. Knowing how to reach agreements with other actors provides a means other than the use of power and force to accomplish one's goal, and, because negotiations are interactive, they fall within the concept of strategy.

The final chapter will take up the problem of relating strategy in politics to the necessity for leadership. The two concepts exhibit some major differences in orientation, as strategy can have pejorative tinges of conniving, manipulative actions, while leadership often connotes illuminating and empowering deeds. Despite the fact that political leaders need to behave strategically, the two behaviors are often contradictory. Thus, the volume needs to conclude by drawing some lines for readers who are aspiring political leaders.

The Essence of Chapter 2

1. The word "strategy" is overused. We need a precise term that defines the struggle by political managers to enact public policies that will implement their vision for a better world, however that is defined.
2. Four ways of approaching strategic thinking can be drawn from military conflict, detailed planning, persuasive communications, and interpersonal dynamics. Each of these approaches will be taken up in a subsequent chapter.
3. "Strategy" is more precisely applied to thinking than to actions. Strategy is then a means—a plan of action—to achieve one's objective or vision despite aggressive opposition.

PART II
ARENAS OF STRATEGY

PART II
ARENAS OF STRATEGY

3
War and Democratic Conflict

> Tactics teaches *the use of the armed forces in engagements*, and strategy *the use of engagements to attain the object of the war*.[1]
>
> —Karl Von Clausewitz

War and politics are both means of resolving social conflict. Words that Christopher Bassford addressed to warfare apply equally well to politics: "a dynamic, inherently unstable interaction of forces of violent emotion, chance and rational calculation on all sides."[2] Understandably, political managers have adopted a warrior-like mindset. Campaign, targeting, zero-sum, victor, terrain, attack, defense, and the like are all terms originating in warfare and used with equal accuracy in political life.

The whole point of democracy is to allow peaceful resolution of conflict. But we cannot escape the fact that hard-fought battles over public policies are inevitable when the core interests of groups collide. In fact, despite a fervent hope for dispassionate leadership, the Founders of the American republic understood viscerally that the machinery of democracy must circumscribe thriving ambition, the individual pursuit of power, and the divisions of faction. Fearing these all-too-human tendencies, they specifically designed the constitutional architecture to contain the struggle over who gets what, when, and how.[3]

In the Discourses, Machiavelli argued that the strength of the Roman republic lay precisely in balancing the internal divisions between the aristocrats and the plebeians. In praising Rome as the perfect republic despite much discord between the Plebians and the Senate, Machiavelli signals that the institutions of government must be capable of surfacing and containing this perpetual struggle.[4] Otherwise the polity will rot, becoming increasingly incapable of dealing with the serious social issues that inevitably have to be confronted and ameliorated in order to avoid a violent explosion or severe repression.

In the five hundred years since Machiavelli's death, we have—presumably—learned more about the capabilities of democratic governance to manage conflict. Occasionally there will be periods of highly polarized partisanship. Anger, antipathy, and hatred spill forth among political leaders and their supporters. Disputes emerging in the legislative process metastasize into the body public. But, if it can be contained, conflict in politics can be viewed positively. It signals the coming to the fore of divisive issues within the citizenry, the real question is whether the institutions of democracy are capable of surfacing and ultimately managing these struggles. If not, anger and disillusionment can fester. The political alternatives—either a descent into anarchy, chaos, civil war, and rebellion, on the one hand, or the emergence of a dictatorship, on the other—stand as stark negative examples. These twin pathologies of politics can emerge when political managers do not observe appropriate conduct and norms of fair play in the processes of government.

The danger of exceeding these bounds is well known: rampant partisanship can become so severe at times that it cripples the functioning of government. The "game" of politics can become so competitive that the participants' efforts to gain an advantage only serve to weaken the institutions themselves. Under extreme pressure, democratic institutions can cease to contain the civil strife and become so dysfunctional that the struggle over political issues devolves into violence, as happened in the United States in 1860. Mindful of this possibility, we can and should conduct our politics within limits imposed by democratic principles. An essential role of political managers should be to prevent political disputes from raging into violence. We want strong democratic institutions that maintain a wall between warfare and civil politics. But, if we accept Clausewitz's continuum of the intertwining of politics and warfare, then perhaps the military can teach us something about strategy that would be useful in political management. The mindset of the warrior and the strategic thinking of the political manager should bear some similarities.

In the United States, military leaders have long recognized the importance of formal training in strategic thinking. All branches of the American armed forces have created institutions that teach strategic thinking to rising stars within their ranks. The US Naval War College in Newport, Rhode Island, traces its founding back to 1884. The US Army established the Army War College in 1901 in Carlisle, Pennsylvania. By the 1990s, both the Air Force and the Marines had established equivalent institutions, and the Pentagon funded the National Defense University at which American and foreign military leaders can study strategy.[5] To quote one mission statement, the Marine War College "prepares officers for future senior command and staff responsibilities requiring exceptional operational competence, sound military judgment, and strategic thinking."[6]

The perceived need to teach strategy rests upon the proposition that general officers will be less effective if they have not acquired an ability to think strategically. The curriculum of the Naval War College, for example, builds upon a core course "Strategy and War," which includes topics such as the political objectives of war and a broad discussion of the geopolitical interests of the United States.[7] The US Army seeks to develop in their officer corps a functional "capability for strategic analysis in support of the development and implementation of plans and policies at the national strategic and theater strategic levels."[8] At both the Army War College and the Air War College in Montgomery, Alabama, students undertake Masters of Strategic Studies degrees. The Marine Corps War College offers an "Art of War Studies" program that seeks to "develop strategic leaders who possess the judgment, creativity, communications skills, and ethical grounding required to assume senior leadership positions within their service or agency." They aspire to produce "military strategists educated in the profession of arms and in the relationships between ends-ways-means who understand the utility (and limitations) of employing force or the threat of force in the pursuit of political objectives."[9]

Along this continuum of conflict, in what sense is strategy in politics akin to strategy in war? If domestic politics can be seen as an extension of warfare onto a civil plane, what can military strategists teach us about functioning adroitly in politics? I believe there are two broad lessons here: the first relates to the scope of leadership and the second to the nature of conflict and competition.

The leadership coursework for officers at military academies emphasizes decision-making in uncertain and unstructured environments. To capture, understand, and formalize the nature of the strategic environment that its graduates may face, the US Army War College incorporates in its curriculum the acronym "VUCA" to summarize the volatility, uncertainty, complexity, and ambiguity that surround action in combat.[10] By identifying these impediments and specifying them as concretely as possible, a VUCA analysis should enhance one's understanding of the difficulties of decision-making in conflict situations.[11] The intent is to encourage the capacity to act even in the face of these difficulties. The same analysis should be applied to the strategic environment confronted by those in public life.[12] *Volatility* suggests that situations of conflict are highly unstable, constantly changing as each of the engaged opponents initiate and adapt in their efforts to achieve victory. *Uncertainty* occurs when the information available to the decision maker is scanty and the predictability of the evolving interaction is minimal. *Complexity* highlights the manifold factors and interconnected variables involved in a situation and the complicated interactions they create. *Ambiguity* results when the causal relationships among the elements of a situation are unknown and, even though appropriate information may be available, the overall meaning of the state of affairs is unclear.[13] Of course, each of these obstructions suggests remedial actions the decision maker can take to address the difficulties they pose. For the military, each of these problems, however, has been magnified as strategic warfare has moved into a "fifth generation" characterized by heavy reliance on information and conflict conducted on cyber battlefields.[14] Similarly, for those working in politics, the digital revolution has complicated each of these environmental characteristics. VUCA is here to stay.

For the military, the concept of leadership demands that general officers have the capacity to adapt and function effectively in highly fluid circumstances characterized by these four characteristics. This demands habits of mind outside of those mastered in the carefully structured, hierarchical environment that most junior officers experience early in their careers. The mental agility taught at the war colleges is essential both in warfare and in the highly entrepreneurial, fluid environment of political life. We would add and emphasize the essential component of courage needed to act in the face of such a confusing, nebulous environment. All of these same skills are essential to strategy making in the political world. The author once heard Jack Valenti, the longtime head of the Motion Picture Association of America and a highly regarded—and highly paid—political manager observe, "Not once in my forty years working in Washington and advising eight Presidents, did I ever hear a President say 'Jack, I have all the information I need to make this decision.' Not once." Yet presidents must act.

Two criticisms of the VUCA analysis are pertinent to its application in politics. First, although they are writing about management in business, Bennett and Lemoine point out that, when it comes to using this schematic as a practical matter, the overall concept may be misleading and even narcotizing. "VUCA conflates four distinct types of challenges that demand four distinct types of responses."[15] The result may be that one just gives up, despairing that she or he should attempt to undertake definitive planning in a VUCA environment. A second critique is that the framework presents an entirely negative viewpoint. Instead, several management theorists have also developed the concept of "VUCA Prime," which flips the concept to focus on the steps needed to confront a tumultuous strategic environment: vision, understanding, clarity, and agility.[16] Of course, what these management authors have done is to take an analytic tool from one circumstance and then criticize it for not being perfectly adaptable to a different realm. Fair enough, but that hardly undermines the utility of this schematic in helping military officers decipher the elements that magnify their confusion and plague decision-making in stressful combat.

VUCA can also serve as a vital framework for understanding the political manager's environment. Suppose, for example, that an environmental organization wishes to advance a government program to restore wetlands degraded by water runoffs from highways and parking lots. The leaders of this organization would confront a strategic environment characterized by VUCA. At first, they might confront considerable uncertainty as to the dimensions of the problem, both in terms of the politics and the level of actual degradation in the land. Progress would depend on the research necessary to reduce this uncertainty.

Given the variety of interests involved, the issue would certainly turn out to be more complex than first envisioned. As they organized activities in different states, they might encounter considerable volatility in political support from state legislators. Then too, public attention and attitudes might shift dramatically depending on news coverage and the salience of other environmental issues. The whole situation demands that these political managers adopt a determined commitment to reduce the level of ambiguity in taking on this fight. Clarifying these problems and reducing their scope would make it easier for them to proceed with their strategy. The mere act of naming these four points of resistance could serve to encourage them to move from strategizing to action. Action could be a tangible first step toward success.

What are the necessary habits of mind that military strategists must possess? First, generals and admirals must be able to remove themselves from the day-to-day minutiae and administrative tasks in order to address factors that will affect their long-term success. They must also be capable of integrating the many distinct forces and functions under their command into a cohesive fighting machine, a task that requires both managing complexity and inspiring subordinates to follow direction. General officers must function effectively in a world of coordinated complexity. The battlefield presents a sea of land mines that can traumatize action. The courage to act in the face of uncertainly without demanding complete information is inevitably and repeatedly required in their job. They must also be able to envision a drawn-out sequence of moves and countermoves as they and the enemy act and interact.

As many studies of leadership have proposed, those directing an organization must be able to focus continually on the overall objective, and they must be able to communicate persuasively to their subordinates a vision of how the world should be. Complex organizations require leaders—both military and political—to be skilled at managing the personalities under them. They must bring about coordinated attention by subordinates to the overall mission. At the same time, they need to avoid micromanaging. Large, complex organizations require leadership that can strike an appropriate balance between direction, coordination, and control of the manifold separate components, on the one hand, and grant them the flexibility necessary to respond to conditions on the ground, on the other.

An instructive example from campaign politics occurred in the 1976 campaign for the Democratic nomination for president by Senator Lloyd Bentsen of Texas. The headquarters developed an elaborate, linear programming model of the actions and tasks to be completed by each state-level organization. The model specified important deadlines for achieving such essentials as hitting specified fundraising goals, hiring staff, and opening regional storefronts for campaign volunteers. The computer at the national headquarters would initiate weekly prompts to remind the state-level staff of these goals and timetables. Political reporters deemed Oklahoma, a neighboring state to Texas, as a "must win" set of caucuses for the senator from Texas. Unfortunately for the campaign, the political manager charged with running the Oklahoma campaign learned that if he simply responded affirmatively to those annoying prompts generated by headquarters, the computer would stop bugging him about incomplete tasks. As the date of the caucuses neared, the national staff arrived in Oklahoma expecting all the necessary groundwork to have already been laid for an effective statewide effort to bring voters to the caucuses. They found little or nothing had actually been prepared for them. When Bentsen did poorly in his neighboring state, journalists interpreted it as a major setback and the campaign folded shortly thereafter. The lesson? Delegation of authority requires monitoring and confirmation by the managers in overall charge, whether political or military.

Whether one is engaged in a policy fight, an effort to shape public opinion, or an election campaign, the excitement of rapid decision-making, the perceived importance of the work, the need to act in the face of uncertainty, and the mixture of personal ambitions and social rationale all serve to drag one's attention down to the daily hurly-burly of politics. The work, the battle, is so enticing, so important, so all encompassing, that it is almost impossible to keep one's ultimate goals firmly in mind. Thus, tactical considerations quickly drive out strategic calculation.[17] It takes a disciplined mind to focus on the higher order and longer-term problems, but this is vital to strategic thinking.

Beyond the need to be able to thrive, take responsibility, and act in an ambiguous environment, the military demands of its general officers a complementary understanding that goes to the heart of both warfare and politics. Both generals and political managers must be able to put themselves into the mind of their adversary. As Edward M. Collins summarizes Clausewitz, in every conflict "each of the adversaries mobilizes all of its means and resources in an effort to overthrow its enemy completely and to avoid being overthrown."[18] War and politics are contests in which calculating, purposeful minds compete to impose their will on others. Opposition is so central in these two arenas that—as argued in Chapter 2—the word "strategy" should be reserved for situations of direct conflict. Overt opposition means that, to prosper in this environment, one must be able to understand the likely actions of a competing individual or group. That in turn requires an ability to discern the motives, abilities, options, and thinking of the opponent.[19]

Political managers can also learn from the military that engaging in a conflict should progress through several orderly stages. First, in addition to assessing explicitly the resources at one's disposal, equal effort and attention should be directed toward those of the opponent. This is simply because it is so much easier to concentrate on actions that we can undertake, so we tend to give short shrift—or ignore completely—the capabilities of the enemy. After all, the pressures to act, to make a decision, to employ one's resources, to do something even in a state of bewilderment are substantial. All this forces attention to our own problems and away from the opponent. That is a serious mistake; failure to consider what the enemy can do—or might do—can be the wellspring from which defeat pours forth.

Classically, military intelligence serves to alert generals to the strengths of the enemy: raw troop strength, battlefield position, array of force components, weapon systems, stockpiles of ordinance, logistical support, and so on. Where intelligence about the enemy's force structure is extensive and accurate, the task of estimating its employment may not be all that difficult. If we know that his armored divisions are full strength and capable, for example, we can imagine multiple ways in which they might be employed in battle. If we know the number of his air-to-ground attack helicopters and fighter planes, we can structure our own ground and aerial forces to meet that challenge. All this, brought together in the mind of the astute strategist, helps to create a picture of what the opponent is capable of doing and what his or her options are. But this does not yet yield an assessment of what the enemy will do, just what he could do. For want of this intelligence, battles can be lost. Consider, for example, General Robert E. Lee marching into the battle of Gettysburg in 1863 during the American Civil War without the essential intelligence as to the Union's troop strength and positioning normally available to him through the reports of General Jeb Stuart's cavalry. Lee committed himself to battle even while largely ignorant of the forces arrayed against him. This critical lack of information contributed to the subsequent battlefield loss, and that loss arguably constituted a turning point for the whole war.

Sun Tzu, the great Chinese strategist, was an avid and repeated proponent of spies who would allow the general to understand how the enemy could deploy his troops. "They are a ruler's treasures... No relationship is closer than with spies; no rewards are more generous than those given to spies, no affairs are more secret than those pertaining to spies... There are no areas in which one does not employ spies."[20]

For much of human history, nations have spied on each other in many ways—behavior that transcends the bounds of propriety in civil politics. Electronic bugging of the opponent's headquarters, as occurred during the Watergate scandal, or dispatching a loyal supporter to work in the adversary's offices can, if discovered, create a serious setback for those working within democratic institutions.[21] This is because in democratic politics the combatants are not alone in their struggle; ultimately, they are competing to win over the minds of the citizens. Substantial portions of the citizenry will have alternative sources of information and perspective. News coverage will indirectly shape public opinion. While the combat is raging between the politicians, organizations built around a particular interest will be communicating with their supporters. All this means that overly aggressive behavior can be counterproductive if the public comes to believe that the norms of conduct have been breached. Whether the battlefield is an election contest or a legislative policy fight, the struggle for dominance is not fought by the combatants alone. The roster of voters or the attentive public will be the ground upon which victory or defeat is determined. Ultimately, democracy means that citizens sit in judgment over the ideas and conduct of political combatants. Notwithstanding

Clausewitz's reminder that wars are essentially political struggles; win, lose, or draw, conflicts on the battlefield are regularly decided by force of arms between the two adversaries. By contrast, in domestic, democratic politics, victory and defeat must be secured within the opinions and behavior of citizens that serve as both active participants and ultimate deciders of the dispute.

Even though information is essential to political strategy, limits do exist that circumscribe the pursuit of intelligence in public life. Contemporary political managers cannot make use of spies because journalists and voters alike deem their use in civil politics to be unscrupulous and unacceptable. Nevertheless, political strategists need to ascertain as much as possible about their opponent's capabilities. Information will allow them to assess carefully the resources and options that the opponent has at his or her disposal. Legitimate means of securing useful information include efforts such as survey research, door-to-door canvassing of voters, requesting logs from TV stations for political advertising, and detailed scrutiny of the opponent's public record. This thinking will lead naturally to a second stage in the cycle of preparation, creating a number of scenarios or "what if" considerations. How might the other side deploy those resources? What if she takes this course of action? And, further, if she opts to undertake a given action, how should we respond? Skillful military commanders and political managers will consider various complex actions that the opponent might choose and seek to work out in advance how each of those possibilities could be countered.

Making a decision on how to act constitutes a second stage of strategic behavior. Emulating the military suggests that one should plan on the basis of possibility but execute on the basis of probability. That is, assessing the capabilities of the opponent is a necessary but insufficient step in the logic of conflict. What one's competitor is *likely to do* yields a different calculation than what she is capable of doing. Accordingly, a shrewd political manager should move to counter how the opponent is most likely to act but should also be ready to react to her other capabilities.

Predicting how an enemy will act can be speculative.[22] Intelligence gathering, on the one hand, should be fact based, whereas moving into projection means one's analysis has become conjectural, on the other. Studying the opponent's past moves—especially those that have yielded him success—is one means of trying to predict his action. Military commanders have also drawn up psychological profiles of opposing leaders in the hopes of predicting what they are likely to select out of the range of actions they could initiate.[23] Ideally, if one is a more careful strategist than the opponent, these predictions will allow the political manager, like a general in the field, to meet the enemy head on. This should not be read, however, as to discount the value of scenario planning, because if the opponent chooses a different, surprising path, then hopefully our side has already thought through how we will respond to this less likely move.

While political managers should be extremely cautious about employing spies, they can, nevertheless, mobilize several tactics designed to give them greater intelligence and facilitate predicting the opponent's likely behavior. We refer to the uses of opposition research, which plays a significant role in both campaign and lobbying politics. Political managers who specialize in "oppo" develop a complete picture of the opponent's public record to assess his capabilities and anticipate his actions. They may even work in the gray area of probing deeply into his private life, including divorce proceedings, personal finances, and credit records, looking for material that can be used in attacks. These same tactics extend into fights over public policy. Opposition research firms take on corporate and interest group clients seeking information on individuals and groups that oppose their policy objectives. Sending observers to monitor the competition's speeches and comments has become acceptable, even expected, as long as the meetings monitored are open to the public. A researcher digging into the opponent's activity on social media may dig up a wealth of material on the words, actions, or values advanced by the adversary.

In the latter half of the twentith century, B. H. Liddell Hart published several editions of *Strategy*, a volume that quickly became the classic treatise on military strategy.[24] In reviewing the history of warfare from the early Greeks to the Arab-Israel War of 1948–49, Hart reached one overwhelming conclusion, namely that success was frequently the result of what he called the "indirect approach."[25] Instead of a frontal assault, battles and wars were almost always won by taking a less obvious method of engagement. In other words, subterfuge and trickery outweighed troop strength. Hart's conclusion duplicates the advice given 2,500 years earlier in *The Art of War* by Sun Tzu:

> All warfare is based on deception. Hence, when able to attack, we must seem unable; when using our forces, we must seem inactive; when we are near, we must make the enemy believe we are far away; when far away, we must make him believe we are near.[26]

Applying this guidance to political management requires a degree of caution on the part of the contemporary political manager. On the one hand, the surprise factor, which deception is certainly designed to achieve, can successfully throw the political opponent off balance and upset his plans. But only rarely can such conflicts in politics be isolated to the two actors alone: protagonist and opponent. Given that the name of the game is to build political support, citizens constitute a critically important third party to every struggle between political combatants. They sit in judgment over the rival interest groups' proposed legislation, characteristics, and conduct in the public sphere. The number of citizens who ultimately decide a political conflict may be large, diverse, and relatively uninformed or they may be small in number, homogeneous, and knowledgeable. But in either case, fights in democratic politics, by their very nature, cannot be isolated from public judgment.

For another of his major conclusions, Hart turned to no less a student of warfare than Napoleon Bonaparte, citing his dictum that in war "the moral is to the physical as three to one."[27] In contemporary terms, Napoleon's wisdom argues that the psychological dimension of conflict between two armies outweighs the concrete array of forces that each side brings to battle. Morale and mental stability count for more than do planes and tanks. It follows that combatants should carefully monitor their own psychological balance and well-being—as well as that of their supporters and allies—all the while seeking to disrupt the stability of their opponents' mindset. Head games can be a critically important aspect of competition, no less in political fights than in warfare. For example, American television stations require three things of political candidates wishing to advertise on their broadcast: they must reserve the time, deliver the ad to be run, and pay for the time upfront.

Issue campaigns supporting legislation pending in Congress can take advantage of the fact that advertising reservations become public. By reserving a large number of broadcast times, an act becomes observable by interest groups on the other side of the fight. If they fail to provide an ad or to deposit the money, however, the ad does not actually run. But the adversary may be fooled into spending down their own budget by buying TV time to counter an ad that never appears.

To cite another example, after the 1993 election campaign for governor of New Jersey, Ed Rollins, the Republican campaign manager, alleged to journalists that they had given money to Black ministers to discourage voting for the Democrat.[28] All hell broke out among journalists and political managers among the Democrats. Then, when threatened by possible prosecution, Rollins retracted this statement, saying he was only seeking to play "head games" with James Carville, the campaign manager for the Democratic candidate. Rollins knew that the two of them would be facing off again the next year in a Pennsylvania Senate race and hoped that Carville would think he would employ the same tactic there. Unfortunately for Mr. Rollins, because of the furor in the aftermath of the New Jersey race, he was fired and missed the opportunity to take on Carville a second time.

Another example. During the 1988 race for the Republican presidential nomination, a staffer in the George H. W. Bush campaign named Jim Pinkerton was given responsibility for vetting potential vice-presidential candidates. He hired staff and began reviewing a list of potentials. Unbeknown to Pinkerton, a parallel effort headed by Robert Kimmit, a Washington lawyer, had the ear of Bush, himself the vice president at the time. The announcement that Bush had selected Senator Dan Quayle was a complete surprise to Pinkerton. He compared his work in the public spotlight to Operation Fortitude, the fictitious decoy maneuver designed to mislead the Germans into thinking the invasion of Europe would take place at Calais.[29] Pinkerton's operation proved to be a smokescreen designed to confuse the Democrats as to the composition of the team they would confront in the fall campaign.

Liddell Hart's research also convinced him that most successful combat operations were the result of the concentration of military force. Assessments of strength—your own and those of your opponents—should allow one to direct any comparative advantages upon the opponent's weakness. The success of this approach can be magnified if dispersed forces are able to converge rapidly to produce a concentrated force that can be focused on the dispersed opposing forces. Hart argues "concentration of strength against weakness depends on the dispersion of your opponent's strength, which in turn is produced by a distribution of your own that gives the appearance, and partial effect of dispersion."[30] In short, one way to bring concentrated force against an opponent's dispersed weakness is to intentionally spread your own forces and then, when the opponent has distributed his strengths in response, quickly consolidate your powers into a coordinated attack.

It does not take too much analogous reasoning to understand that a candidate might launch appeals to a wide array of social groups before narrowing down to one key demographic or that she might raise an entire range of policy issues before zeroing in on one major difference with her opponent. Until the battle is fully joined, one should endeavor to keep the opponent guessing as to the grounds on which one will mount the principal attack. In this case, for the political manager, the "grounds" for attack could equally apply to the issues raised during a public policy fight, or to the narrow segments of citizens that may be brought to support the cause, or to the selected group of politicians who hold power over the issue, or even to the physical territory in which one will mount major efforts to build support.

This back-and-forth, action-and-reaction cycle that characterizes so much of strategic thinking in the military has prompted Edward Luttwak to propose that a paradoxical logic pervades the conduct of war.[31] He argues, for example, that if a general can choose between two routes toward engaging the enemy—one short and easy, the other long and difficult—he should choose to attack through the latter. The enemy will be expecting him to take the easier way because the harder road will mean a greater expenditure of effort and more dislocation in the fighting strength of the army that arrives on the battlefield. So, the enemy's expectations dictate that the hard route becomes the best route; the less desirable becomes the more desirable. Paradoxically, the defender should concentrate on confronting that tactic directly while leaving the easy route relatively weakly defended. But the defender must be wary of the possibility that the attacker will comprehend the weakened defense of the easier route and exploit that opportunity. The logic of action and reaction choreographs for us a scenario of two opponents, facing each other, endeavoring to predict the opponent's move, each trying to outthink the other. Each may be waiting for the other to make the first move.

If political managers were alone on the battlefield, Luttwak's analysis might apply equally well to struggles in politics. In fact, one can imagine circumstances in which competition in domestic politics can be isolated to the two actors and kept out of sight to the public. Negotiations behind closed doors could be one such arena.[32] But these conflicts are likely to be rare given that the major battles in politics are fought over the attention and support of citizens. The processes of public communication and persuasion are so burdensome, the effort needed to penetrate the consciousness of citizens so taxing, that politicians are likely to find building the easier and straightforward attack to be more fruitful. Thus, in democratic systems political managers are predictably likely to surrender surprise in order to achieve effectiveness. Deviousness can be carried too far in public life.

Having surveyed centuries of armed conflict, B. H. Liddell Hart provides a succinct chapter[33] in which he offers, "a few truths of experience seem so universal, and so fundamental, as to be termed axioms." Here, in condensed form, is his direct advice for military strategists (italics in the original):

1. *Adjust your end to your means*. . . . [T]he beginning of military wisdom is a sense of what is possible . . .
2. *Keep your object always in mind*, while adapting your plan to circumstances.
3. *Choose the line (or course) of least expectation*. . . . . [W]hat course is it least probable he will foresee or forestall.
4. *Exploit the line of least resistance* . . .
5. *Take a line of operation that offers alternative objectives.* For you will thus put your opponent on the horns of a dilemma, which goes far to assure the chance of gaining one objective at least . . .

6. *Ensure that both plan and dispositions are flexible—adaptable to circumstances.* Your plan should foresee and provide for a next step in case of success or failure . . .
7. *Do not throw your weight into a stroke whilst your opponent is on guard.*
8. *Do not renew an attack along the same line (or in the same form) after it has once failed.*

Much, but not all, of this advice can be applied to the world of politics. There can, however, be other dangers in the field of politics that may not apply to warfare. Consider, for example, the difficulties that would be incurred by a political candidate who had consistently supported abortion rights for women but then (following axiom number 3) suddenly announced a change of heart. That act would certainly disrupt his opponent's plans, but it would most likely also significantly unsettle his own support base.

Of course, we can find many examples in which the advice of doing the unexpected does hold true in politics. Hillary Clinton's senate campaign in 2000 in New York State provides one instructive example. Initially, she thought she would be running against Rudy Giuliani, a popular Republican mayor of New York City. Given that his support from within the city would be stronger than most Republicans could hope to achieve, Ms. Clinton started by giving much more attention to parts of upstate New York where Democrats had traditionally fallen short. When Giuliani announced he was dropping out of the campaign for a variety of personal and political problems, the Republican nomination went to Congressman Rick Lazio from Long Island. The Clinton-Lazio contest took on the character of a more traditional "R versus D" inter-party competition in the Empire State. In that context, Ms. Clinton's unexpected efforts in upstate yielded a margin that gave her a more substantial victory than would be expected for a New York City Democrat running against a Long Island Republican.[34]

Another, more visible and more consequential about-turn, occurred when Richard Nixon, the American president and long-term anti-Communist crusader, suddenly reversed course and made a historical visit to China. By that surprise initiative, the United States was able to change the strategic posture of the Cold War, confronting the Soviet Union with a potential potent alliance of the United States and China.

Adroit political managers will discern other ways in which Hart's axioms apply aptly in specific politics situations. Here, I will only make one additional observation, drawing upon his last point of advice. Certainly, when a line of attack has been tried and failed, continuing on the same course might be seen as futile. After all, the opponent will be alerted to this approach and will be prepared to defend against a renewal. But what constitutes "failure" can be subject to dispute. Whether one is taking about grassroots lobbying or a referendum fight, modern politics demands significant repetition before a message begins to infiltrate and shape the thinking of voters. An advocacy campaign that does not bear much fruit in the early going should not be abandoned just at the point at which the electorate is starting to get the message.

The military's approach to strategy—in this case the US Air Force—offers another concrete idea adaptable to the political environment. In 1995, Colonel John Boyd (USAF) publicly released a set of teaching slides in which he presented his ideas on rapid decision-making during an engagement with enemy pilots.[35] Boyd proposed teaching pilots to employ an "OODA loop," an acronym that stands for a sequence of stages that one should go through in the midst of aerial combat. The approach has subsequently been applied more generally in the conduct of warfare. Boyd proposed a cycle of Observe, Orient, Decide, Act, and then loop back to the Observe stage. To be unconscionably brief, Boyd's instruction was meant to drill into the pilot's brain a sequence of actions to the point that they would become automatic. Once in combat, a pilot should first *observe* the whole environment of the conflict including the actions of the enemy; then *orient* himself to that situation by filtering the observation through cultural norms and prior experiences; then *decide* what to do in response to that interpretation of the incoming data; and then *act* upon that decision. The next and crucial step was to shift right back to observing the situation that had changed as a result of one's act. Notice that the first crucial step, "observe," brings the actions of the enemy squarely to the pilot's attention. Boyd wanted his student pilots to go through this decision loop as fast as possible in an attempt to make quick decisions and to act more rapidly than the opponent. By doing so, he hoped the pilot would get inside the enemy's own decision loop causing confusion and disrupting his decision process. By continually changing the situation faster than the opponent could process the situation, pilots could stay on the offensive, constantly attacking with an ever-adapting strategy. In aerial combat, faster action should result in American pilots making tighter loops to get behind the enemy, the best position for shooting down the other plane.

The import of Boyd's strategic contribution is that it provides a concrete method for maintaining the initiative in warfare. The principle is the same in political engagements; the side that moves faster and commandeers the initiative is likely to prevail. Forcing one's opponents onto the defensive and making them react to an environment that one is constantly changing proves to be a decisive strategy in many situations. Yet, it is important to keep in mind that politics, like warfare, needs to be fought as a continuous, ever-changing loop. Completing one cycle does not mean enjoying a small victory; it should mean leaping ahead into the next round of decision-making. Only then, can one maintain the initiative.

We conclude this discussion with a pair of ideas on war and politics drawn from the nuanced thinking that Karl von Clausewitz brought to leadership in warfare. He is justifiably famous for his twin notions that affect the conduct of war: "friction" and "fog." Friction denotes all those little resistances that inexorably creep into the implementation of any plan in a complex organization. The examples are legion. Supplies don't arrive on time; an order is misunderstood; helicopters staging in the desert get sand in their motors; stomping through a field of mud exhausts the knights marching in full body armor to meet the enemy; a convoy must proceed at the speed of the slowest ship; a division commander decides that, since night is falling, he'll make the attempt to capture a strategic hill in the morning only then to discover that the enemy has seized the opportunity to reinforce the hill's defenses. The same chafing problems will occur in political management. The communications team wants to revise the talking points put out by the policy shop; the brochures do not arrive back from the printer as promised; the paid ad doesn't run where designated; the field staff starts to canvas on the wrong street; a typo changes the meaning of a press release; a volunteer team doesn't show up when planned. These are all tactical annoyances that can add up to complicate strategic plans. They necessitate that the political strategist must allow some contingency into the execution of the most carefully conceived blueprint.

Clausewitz's other concept of the "fog of war" confronts the political manager with a similar implementation problem, only partially extrapolated by the VUCA delineation.[36] In the heat of battle, confusion, lack of information, and fear become disorienting. The importance of the values at stake in domestic politics leads participants to devote eighteen-hour days to the struggle, only to fight exhaustion and the deterioration of judgment that it brings. The number of variables at play and their interrelationships create a complex environment that cannot ever be fully comprehended. Our commitment to a "just cause" transforms the opposition in our minds into a conniving, deceitful, unscrupulous, band of wrong-headed thugs. Their bad behavior justifies our getting lost in the passion of the moment and transcending the bounds of propriety we would normally observe. All these factors are inevitable in politics. They cloud our judgment and, yet, understanding and indeed tolerating them must be part of the political manager's strategic mindset. They also mean that contemporary political leaders must be comfortable operating in a highly uncertain environment. Like Clausewitz, our advice here is akin to shouting, "Get used to it; it's inevitable!" That's not extremely helpful, I realize, but there it is.

A famous quote has been handed down from Clausewitz, translated variously as "War is an act of violence pushed to its utmost bounds" or as "War is an act of violence which in its application knows no bounds." A crude synopsis of strategic advice resulting from this observation suggests that the first rule of warfare is to do whatever you have to in order to win. Here we come to a fundamental divide between the military combat and civil, democratic politics. In politics, strategists have ethical boundaries that should not be transcended in the pursuit of victory. There are laws that regulate their conduct. There are norms to be upheld and expectations of other actors and the citizenry that govern the behaviors of those engaged in civil politics. If you must, consider these as indicators of the long-term consequences of bad short-term efforts to win at all costs. That is, improper behavior may be counterproductive in the long run. But I think they are more than that. Political managers have an obligation to maintain and strengthen the institutions that provide for democratic politics. It is perilous to assume that democracy is firmly established in perpetuity; instead, it is always a work in progress. As we will argue in Chapter 9, each generation of political actors has a duty to the future to safeguard the norms of civil conduct that make democratic politics possible.

The Essence of Military Strategy

1. Military conflict and politics should be thought of as two ends of a spectrum of coercion. Just as Clausewitz saw warfare as a projection of politics onto a domain of violence, so too is politics a projection of war onto a domain of civility.
2. Strategic thinking, an essential element of military leadership, starts with a focus on long-term, higher-level goals and the necessity of bringing multiple units into coordinated action. In both war and politics, it is essential to rise above the day-to-day tactical complications and focus upon larger and enduring objectives.
3. Military campaigns and civil politics should be planned on a calculation of the enemy's capabilities but executed on the basis of the probability of his actions. Reliance upon predictability of the opponent's movements, moreover, focuses one's attention squarely on the aspects of the conflict that one can control and those that one cannot.
4. Both military leaders and political managers must learn to function in the face of substantial volatility, uncertainty, complexity, and ambiguity. Moreover, minor flaws in execution—as in Clausewitz's notion of "friction"—can add up to major shortcomings in implementation. Vagueness under circumstances one faces—"fog of war"—creates an environment of uncertainty surrounding most conflicts. While a VUCA analysis may serve to reduce somewhat a pervading sense of indecision, ultimately one must act in the face of confusion and lack of necessary information.

4
Strategic Planning

> Failing to plan is planning to fail.
> —Benjamin Franklin

In its most common conception, strategy is an exercise in planning. At a minimum, planning involves bringing together four critical elements: a precise statement of the objective to be achieved, the available resources that one can deploy in pursuit of the objective, actions one can take in hopes of attaining one's goals, and the assumptions upon which the proposed actions rest. These elements can help the strategist undertake a variety of conceptual tasks from rational allocation of resources, to scenario building, to directing attention to events that will take place over a long-term horizon.

To start with a definition of strategic planning rooted in military theory, Carl von Clausewitz offers us this conception of strategy: ". . . the art of the employment of battles as a means to gain the object of war. In other words, strategy forms the plan of war, maps out the proposed course of the different campaigns which compose the war, and regulates the battles to be fought in each."[1]

This definition complements that of Fred Nickols, a business consultant, who notes, "Strategy is the bridge between policy or high-order goals on the one hand and tactics or concrete actions on the other."[2] Arthur Chandler, Jr., "who gave the concept of strategy prominence in a business setting," tied his perception of strategy closely to the notions of planning and implementation.[3] For Chandler, strategy determined "the basic long term goals and objectives of an enterprise and the adoption of courses of action and the allocation of resources necessary for carrying out these goals."[4] Thus, thinking and plotting long term appear to be central ideas of strategic planning. While there is more involved than these ideas, they provide the core of a rudimentary conception of strategy in the sense of planning.

The Nature of Planning in Political Settings

Political managers must be mindful of a trio of difficulties that can limit the effectiveness of planning. First, consider the fact that planning should include both the resources one can bring to a political skirmish and the options one has for employing those resources. Thinking strategically can then include linking propositions as to how the employment of those resources will lead to preferred outcomes. "If I do 'X,' then 'Y' should result." These are predictive and contingent statements of cause and intended outcome. As such, they may be inaccurate. They are, moreover, grounded all too often in assumptions that are unexamined, a fact that should give the strategist pause. To plan effectively, the strategist must pierce his own logic and explicitly surface the assumptions that underlie his thinking.

Second, planning tends to focus attention on the resources, options, and tactics that the planner can control. It drives one to ask, "What am I going to do?" As such, planning tends to blind one to the equally important actions and reactions of an opponent. Where strategy should be a cerebral activity, planning may push heavily toward action. In addition, political managers must always be vigilant not to get so carried away with their own actions that they are surprised by unanticipated and unexpected actions of competitors.

Bill Greener, a successful, veteran political consultant, describes an approach to strategic planning that leads us to consider a third issue that can limit successful planning. His view of strategy is defined as follows: "Strategy is the road map of how you are going to get from where you are now to where you want to be. It's a statement of how you're going to win."[5] Given that Greener's job is to help his clients win elections, we might wonder if he passes too quickly over the need to specify precisely the defined objective. But Greener readily accepts the fact that just declaring that the goal is "to win the election" is entirely inadequate. Instead, he argues that campaign strategy begins with a clear and operational goal that delineates how many votes will be needed from what parts of the constituency and from which demographic groups. Then, his roadmaps specify which appeals, issues, policies, and/or proposals will motivate performance by enough voters from those demographic and regional groupings to constitute that winning number. Frequently, political managers give too little careful thought to defining exactly what they hope to accomplish. So, our third lesson is that goals should be concrete and explicitly delineated.

Strategic planning is essential in all arenas of politics. There are, however, several benefits to observing that process through the lens of an election campaign. Campaigns are temporary organizations; they come into being to contest a specific election. Because campaign organizations have a start, an execution, and an ending, they offer strategists opportunities to plan before the action really gets underway, to work toward a definite conclusion, and to assess after the fact the reasons for defeat or victory. In so doing, they provide insights as to internal processes that can be more difficult to perceive in organizations engaged in policy fights. In the latter, strategy must be developed in the middle of a flow of events, pressures, problems, prior successes, and partial outcomes. In addition, struggles over public policies are rarely static. They evolve and endure. From the complicated decision-making of a legislature, the conflict can move to the executive and, often, to the courts. Losers in one round can regroup and retool their strategy, carrying the battle back to the legislature. And so, it becomes as difficult for observers to call an insightful halt as it is for participants to plan in the midst of a torrent of response-demanding events. Clausewitz argued for much the same idea as follows: "Lastly, even the final decision of a whole war is not always to be regarded as absolute. The conquered state often sees in it only a passing evil, which may be repaired in after times by means of political combinations."[6]

While election campaigns provide a focus for observations, we should acknowledge the differences between campaigns contesting primary elections and those seeking to win in a general election. Political managers involved in primary campaigns must keep in mind the dynamics of the general election contest that will follow if their candidate wins the primary. Completely alienating supporters of the primary opponent could weaken their candidate in the general election. In addition, they should also be mindful that policy positions taken during the campaign—primary or general—can subsequently complicate the tasks of governing for the winning candidate. Of course, campaign managers must consider all that has happened in the past, but they initiate their activity and assemble their organization de novo. They do so in the knowledge that, ultimately, there will come an endpoint. When that happens—win or lose—everyone involved will move on to other things. This remains true even though the permanent campaign has become a reality in the United States.[7] To some extent, therefore, victories are temporary.

In countries with multiparty systems, the sequence of elections often creates similar dynamics. Election laws mandate that to be declared elected, the winner must receive a strong plurality, often a majority. If no one passes the threshold in the first round, a runoff election occurs between the top two candidates. As in American primary elections, political managers must be aware of how their actions in the first round will affect their candidate's chances in the subsequent election and in governing after the election. For the top two vote-getters, the campaign rolls on. But ultimately, the runoff election takes place and the campaign organizations fold.

In the arena of elections, political managers can undertake strategy formulation and actual execution as discrete processes. The same is not true for efforts in issues management or legislative politics. There, political managers confront an ongoing flow of events, competition, and partial victories or setbacks, such that management occurs within a stream of interactions that is inevitably continuous. Strictly speaking, campaign strategists, in contrast, do not have to plan while simultaneously managing an ongoing situation. The fact that most campaigns are temporary and end once the vote is counted also allows political managers to assess the success of their planning retrospectively. The goal has been achieved or not, and, while life goes on, closure has been obtained and the campaign as a discrete entity has a concrete result against which to judge its efforts at planning. In some ways, this simplifies the task of strategic planning, for there should be time to scheme beforehand and time to reflect and assess afterward.[8]

In reality, much of life takes place within a constant stream of events. Accordingly, those working in issue politics may have difficulty finding a starting point from which to initiate a calculated strategy. Particularly in the politics of governing, the flow of events and incoming information may overwhelm their capacity to plan. In contrast, election campaigns—with their initiation, implementation, and definite conclusion—provide insights to the planning process precisely because they allow us to isolate the planning process within the stream of events.

While we take advantage here of the unique characteristics of campaigns, this should not blind political managers in legislative politics to the necessity of stepping back from the velocity of interactions in political life. Planning demands from them attention to the longterm dynamics of their current situation. Acting within a continuous flow of events, those political managers working in governance must pursue enduring goals that drive their never-ending quest for policy outcomes. They often use the phrase "drinking from a fire hose" to describe their sense of the pace of events that commandeers their attention and the resulting difficulties of carving out the time necessary to the luxury of planning. In other words, the model presented here, based upon election campaigns, may present an ideal that those working in issue politics may find difficult to implement in practice.

In whatever type of political maneuvering the reader finds herself, she needs to appreciate that the best planning may go out the window once implementation starts. An aphorism in military thinking proposes that "plans are great until the first shot is fired." Perhaps this thought derives from the writings of another German theorist of warfare, Field Marshall Helmuth Karl Bernhard Graf von Moltke, who wrote, "No plan of operations extends with any certainty beyond the first contact with the main hostile force."[9] That idea may cause our reader to wonder, if our plans dissolve at the first instance of engagement, what good is all the effort put into creating them? Perhaps General Dwight Eisenhower provided a better perspective: "In preparing for battle I have always found that plans are useless, but planning is indispensable." It is probable that he expressed the same thought on other occasions, for in a pithier version, he is often quoted as saying, "Plans are worthless, but planning is everything."[10]

Undertaken seriously, planning—as distinct from the resulting plan—not only forces one to define precisely what one wishes to achieve, it also prepares one for the employment of available resources in a rational manner. A complete survey of the situation in which one must act should provide an inventory of one's strengths and weaknesses. It should also endeavor to determine how strengths should be deployed and weaknesses minimized. The stages of a rational decision-making process are set out in Table 4.1.

This process may seem to be straightforward and easy to implement. But it does contain a glaring omission. Since strategy in politics must be formulated in the context of being over the opposition, we must calculate the actions of other willful actors. And we cannot assume that our competitor will always be rational. In fact, as Julia Galef points out, rational planning often goes array by assuming that others will also behave rationally.[11]

What benefits should planning deliver to political managers? Before one gets lost in the heat of battle, planning should force a political manager to define her objectives precisely, think through the probable scenarios that will be encountered, assess the resources that will likely be available, estimate the most effective means of employing the resources in hand, develop contingencies for how the confrontation may evolve, and generally prepare psychologically for the conflict at hand. Of course, every political manager will confront a lot of guesswork in making these calculations.

Political managers must guard against two hazards in planning for political combat. First, it bears repeating that they must constantly remember that the planning process unavoidably encourages them to direct their attention toward what they must do to achieve their goals. It drives them to ask questions such as the following: What messages

Table 4.1 Stages of a Rational Decision-Making Process

---

1. Define goals in as much detail as possible.
2. Identify alternative actions that will achieve goals.
3. Calculate consequences (positive and adverse) of each alternative action.
4. Decide most favorable (benefits to costs) possible course.
5. Monitor implementation as actions proceed.
6. Repeat this process.

---

do I want to communicate? What actions will I take? How should I commit my scarce resources? When do I need to make the critical decisions? And when do I need to act? Of course, these questions must be addressed. In fact, they constitute the core process of achieving one's goals. But as a practical matter, these details of planning may push political managers to ignore the actions and responses of competitors. Planning must not blind one to the equally important tasks of assessing the likely actions and reactions of one's opponent. We must always be vigilant not to get so carried away with our own actions that we are surprised by unanticipated and unexpected actions of competitors.

Planning also tends to limit one's attention on "What am I going to do *now*?" The need to act and react can result in a short-term perspective that downplays the greater importance of longer-range strategic decisions. Furthermore, the pressure that planning places on the need for immediate action tends to focus one's attention on the resources, options, and tactics that the planner can control. Often, factors that political managers cannot control will prove to be the more consequential drivers of outcomes. Political managers can certainly work to predict and influence the actions of their competitors, but they cannot control them. Political managers must discipline themselves to think like chess players, envisioning their moves and the opponent's countermoves through several stages of interaction. The American Secretary of Defense, Robert Gates, once identified the three words "And then what?" as the least-asked question in Washington.[12] He was referring to both the absence of thinking about a follow-up plan and the failure to understand how opponents and critics would react.

Given the fact that events are unlikely to unfold exactly as our plan has specified, we should ask again, why we need a plan at all? There are several answers. In the first place, the whole purpose of a plan is to allow one to allocate scare resources more efficiently and effectively. In terms of maximizing impact, those with an explicit plan of attack are likely to be more effective than those who merely "wing it." The planning process requires that one assesses comparatively the costs and benefits of different allocation schemes. Second, if well-conceived, a plan is likely to assist political managers in maintaining a focus at the level of strategy rather than on tactical considerations. In the fog that envelops any sustained political encounter,[13] the tendency is to concentrate on what one can *do* now rather than maintain a firm grip on what one is trying to accomplish. Certainly, day-to-day action often drives out attention to longer-range foresight. A well-conceived plan—particularly one that is written down—would help one concentrate on the overall objective. Third, planning helps to prepare one for the political fights that will occur simultaneously at macro and micro levels. "Macro" refers here to the struggle with external competitors and "micro" to the likely internal conflicts. Within every complex organization, people will have different priorities based on their individual responsibilities to the organization's mission and their perception of the best way to achieve the organization's goals.

Having a plan that has been thought out in advance can serve as an internal peace treaty helping to resolve disputes over power within and direction without. This may not always be successful, especially if it becomes clear that the strategy is not heading the organization toward a clear victory. Nevertheless, having thought out as carefully as possible the goal to be achieved and the means of achieving it will help keep the organization on track during the thick of battle.

An insightful lesson can be drawn from the 2008 presidential campaign of Senator Barack Obama. In his book *Audacity to Win* about Obama's first presidential campaign, David Plouffe, the campaign manager, described how, early in the campaign, the candidate told him that he was under a great deal of pressure from African American politicians to organize more events specifically targeted toward energizing Black voters. He asked Plouffe to divert some funds from the agreed-upon strategy focused on the Iowa caucuses.[14] Plouffe reminded Obama that they were devoting all available resources to the Iowa caucuses as the essential first step to an eventual nomination. They could take resources away from that effort, but it would weaken that first essential step toward victory in the nomination phase of the campaign. Obama backed down; they stayed with the plan and went on to win.

Before delineating the specific elements of a campaign plan, we should start with an urgent plea that the plan be written. To be sure, sloppy thinking is still possible with a written plan, but it is almost inevitable if the plan exists only in one's head. Without a concrete document, it is much easier to allow imprecision to enter the planning with much less implementation, fuzzing the lines as to how resources should be deployed, responsibilities allocated, timing determined, and decisions made. Having to commit the plan to writing should force consideration of these points. In addition, the concreteness of a written plan means that during actual engagement, when one is confronted by uncertainty, the document can be consulted. In short, a plan that has been written down is more likely to be precise and accessible during the heat of battle.

In the context of an election campaign, there is an additional reason why planning is valuable. Since campaigns are transitional entities, relatively short lived yet instrumental in achieving an office, they tend to exhibit an ongoing internal struggle among their staff for power and resources and a position in what may follow the campaign, especially if they win. A written campaign plan should be seen as an agreement as to how the inevitable internal competition will be managed. The document can be referred to when the mad pace of day-to-day events overwhelms strategic thinking. The plan should help to ensure persistency and endurance in the heat of conflict.

Finally, as I will discuss below, a written plan will provide help in making a judgment call as to whether circumstances warrant a dire change of strategy versus a short-term bump in the road that calls for persistence on course. All these benefits are enhanced if the plan is actually written down, in part because one thereby avoids the natural tendency to glide over difficult parts of the logic or areas of uncertainty.

Strategic Elements of Planning in Politics

The first part of a campaign plan provides a strategic analysis, bringing together four critical elements: Situation, Objectives, Assumptions, and Resources. They lead us to propose the acronym SOAR as in Table 4.2 as a useful mnemonic. Each of these dimensions exhibits some unique aspects when applied to democratic politics.

Situation. First, campaigners must assess and describe the strategic situation in which they will be operating. They often do this before deciding to enter the race. Potential candidates should create a campaign plan as a precursor to a decision to run for office. A formal written

Table 4.2 SOARing in Planning

Situation—a summary of the present strategic circumstances.

Objective—a detailed statement of the goal(s) to be achieved.

Assumptions—conditions that will shape the strategic environment.

Resources—critical and limited assets that should be allocated rationally.

---

statement has a great deal more cogency and usefulness than a half-hearted informal discussion of "Should I run?" or "What will I be up against?"

Summing up the strategic situation is much like a SWOT analysis that businesses and other organizations frequently use as an aid in decision-making. That analysis facilitates assessment of one's environment by explicitly considering four elements: Strengths, Weaknesses, Opportunities, and Threats.[15] Evaluating one's strengths directs one's attention to those factors that give an organization an advantage over its competitors, while under "weaknesses" one would list factors that put it at a disadvantage. These two dimensions direct one's attention to factors internal to the campaign organization—how many staff members are there, how much money has the campaign raised, does the campaign have the support of their political party apparatus in terms of endorsements and funds, etc.? These elements should be measured directly against the strengths and weaknesses of the other players in the game. They should not be compared against past campaigns, campaigns for other seats in other regions, or anything other than the challenge at hand.

Opportunities and threats, on the one hand, are external to the organization. Explicitly considering possible opportunities serves to nudge one's thinking toward actions in pursuit of the campaign's goals. In assessing threats, on the other hand, look for dangers that could harm the organization or stand in the way of accomplishing its goals. Because these include actions that competitors or opponents might take, it is a smart move to turn the SWOT analysis around and look at the situation from the opponent's viewpoint. What would be the effect of your opponent unexpectedly receiving, for example, the endorsement of a former president who should be supporting your campaign? Then too there are possible threats—like natural disasters, riots, or sudden adjustments in the economy—that can materialize unpredictably in the general environment. While these types of risk are neither under your control nor that of your opponent, they can certainly affect the competitive environment you are confronting. Therefore, they need to be included within your situational analysis.

Examining the opportunities involves identifying different scenarios through which the organization may seek competitive advantage. If you have a clearly defined objective in mind, there may be multiple paths toward achieving your goal. In some respects, these opportunistic scenarios lie across the divide between strategy and tactics, given that they are likely to be complex composites of multiple tactics.[16] Identifying opportunities that one might capitalize upon brings with it optimism about what your campaign might be able to accomplish.

In elective politics, with its overt, winner-take-all competition, a SWOT analysis should include assessing the strengths and weaknesses of one's opponent. Campaigners have long used consultants who specialize in "opposition research": firms that examine mostly public records to discover any potential political vulnerabilities of those running for office.[17] Such records might include newspaper reports and media appearances, internet posts and tweets, website content and presentation, prior statements and speeches, voting records, lawsuits, legal proceedings and criminal records, bankruptcy proceedings, and the like. The more unscrupulous opposition researchers may dig through its opposition's trash or pay for reporting services that give them access to credit records. Some of them may be akin to computer hackers trying to retrieve online personal information or behavior that can be cast in an unfavorable light.

Careful political managers will hire an independent "oppo" firm to dig up dirt on their *own* candidate or cause. It is better to be prepared for whatever the opponent's opposition research may discover about your candidate or organization. Then these professionals can at least prepare a defense in advance in case that becomes necessary. To be useful in guiding the campaign through the areas of exposure, the plan must be brutally candid. A hard look at the weaknesses and vulnerability of your own candidate is essential. For this reason, the campaign plan will normally be a carefully protected document accessible only to the higher command of the campaign. If it should fall into the hands of reporters or the opposition, not only will the strategy be revealed in advance, but a forthright assessment of the candidate's weaknesses will also give ammunition to journalists and competitors alike.

The major reason for undertaking a careful assessment of the strategic environment is to enable the campaign to consider the various decisions it will have to make, the options it has before it, and the timing of those decisions. To achieve this, the plan should explicitly consider those factors that are under the control of the campaign for they serve to pinpoint the upcoming choices. These dynamic elements would naturally include the messages that the campaign plans to convey to voters, the expenditures of available resources, and the timing of many campaign events. There are also aspects of the evolving contest that cannot be controlled by the campaign. Yet, insofar as it is possible to predict their occurrence, these events need to be comprehended by the campaign plan. Two examples will make the point. Large-scale forces such as the health of the economy or emerging international conflicts will certainly influence the dynamics of an election, but they are well beyond the capacity of most campaigns to predict or influence. To cite another example, if debates between the competing candidates have become a standing expectation of voters and journalists alike, then the campaign may not really be able to opt out. Avoiding a debate in these situations would certainly open a candidate up to an attack.

Even though the campaign plan is intended to map out the strategy to be followed, much of the written document will be constructed at the level of tactics. The essential interplay between tactical considerations and strategic aspirations cannot be overstated. The document must address both, moving back and forth as the two levels interact and shape each other. In general, the sections on goals, the SOAR analysis, assumptions, messages to be communicated, and targeted audiences address the strategic layer of the plan. Tactical considerations address the practical actions the campaign will actually undertake. If, for example, the campaign plans to rely heavily upon one-to-one contacting, that conclusion lies at the level of tactics. But the supporting reasons for banking on personal contacts exist on the strategic plane. The available resources, the complexity of the messages to be communicated, and the nature of the audience all argue for the tactic of door-to-door canvasing. At the same time, the tactic is rooted in a strategic assumption that personal contact will be an effective means of influencing voter choices. The political manager is also assuming that the campaign will be able to attract numerous volunteers to carry out such an approach to voter contact.

Evaluating the critical elements of one's present situation is a natural starting point for campaign planners because it directs their attention to where they are now. And that assessment leads to the next step: a delineation of where they want to go.

Objective(s). The next essential task of strategic planning—in whatever context—involves carefully defining the objective(s) you want to achieve. As Yogi Berra, one of baseball's great characters, once opined, "If you don't know where you are going, you'll end up someplace else." This cannot be emphasized enough. The more effort that goes into clarifying and stating the goal precisely, the easier it will be to measure progress toward it. Equally important, if the goal changes for whatever reason, the strategy for attaining it will also have to change. Establishing a concrete goal is so critical to the entire process of planning that some consider that the first "rule" of successful planning is to get the goal right.

Too often goals are hurriedly drafted or skimpily defined. The same is true of the attention given to delineating the assumptions upon which the analysis rests. Together, these inadequacies in drafting strategic plans should alert the reader to a genuine issue, namely the strong pull of tactical elements. Attention naturally drifts toward action—things that need to be done—and away from the higher-order, strategic considerations. All too often, short-term necessities drive out longer-term dynamics. Successful political management demands that practitioners give due attention to the tasks at the level of strategy. These are going to be cerebral, contemplative rather than action oriented.

In politics, this task is more complicated than it might appear. It is entirely too easy to set a superficial goal such as "winning the election" or "enacting a given piece of legislation" or "shaping public opinion to our advantage." While these might generate the reason for undertaking a strategic fight, they cannot provide the measurability that is necessary to assess progress toward victory. To be an effective guide to action, goals need to be concrete and precisely defined.

For example, in an election contest, the goal should be stated more precisely than just getting the most votes possible or more than the other candidate(s). In contrast, a concrete campaign goal would specify how many votes will be needed to win and where they will come from in terms of geography, demography, and psychographic characteristics. Based upon an analysis of elections in the past and whatever information is available about the voters, political mangers should calculate the number of people who will actually vote in an upcoming election. The campaign's strategic plan should then proceed to provide a statement of how that goal is to be achieved: a specified number of votes, composed of an identified roster of voters, mobilized by an itemized list of tactics of outreach, and persuaded by a specific set of arguments or appeals. Consider the following hypothetical illustration: "The election in this congressional district will be won by mobilizing 225,000 suburban voters including 147,000 base Republican voters combined with 33,000 married independent women ages 30 to 60 years old and 45,000 church-going Catholics energized by an emphasis on the importance of generating wide-spread improvements in education and job growth in order to reduce income disparities and a sharp reduction in street crime." Definitive figures like those in this statement provide benchmarks against which progress can be measured.

Assumptions. The next most important and possibly the most challenging task in strategic planning is to articulate the assumptions upon which the campaign strategy will be built. By their very nature, assumptions tend to be unstated, as they are often rooted in preconceptions or biases. But there is a critical reason for bringing the assumptions to light, even though that may require some incredibly careful and time-consuming thought. Suppose, for example, that the above strategy statement was developed a full year before the election in circumstances in which the congressional district was experiencing stagnant economic growth and high unemployment. An assumption of that hypothetical campaign—one that is unlikely to be articulated—might be that the poor economic conditions would remain true throughout the election. That could be the basis for believing that an emphasis on job creation and street crime would be effective arguments to mobilize the targeted groups of voters. But, if the assumption is unstated, the campaign is likely to miss the logical connection between arguments advanced and electoral support. When nine months before the election, Walmart announces plans to build three new stores in the district bringing with it construction jobs and subsequently retail employment, the job creation argument will lose its potency.

We know that the state of the economy is often a crucial factor shaping voter decisions during an election campaign.[18] But, even for most incumbent officeholders, their ability to affect economic conditions, especially in the short run, is minimal. As a result, they tend to ignore that factor in developing their campaign plan. The import of this observation? One of the important dynamics in careful planning is likely to be ignored. Another critical assumption often gets downplayed or ignored completely. All too frequently we just assume that we know what the opponent is up to. Without giving it much attention, we simply presume that he or she sees the strategic situation as we do and will behave accordingly. This error may reflect our side's biases or disdain with which we view the opponent. Instead, political managers should endeavor to observe the opponent objectively and give careful attention to the options and strategies that the competition is most likely to adopt. It may be helpful to profile the opponent's character and past behaviors and endeavor to view the dynamic of the joint competition through his eyes.

In considering the importance and yet the difficulty of teasing out the assumptions made during planning, we can learn from the words of Donald Rumsfeld, the former US Secretary of Defense:

> [T]here are known knowns; there are things we know we know. We also know there are known unknowns; that is to say we know there are some things we do not know. But there are also unknown unknowns—the ones we don't know we don't know.[19]

Many of the assumptions made by campaign planners fall into a fourth category that Rumsfeld overlooked: unknown knowns. That is, they are known in the sense that we believe them to be true, but, at the same time, they are unknown because they are unstated in our planning. The planner has not bothered to articulate all his beliefs about the looming political conflict. But they are knowns because, although they are unspecified propositions, they are still beliefs about those factors that will have a major impact upon future interactions. As such, they underlie and circumscribe our planning. Yet we avoid taking the time to reflect and articulate them. By formulating these beliefs in a campaign plan, however, we at least make them observable and capable of being monitored. By observation and measurement, they could become "known knowns."

At the very least, careful thinking can result in identifying the "known unknowns" that will be confronted by our campaign. We will be made aware of what we would like to know. Nevertheless, these issues continue to pose a challenge for planning, as they demand more knowledge.

Unless articulated, assumptions lurk in the background of our thinking, blindsiding our efforts at careful strategic planning. They require political managers to recognize the nature of the assumptions that frame the analysis, even though one may not be able to place a value or measurement on these factors. Nevertheless, recognizing that they exist will sharpen the planning. Those elements that may critically affect the strategic plan need to be brought, as much as possible, into the domain of known unknowns. As such, they are less likely to be complete surprises when they suddenly surface during implementation.

Why should it be so critical to spend the time to tease out the assumptions that are implicit in the formation of our strategy? Consider that knowing when to abandon a strategy that is not working must be one of the most critical issues faced by political managers. But, in implementing their plans, political managers may face a critical dilemma. How should they know when it is time to change the plan? Clearly if things are not working out as planned, one should consider altering one's strategy. But abandoning the strategic plan at the first sign of trouble is tantamount to not having a plan at all. Instead, one is reacting to events as they unfold. One is in reactive, not proactive, mode. Yet, sticking with a campaign plan that is not achieving success can put one on the path to losing. Campaigners must bring judgment to bear on this difficult choice.

A strategic plan should be a document intended to guide the political manager through the fog of conflict. Long-term calculations and careful thought as to the significant factors in victory should take precedence over short-term disruptions or setbacks. But persistence in the face of continuing poor performance may be quite foolish and lead to defeat. If the plan is not working, it may be necessary to abandon it. So, how should we draw an appropriate line between being overly reactive versus being overly steadfast? Having a well-defined set of assumptions can help this judgment because if the assumptions are invalid, then it is appropriate to change the plan.

Suppose that an association of banking interests has been trying to convince the Federal Reserve to lower interest rates based on the assumption of a looming economic slowdown. If concern over inflation starts to accelerate in the middle of their pressure campaign, the association will have to advance a different rationale supporting their demand for easy money. Or consider a situation in which an incumbent running for re-election has assumed that the economy will be in decent shape but as the calendar unfolds, it becomes clear that the economy is slowing down markedly. In this case, it should be appropriate to re-evaluate the campaign plan. When the assumptions imbedded in the planning continue to accurately describe the evolving situation, however, it is probably better to stick with the campaign plan even if events in the short term seem to be going south.

Articulating and writing down one's assumptions made while drafting the campaign plan also allows one to monitor whether events are proceeding as predicted. That is, an important reason for explicitly stating the assumptions of a campaign plan is because when assumptions are proved wrong, the strategy may have to be revised. Describing the assumptions of a strategy unambiguously will allow the political manager to monitor whether reality is aligning with forecast and thereby detect whether it is necessary to revise the strategy.

Resources. Five different resources constitute "spines" of the campaign plan in that they run through every aspect of campaign activity. They serve to define the tactical activities that correspond to sections of the plan. In effect, as political managers draft the campaign plan, they are making dispositive strategic choices allocating these precious and limited resources.

Money. In the middle of the 20th century, Jesse Unruh, the powerful Speaker of the California State Assembly, coined a famous quote about the importance of political money: "Money is the mother's milk of politics."[20] He knew that everything a campaign undertakes requires money and that the efforts required in reaching and involving the public are very costly. Even the pursuit of press coverage, which is sometimes referred to as "free media," requires funding for staff salaries, press releases, office space, telephones, and the like. A well-constructed campaign plan will have separate sections on budgeting and fundraising. Strategic planners should realize that the campaign cannot undertake all that it would like because most things will draw from a limited campaign treasury. A campaign plan should not be a wish list of things that would be good to do, but a realistic statement of activities that the campaign can and will undertake. As such, it must confront the hard choices of what can be undertaken.

Geography. Campaigns are rooted in geography for the simple reason that an elective office represents a specific set of communities in which voters reside. The campaign will confront differences among citizens across the relevant territory; differences in a range of social indicators like income, education, race, religion, age; and, in some cases, language and tribal heritage. Party preference and likely vote intentions will vary among these different clusters. Early in the 21st century, journalist Bill Bishop discovered that these clusters were intensifying.[21] Driven by community values, media differentiation, and mobility, Americans were gathering increasingly into like-minded communities. Whether this trend will continue into the future or not, political managers understand that some geographical areas will be more hospitable to their campaign and some more hostile, some areas will be more fertile grounds for reaching swing voters, and some communities will be extremely difficult to mobilize into actual voters.

Normally campaigns adopt a "triage" system, like that employed by battlefield hospitals. They will largely ignore some areas either because either they will perform well for the campaign even without much attention or because they will never be congenial even with a major campaign effort. In between these neglected areas, there will be terrains that require a variety of tactical approaches. Some areas will be appropriate for mobilizing friendly voters and making sure they vote. In other precincts, the campaign will need to direct persuasive messages toward undecided or swing voters, those critically important voters that may make the difference between a winning campaign and a failed effort. In those areas where most voters will be hopelessly committed to another candidate and thus not terribly amenable to persuasion, the campaign plan may call for maintaining a low profile lest its efforts inspire a reaction that could increase turnout of voters for the other candidate.[22]

Accordingly, campaigns will need to plan with these differences in mind: where the candidate will travel, where the staff headquarters will be located, where the campaign will purchase advertising, where volunteers will be sent to knock on doors or display signs, where campaign posters will be placed, and so forth; all these decisions will be shaped by the geography of the constituency.

Time. Because Election Day looms at a definite point in the future, campaigns face a sharp limitation on the amount of time they have at their disposal.[23] Planning the use of time for key campaign personnel—the candidate and family, the important surrogates, the upper-level campaign staff—should be given deliberate attention in the campaign plan. Start by figuring out how much is available. If, for example, there are 100 days to the election and if the candidate needs 7 hours per day for sleep and resting, the campaign has 1,700 hours of her time to allocate. Some of this calculation will be made based on geography. Another division of effort should be made on functional grounds: how much of the candidate's time should be given over to fundraising, meeting with party activists, talking to the media, maintaining staff morale, meeting voters, preparing for debates, and so forth. Adroit campaigners will undertake the same sort of calculations in determining the time constraint for other key campaign personnel. The overall point is that—like money—time is a limited commodity and should be expended according to some logical connection to achieving the goals of the campaign.

Campaign Personnel. How to deploy the available campaign personnel, whether they are paid or volunteers, should also be considered methodically throughout the campaign plan. For example, a campaign that is fully funded by the personal wealth of the candidate can devote less staff time to the tasks of fundraising. A candidate running in a district where television advertising is prohibitively expensive may decide to recruit a robust roster of volunteers needed to conduct a door-to-door canvas of voters. Whatever activities the campaign plans to undertake will require staff to accomplish and recognition that staff time is also limited.

The same kinds of calculations that the plan directed toward money and candidate time should be applied in allocating staff time. There will always be a limited amount of energy in the form of effort available through volunteers and paid workers. Undertaking some tasks will mean not being able to mobilize other efforts. In drafting the campaign plan, political managers should develop a list of priorities in the tasks to be undertaken. Of course, these will be shaped by the calendar of the campaign. For example, it may not be the most effective use of volunteer time to send them out to knock on doors during months when many citizens are on vacation. Note that in other areas of politics such as a fight over legislation, the endpoint might not be so clear cut. Yet, even so, thinking through the demands for allocating staff time is essential.

Campaign Messages. In campaign politics, words are not cheap. Many inexperienced political managers might dispute this, pointing out that, while the above factors of money, staffing, time, etc., are limited quantitative variables, the campaign's messages are more likely to be qualitative. Politics seemingly offers endless opportunities to talk. Talking about one issue does not appear to detract from the campaign's ability to raise other matters. Suffice it to say, however, that there is a sharp limitation upon the number of messages that can be *effectively* communicated during an election campaign. As we will argue in the next chapter, thinking strategically, political managers need to impose message discipline to keep the campaign focused on communicating very few ideas. Most practitioners of political communications believe that with all the media, noise, and commercial messaging competing for the attention of the voters, no more than three messages will penetrate the communications process. A longer list will result in a diffused picture of the candidate or campaign, causing confusion in the minds of voters.

Earlier in this chapter when discussing the need for clearly stated objectives, we provided a one-sentence example of strategy for a fictitious congressional campaign. If the reader will think back to that statement, it should be clear exactly why the messages to be conveyed are a critical component of the campaign plan at the strategic level. In the context of an election campaign that needs a given number of votes to win, persuasive messages define how the campaign hopes to achieve its goal.

Tactical Elements of Planning in Politics

The four elements of a SOAR analysis—Situational assessment, Objectives sought, Assumptions made, and Resources allocated—constitute the strategic layer of the campaign plan. But attention to the allocation of resources also serves to link strategy to the tactical components because every undertaking will implicate the commitment of finite resources. We turn now to the sections of the campaign plan that address activity at the level of tactical operations.

The rest of the campaign plan should normally be composed of a long roster of sections addressing action plans for various activities that the campaign will employ to implement its strategy. We need not discuss some of these sections further as they were presented above in addressing the strategic layer; those that are purely tactical will be discussed briefly below. Table 4.3 contains both the strategic and the tactical elements of the campaign plan.

Voter Analysis. We noted above that the campaign plan should specify a concrete objective based on an analysis of the pool of possible or likely voters. There are several techniques for conducting this analysis. The most common is "past performance targeting," which examines precinct-level data to discover geographical areas that consistently vote for the candidate's party. The campaign wants to know how many votes it can pretty well count on from these polling stations, and what would be the likely yield of a vigorous get-out-the-vote (GOTV) effort. In many races, persuading swing voters can make the difference between winning and losing.

Polling or survey research provides the campaign plan with a different cut at the electorate by allowing political managers to understand the distribution of opinions over demographic groups. Distinct groups

Table 4.3 Sections of a Campaign Plan

Strategic Elements
1. Situation Analysis
2. Objective(s)
3. Assumptions
4. Resources

Tactical Elements
5. Voter Analysis
6. Policy Research
7. Messages and Themes
8. A (Realistic) Fundraising Plan
9. The Campaign Budget
10. Scheduling Considerations
11. Paid Advertising
12. "Earned Media"
13. Online Communications
14. Campaign Staff

such as male versus female voters or married versus single may have marginally different rates of support for the competing candidates. Depending upon the number of voters polled, the campaign analysts can dig down deeper into groups defined by several characteristics. This analysis may point out certain social groups that are up for grabs, making them targets for the persuasive efforts of all candidates. For example, at a certain point in a given campaign, married, suburban women with children in the household may be undecided as to which candidate they are supporting. Often such groups are given catchy, descriptive names, as in this case, "Soccer Moms." Savvy political managers recognize that they are unlikely to win over every voter in these groups. The strategy should be to improve on the margins. If, for example, a campaign can attract some voters from the opponent's base, bringing the opponent's support down to 70 percent from a norm of 85 percent, that can be the fountain from which victory flows.

Analysis of large databases composed of numerous variables can be combined with polling data to improve the sophistication and precision of this analysis. So-called big data allows political managers to aggregate indicators from a variety of sources to create a defined picture of persuadable voters. For example, home and automobile ownership, consumer purchases at the grocery store, magazine or newspaper subscriptions, and the like are all bits of information that can be purchased about citizens and merged into a database with indicators of political behavior and persuasion. The intent of this analytic technique is to narrow the targeted group of voters—targeted either for persuasion or mobilization—down into smaller and smaller clusters, presumably increasing the efficiency of the campaign's efforts.

When citizens use an online search engine to retrieve information, they are also giving away useful information about their interests and needs. Social networking software ties individuals into a fabric of relationships that may be revealing of political preferences. If campaigns can get access to these data—whether by asking supporters to allow them access or, in some case, through commercial vendors—they can become a powerful tool for narrowing the campaign's focus upon a roster of voters that can decide the outcome. This facility became quite controversial in the aftermath of the 2016 US presidential elections. Back in 2008, the Obama campaign had requested that their online supporters grant them access to their contacts list and their roster of friends on Facebook so that they could ask those same supporters to follow up by communicating with and trying to motivate their friends to support Obama. By 2016, the Trump campaign had carried this one step further by hiring a firm, Cambridge Analytica, that had obtained a detailed database of some 65 million Americans. Where the Obama campaign had asked for permission to access supporters' friends, the Trump effort to collect this data began with a questionnaire that when submitted, unbeknown to those filling it out, gave the firm access to the respondent's friends on Facebook. As a result, policy makers on both sides of the Atlantic came to understand that strengthening privacy protections was necessary.

Policy Research. Theoretically, political campaigns have complete control over the messages they wish to communicate to the electorate, unless, of course, they are operating in a governmental system that imposes restraints upon the content of their rhetoric. In practice, however, the range of messages will be narrowed to those which have a chance of maximizing the vote or producing electoral victory. While a campaign may decide to center its message on factors such as the personality and talents of the candidate or an attack on the character of the opponent, inevitably the candidate will be asked by voters and journalists about her stands on public policy issues. To be prepared, the campaign must delve into the nuances of the numerous issues of public policy that are likely to arise during the election contest.

The section on policy research should provide an initial statement of those matters about which the candidate feels very committed. These will constitute the limited number of issues that can be effectively communicated to voters in the conduct of the campaign. It should also establish a commitment—in terms of funding, personnel, and attention—to a mechanism for researching other issues of importance and for allowing the campaign—if not the candidate—to respond to questions from within and outside about the public policy preferences of the candidate. In the final decade of the 20th century, as the daily cycle of news speeded up, American presidential campaigns established so-called rapid response units to furnish quick reactions to the opponent's attack or questions from journalists. Though the evidence is scanty, most campaigners believe that a charge or attack left unanswered will be believed by voters and can, therefore, become a serious difficulty for the campaign unless rebutted instantly. Given the emergence of constantly available, 24-hour news, the necessary speed of reply accelerated with consequent demands for advanced preparation to be in a position to respond within the same news cycle.

Messages and Themes. While the campaign needs to be informed on a variety of issues on the minds of voters, contributors, and journalists, those drafting the campaign plan will endeavor to decide the essential messages they wish to communicate to the voters. In the rush of either an election contest or a drawn-out issue campaign, you may be only able to communicate effectively only a select few messages, and those are usually brought together under a single theme.

Fundraising Plan. In many circumstances, there will be laws that regulate the amount of funds that campaigns will have available to them and serve to limit how they can spend it. Understanding these laws and working within those permissible limits can be a critical ingredient of success. Unless the campaign is totally self-financed by the candidate or through some program of public funding defined by law, you will need to raise the money needed to undertake a campaign. That important task should not be left to chance; it requires a carefully defined and dedicated effort to achieve success.

The normal rule in fundraising is that a sizable percentage of the money collected will come from a relatively few sources. Political managers think in terms of a pyramid that represents the number of contributors giving different amounts. At the top will be the few sources of substantial funds; the wide base represents a large number of contributors of lesser amounts. In between, the norm is to find fewer and fewer donor sources as the amounts contributed increase. The amounts collected from each layer will normally be a declining percentage of the total. That is, the few large donors will generate a larger percentage of the total than the many small donors. Except for unusual candidates who can inspire a crusade-like cause, this standard rule holds true, despite the recent enthusiasm for tapping a vast pool of small contributors through online media. Even though technology has greatly expanded the number of donors and the amount of funds that they can be induced to contribute, the largest share of campaign funds still come from a small group of wealthy people and interest organizations.

A complete fundraising plan will include a variety of procedures for bringing in the necessary funds. Direct personal appeals by the candidate to potential donors are an essential element, even though the candidate may be very reluctant to ask friends, family, and acquaintances for money. Solicitations online or through the mail or by telephone calls to lists of individuals that are known givers will certainly be part of the mix. Small receptions in supporters' homes for cocktails, exclusive dinners for large donors, or large concerts or events for small donors should all be considered. It takes substantial effort to raise money in politics, but it needs to be done and it should be undertaken with a degree of careful planning and creativity and, importantly, a commitment of the resources necessary to achieve fundraising success. That is, it takes money to raise money.

Thinking strategically about fundraising requires one to confront the potential motivations of those who will donate to the campaign. Some donors will be personal supporters—friends and family—of the candidate; they give because they like and respect the individual running for office, and they think he or she will do a respectable job once in office. Others will be motivated by ideology; they believe strongly in the issue positions on which the candidate is basing her campaign. Still others wish to be on the winning side, to be associated with powerful and successful politicians. They like the glamour and the attention focused on them as insiders, close to the candidate. Finally, the reality is that some donors will expect to have influence over the candidate's actions once in office.

Political managers must identify why certain individuals are contributing to the campaign and to build these motivations into their different approaches to soliciting contributions. The best advice concerns dealing with the last type of self-interested giver in which the interchange may come perilously close or over the line into bribery. To stay on the safe side of that line, it is essential that there not be an explicit quid pro quo involving an official act by the officeholder in return for a donation. The candidate or her staff can certainly discuss with the potential contributor her general philosophy or approach to public policy. That aligns the general directions of policy preferences of the candidate with those of potential donors. But in this relationship, only the candidate can make firm commitments and those should remain general.

Campaign Budget. As has been noted several times, strategy is inherently situational: a statement that is nowhere clearer than in formulating the campaign budget. How the available funds will be used must be responsive to many factors among which the most important are the amount of funds that can be realistically raised, the unique strategic situation of the campaign, and the options for expending the available funds. Suffice it to say that a detailed budget lies at the heart of the strategic plan. Since almost everything the campaign wishes to undertake will cost money, drafting an explicit statement of how the money should be spent, and then keeping to it, is—simply stated—essential.

Thus, a complete campaign plan will include a careful statement of how to the campaign's dollar will be allocated. Consideration should also be given to such topics as when the funds must be available to be used effectively. For example, buying time for television advertising simply cannot be done without delivering the necessary funds before the desired time slot. The campaign managers may also have to consider whether the campaign will be allowed to run up a deficit that the candidate will be obligated to repay once the campaign is concluded, something that has proven to be much easier to accomplish if the candidate wins than loses.

One additional warning is necessary here, one which goes to the nature of a campaign and involves both the self-discipline of the campaign's financial manager and the need to control others within the campaign. Earlier, we observed how Barack Obama wanted to divert funds from the effort to organize the Iowa caucuses and David Plouffe, his campaign manager, resisted and persuaded the candidate to stick to the plan. That anecdote stands as a poignant example of the internal pressure on the campaign budget that must be managed in the heat of battle.

But achieving self-discipline on the part of campaign decision makers may not be the most severe problem in imposing budget control. As temporary organizations constructed in pursuit of political power, campaigns attract individuals who are ambitious, entrepreneurial, task oriented, and anxious to win. Accordingly, in their pursuit of what they see as a greater good, not to mention the personal benefits that might accompany working on a winning campaign, they are likely to "cut corners." Unauthorized bills that have flooded in after Election Day have surprised numerous campaign budget managers. In other words, creating a thorough campaign budget is only part of the problem; enforcing it upon an ebullient staff requires diligent and continuous attention.

Scheduling Considerations. The discussion above as to the need to consider the available days and hours of candidate and staff time should be mostly sufficient. Yet one should emphasize that there will be conflicting demands upon the candidate's time from the various parts of the campaign. A full-blown campaign organization is just tailor-made to develop demands on the candidate's schedule, no matter how far off is Election Day. At times, these battles can become quite heated, as various staffers and indeed the candidate herself press for attention to their needs and challenge the wisdom and authority of the scheduler. All this day-to-day conflict makes a rationally calculated scheduling plan all the more essential.

Communication Vehicles. Paid Advertising, Online and Earned Media. A complete campaign plan should include sections that consider the different tactical means of reaching voters. We will address these means in the next chapter. The plan should address how best to get the campaign's message to its target audiences by employing a wide variety of vehicles or channels that could be put in service. Here again, the unique situation in which the campaign is conducted will define the viable options based on the available media and the budget.

The campaign plan should plot the use of specific media. For example, under paid media, the campaign could consider billboards, yard signs, direct mail, and ads placed on radio and television. "Social" would include the use of Facebook, Google +, and other networks in which pools of potential supporters are linked in affective networks. Online media refers to website development and email outreach to targeted audiences. We could debate endlessly whether advertising online through such vehicles as Google AdWords should fall under paid media or online, but the point here is that the campaign plan should consider how this channel to voters will be used.

Conclusion

Campaigns allow a window into the dynamics of planning that can be obscured in ongoing organizations. The lessons of this chapter also apply, however, to other political arenas. Consider an issues management engagement, for example, an immigration rights organization seeking to raise awareness among citizens of brutal treatments dished out by local authorities. They would go through most of the same analysis to organize their public communications. They might ignore the dividing line between voters and nonvoters, but they would certainly undertake an effort to delineate their audience akin to an election campaign's voter analysis. They would, moreover, work through exactly the same issues such as fundraising, budgeting, the effective deployment of limited resources, and so forth. Meanwhile, a coalition of corporations seeking to advance "beneficial" tax legislation would map out their efforts to lobby the legislature much as a campaign would develop its plan. Assessing the ongoing political climate, defining their goals, delineating their underlying assumptions, estimating their opposition, and totaling up the available resources would all be aspects of their planning. The political managers involved would draft a formal document that would calculate how the coalition members would participate and what each would contribute to the effort. The resulting document would certainly address the internal and external management problems that the coalition might face. But the biggest difference between the strategy-making efforts of these differently situated actors is that they would have to plan in the context of an ongoing stream of events, interactions, history, and evolving disputes.

In practical terms, we should reiterate here that much of a written plan will be addressed to the tactical level of actions the campaign will actually undertake. The strategic components of the plan relate to (1) defining the overall situation in which the battle will be found, (2) the objective to be attained, and (3) the assumptions and (4) resources embedded in a simple statement of how the political managers will endeavor to secure the goals.

The Essence of Strategic Planning

1. Strategy involves rational decision-making based upon careful deliberation as to four key factors that we refer to as a SOAR analysis: Situation, Objectives, Assumptions, and Resources available. These elements define the strategic layer of planning in a political context.
2. A written, candid, and confidential plan is essential to guide the internal and external conflict that will inevitably emerge within an organization pursuing political goals.
3. Political managers need to devote both time and attention to the difficult, conceptual tasks of defining in considerable detail the objective(s) to be achieved and the assumptions upon which the

strategy rests. If the assumptions prove to be wrong, the strategy will probably need to be revised.
4. On the tactical level, the strategic plan should have five "spines" that run throughout every action planned as a means of achieving the objective(s): money, geography, time, staffing, and messages.

5
Strategic Political Communications

> In a democracy, the bedrock of political power is public support, so one of the most basic requirements for a public official is the ability to influence public opinion, and the journalists who mold it. None of the lower arts of politics is more essential to the politician than the ability to obtain favorable publicity.[1]
>
> —Robert A. Caro

Communication is an essential skill of politics.[2] Even in autocratic systems, dictators must communicate their decisions—however arbitrary—to their subordinates.[3] In democratic politics leaders must build followings or constituencies, a task that necessitates communication. Recent developments in communications technology have, moreover, increased the importance in democratic systems of reciprocal communications between politicians and their supporters. The ever-changing mix of communications media means that the channels through which messages flow will inevitably vary over time. But the essential dynamics of the public communications process will remain more or less the same.[4] Tactics will evolve but the strategy of communications that lies behind the employment of emerging technologies will endure.

In this area of political combat, separating the tactical from the strategic can prove to be quite difficult, perhaps because of the temptation to leap immediately into action and to start talking. In response, we should recall that strategy is an analytical and cerebral task, while the tactical involves implementation and doing. Political consultant Bill Greener[5] suggests that to keep your focus on the strategic level, political managers should concentrate on answering two questions: "With whom do I need to communicate?" and "What message do I need to deliver to those different audiences?" To these, we must add a third: "What vehicle of communication should I use?" Whatever problem you face, whatever goal you wish to secure, if addressed at this level, you will be thinking strategically, not acting tactically.

Delineating the Audience

In practice, one often encounters difficulty in maintaining a focus on the level of strategy. In the first place, in politics there is not one audience but many, each with its own concerns, amount of knowledge, depth of interest, and level of engagement with the subject matter of the communication. Puzzling out the messages to be conveyed to the relevant subgroups requires considerable thought about the nuances of what each community is prepared to hear and how it will likely react. That trick must be accomplished, moreover, without treading into self-contradictions that would open one up to attacks from the opposition. A well-established truism dictates that in an electoral context, not all voters are similar. Not only are voters divided by partisan sentiments, there will be differences in the degree to which they are paying attention to the political discourse. All these aspects complicate the strategic tasks in communication.

Consider the following fictitious scenario. Josh Jones, a 35-year-old former Marine, is contesting a primary election for Congress against an incumbent with 30 years of service in Washington, DC. The race has generated much national attention, which has meant that a lot of money has recently flowed into the coffers of both candidates. With one week to go before the primary, the polls have been moving toward Jones, who has closed to about 5 percent behind from a 28 percent deficit when the campaign began. At about 3 p.m. one day, Jones's campaign press secretary receives a call from a reporter from the local newspaper requesting reactions to a story they are about to put out that Jones did not file his income tax 12 years ago. The subsequent back and forth with the reporter reveals that the source of the information now in the newspaper's hand is mostly likely the opponent's campaign. Based on the strength of the relationship between reporter and press secretary, the newspaper has agreed to hold off on releasing the story until 7 p.m., four hours from now. What should be the communications strategy pursued by the press secretary?

Obviously, the first task is to ascertain what actually happened. Speaking with Jones on an emergency basis, the press secretary learns that it's technically true. Thirteen years ago, not 12, while deployed overseas in a battlefield situation with his Marine brigade, the 22-year-old Jones failed to file his income tax returns by April 15th. Upon returning to the United States in October of that year, he then filed a late return for the missing year and paid a fine that consumed most of the refund he was due.[6] He has since filed every year on time and there have never been any questions about the accuracy of his returns.

Armed with this information, what should the press secretary now do? Again, obviously, contacting the reporter with the mitigating facts should be high among the priorities. But that's tactical. What else? What should be the appropriate communications strategy?

At this point, strategic thinking becomes important. For many political managers, the first instinct would be to call a press conference to explain Jones's actions. But that is doing, and strategy, remember, is cerebral. One should first react by thinking—not doing. In terms of the content of messages, this case may seem an easy one to handle. True, a press conference could lay out the facts but may not convey the message to some critical audiences. News reports will undoubtedly contain both the campaign's response and the original charge. Meanwhile, a variety of allies and supporters need to hear the campaign's side of the story first. With a bit more thought, the press secretary could go beyond a firm rebuttal. This back and forth could be viewed as an opportunity to accentuate Jones's military service and put the opponent on the defensive for dredging up such a minor, ancient, and understandable mistake.

So, let's suppose that the negative story is more challenging. What if Jones's ex-wife has come forward to accuse him of spousal abuse? Suppose this is the first time in the 10 years that they have been divorced that she has mentioned it? Jones has denied the charge, and nobody who knew the couple back then has come forward to corroborate the story. Substantively, this is trickier for a couple of reasons. First, the fact that the opponent is behind the release of this charge is likely to be seen as totally secondary to the facts of the matter. Second, much of the public will view Jones's denial as a "she says, he says" story. Now, it's become a public spat between a divorced couple. Third, and most harmful, even rebutting this story will give it a much wider reach. A back and forth between Jones and his ex will likely result in a story in the news for several days.

This more subtle and complex problem demands a strategic approach. What audiences need to be reached? In this context, the campaign should endeavor to communicate with important groups like its financial contributors, campaign volunteers and paid staff, and important party leaders. The campaign must contact these significant supporters first so they are not completely blindsided. Other onlookers will undoubtedly press the individuals associated with the campaign for their knowledge and opinion about the news coverage that will surely follow. They need to know how they should respond. To contain the damage, the press secretary will also want to reach out to other journalists presenting Jones's side of the story. The campaign's "spin" will undoubtedly emphasize those aspects of the situation that mitigate Jones's behavior. Reaching out to the primary electorate, the campaign should differentiate between all likely voters and the group that social scientists refer to as the "attentive public." Loyal voters who have been identified by the campaign and undecided voters constitute further discernible clusters. And the campaign's leadership must also consider whether it would be worth the effort to try to communicate with nonvoters and the voters loyal to the other candidate.

For each of these groups, the campaign should consider both the nuanced messages to be communicated to these various constituencies and the most appropriate channel to reach them. For example, the state party chair and major donors need a personal call from the candidate. On the other ends of the spectrum, the campaign might consider whether it would make sense to cut a radio or television ad to reach those in the electorate for the party primary.

Noting that there are different audiences that need to be reached does not mean that political managers can be deceitful, conveying to different audiences dissimilar messages that contradict each other. A better way of thinking strategically about political messaging is to keep in mind that different audiences will have different expectations as to the content of your messages. The essential task of a political manager is to marry advocacy—as in the candidate's or campaign's essential message—to the necessity of responsiveness to the audiences' interests and capacity. Balancing these somewhat contradictory requirements is an essential task of political management. Adherence to the principles of simplicity and repetition should go a long way toward ensuring against duplicity. A third commitment to responsiveness should ensure that the communications are relevant to the needs and interests of the audience. As we shall observe momentarily, the development of social networking early in the 21st century has accentuated the necessity of responsiveness in communicating effectively with multiple audiences. The arrival of a true, many-to-many communications structure altered the expectations of politically active citizens, allowing them to require greater responsiveness from political leadership.

The major point here is that a lot of thinking—call it strategizing—needs to take place in designing a responsive strategy, well before someone starts to arrange the details of a press conference. The campaign must engage in the essential thinking first; only then should it move on to the tactical implementation.

Consider another example drawn from the arena of public advocacy. Early in the 21st century, Planned Parenthood, an organization providing a range of reproductive health services for women, was hit by a heavily edited video recordings released to the news media by the conservative group Project Veritas.[7] Long before Planned Parenthood could document how heavily and deceptively the video had been edited, the damage was done. Legislation was introduced in Congress to defund Planned Parenthood entirely, even though no federal funding went toward abortion services. Key partner organizations and funders threatened to pull back. Reporters clamored for reactions. The crisis threatened to kill the organization. In terms of strategic communications, however, the crisis was similar to the hypotheticals above. Planned Parenthood needed to reach out to a substantial variety of supporters and allies with their side of the story. Key members of Congress needed information to rebut the sensational charges of their peers. Foundations that provided funding needed to be reassured those statements on the video by Planned Parenthood staff had been distorted by taking them out of consequence. Millions of patients and supporters needed reassurance. The Planned Parenthood staff needed to sort through all these various audiences and share with each a tailored and nuanced message.

Targeting. In political parlance, the operative term for addressing different messages to different audiences is "targeting," a logical process by which the campaign will separate the whole citizenry or sum of likely voters into segments that will be treated differently. While the overarching strategy has remained unchanged, the last 80 years have seen a significant transformation in the means of deciphering whom to contact with what messages and through which media channels. Back in the days of powerful party machines, the ward heelers knew exactly who they could count on to vote for their chosen candidate. They maintained lists of regular and reliable supporters even while they took steps to expand their supporters through small favors and minor graft. As these party organizations deteriorated, however, candidates were gradually deprived of the intelligence provided by the party cadre. In its stead, targeting became probabilistic, based on data drawn from previous election returns. While campaigns could not know how individual voters cast their ballots, they could determine that the voters in a given precinct were more or less likely to vote for a particular party and, almost as important, whether turnout in a particular neighborhood was consistently high or low or fluctuated dramatically. Sharp political managers used this "past performance targeting" to decide where they should concentrate their persuasive and voter turnout efforts and, not incidentally, which areas to ignore. A precinct that normally voted overwhelmingly for their party would be "targeted" for GOTV efforts, while a ward that had proven over several past elections to be volatile in party support would be the object of persuasive messages. Voters who live in neighborhoods in which turnout fluctuates widely could be approached with persuasive messages and GOTV outreach to those who the campaign was able to identify as supporting its candidate.

Significant changes in communications strategy have come about in the 21st century driven by a markedly enhanced ability to tailor audiences to ever narrowing groups. Where during the 20th century the "mass media" used to be truly mass—as in reaching a broad audience of undifferentiated citizens—changes in the technology of communications have allowed political managers to reach smaller and smaller groups defined by demographic characteristics or even attitudinal and behavioral variables. At the same time, the increasing power of computers has enhanced the ability to develop and comprehend greater amounts of information about the individuals that make up the audience so that messages can be precisely targeted. By 10 years into the new century, political communicators could carry on distinct conversations with literally thousands of individual citizens. Though definitive proof is not yet available, presumably if a given conversation contains specific information tailored to the recipient's interests and desires, the persuasive effects on his or her preferences and behaviors are likely to be enhanced.

As a result, political managers have recently learned how to target voters more precisely using the ever more generally available socioeconomic and commercial data. Citizens who exhibit certain demographic characteristics such as the "soccer moms" of the 2012 cycle could be singled out for intense efforts at conversion communications. As more and more data has become available, these groupings have become ever more narrowly defined by multiple crosscutting indicators, leading to so-called micro-targeting.[8]

The American presidential campaigns of 2012 and 2016 ushered in an era of "big data" that provided a rather different approach to targeting in political communications. In part, this development amounts to a further move in the trend toward ever more granular information about citizens, allowing a more exact delineation of smaller and smaller groups of similar individuals. Targeting decisions have become based on more than probabilistic inferences about voters who fit a given model. The tactical difference is that the political manager starts with a computer record of every known eligible voter and then adds a myriad of other data to that record. Information about individual citizens has become so extensive and rich in detail that the range of known "facts" about individual citizens allows a political communicator to learn a great deal about each specific individual voter. Based on this information, the campaign can create an individually tailored message designed to influence his/her behavior. Instead of inductively selecting individuals who exhibit characteristics that make them likely to be supporters, now campaigners can communicate directly with a given roster of known supporters.

In some ways, this strategy constitutes a return to the detailed knowledge of voters in a given community that was provided by the party ward heelers of old, except that computers now have replaced those party cadre. The inference has shifted away from one in which, based on polling, focus group research or past voting data, a particular grouping of similar individuals can be projected as likely supporters of our candidate. Instead of deciding based on a few indicators (residence, gender, race, home ownership, etc.) that an individual is probabilistically a supporter of a given candidate, the political managers are amassing ever more extensive data about particular individuals. By the election of 2016, political managers had learned how to monitor individual Facebook, Twitter, and Instagram accounts so that they could add to these data sets information about issues that most concerned individual voters as well as, in some cases, their declared voting intentions.

Delineating a Message

Having a precise definition of the audience(s) to be reached helps determine the messages to be communicated. Like most aspects of strategy, messaging is entirely situational. Nevertheless, there are some general guidelines that serve to allow the political manager to maximize the effectiveness of messaging.

Limitations on political communications. Political managers across the spectrum have concluded that a critical limitation exists in the number of topics that political managers can advance in their quest to shape the thinking and behavior of citizens in their audience. Whether the goal is mobilization of committed supporters of a policy initiative or persuasion of voters during an election, communications with the audiences within the public are, simply stated, more difficult to conduct than private communications with a finite number of individuals. No more than three messages can be successfully communicated to the public over the course of an election or public relations campaign. In large part, the limitation is a consequence of the fact that political communications must compete with a massive flow of public and commercial communications to citizens and consumers through a manifold set of channels. Political messages tend to be eclipsed. In this context, more than three ideas are likely to diffuse the campaign's message and fail to penetrate the voters' awareness. When messages are actually perceived by the public, more than this number will tend to confuse the audience as to what the issues are in the campaign and what the sponsoring organization hopes to accomplish.[9]

Simplicity and Repetition. To surmount these difficulties, every political manager should take the time to listen to and contemplate a recording of *Bolero* by Maurice Ravel. The piece presents a nearly perfect analogy to the tasks of political communications. Bolero starts with a flute playing a simple melody that lasts approximately 50 seconds and then repeats and repeats and repeats practically until the listener is ready to beg for an end. Over the 18 minutes of the piece's unfolding, the tempo speeds up, the volume grows, the percussion become more demanding, and more and more of the orchestra's instruments enter, making the melody increasingly complex. Each repetition involves a slight variation on the basic theme, so that while the essential message remains the same, variation serves to retain the listener's interest. Then, at the end, the piece comes to a loud and crashing finish on one blaring, dissonant note. There could be no better metaphor for the task of communicating in political competition, whether election campaigns or policy fights. They exhibit the same dynamics of simplicity marked by variation and acceleration. Public communications battles can have dramatic endings, often on a discordant note.

Even with a sharply reduced number of messages, repetition is essential. As Election Day looms ever closer for a political campaign, strategists work to speed up and increase the volume of their communications with the electorate. Yet to maintain the attention of those in the audience, they must innovate. Doing so will allow them to keep their messages interesting. Exact repetitions are likely to have diminishing effectiveness. In fact, watching the same ad repeat over and over on television can take the viewer beyond boredom to annoyance.

Content: the Leesburg Grid. In the mid-1990s, a gathering of political managers from the Republican Party met in Leesburg, Virginia, to improve their ability to provide strategic messaging advice to their candidates. Collectively, they came up with a device that came to be known as "the Leesburg Grid" and has become a staple of communications strategy on both sides of the American political divide.

The grid is a two-by-two table with a column for each candidate and rows dedicated to the messages each communications team is likely to apply to those candidates. The boxes of the grid require the communicator to address four questions about the content of messaging: (1) What will *we* say about *our* candidate; (2) What will *the opponent* likely say about *our* candidate; (3) What will *we* say about *the opponent*; and (4) What will *the opponent* likely say about *himself* or *herself*? Examining the content of the two columns should make it clear to the reader that effective messages cannot simply be developed in isolation. Whatever messages you hope to communicate to an appropriate audience must be crafted in part based on an assessment of the ideas that the opposition will be endeavoring to communicate. The reader should remember that political managers are not engaged in a power struggle in splendid isolation. Citizens affected by policy determination and voters engaged in elections will, to some extent, be exposed to both presentations and will stand in judgment of the work of the competitors. If they wish their messages to be effective, political managers must develop them with an eye toward what the opposition will be saying.

The height of message confrontation occurs when the candidates agree to debate one another. Normally journalists take part by asking the two candidates a series of probing questions. But if the political managers are doing their job, they will have engaged the services of an effective opposition research firm to anticipate everything the opponent will probably say. Knowing that, the candidate staff can tailor the words their candidate will utter to advance the campaign's agenda while contrasting their position with the disastrous ideas of the opponent.

Two concrete examples will help the reader understand the use of the Leesburg grid. The first is drawn from an American presidential election in 2004 in which the military service records of the two candidates became an important issue.

This overly partisan perspective of the messaging during the 2004 election between President George W. Bush and Senator John Kerry was developed by a Republican consulting group named "Your

Table 5.1 Leesburg Grid of Messages during the 2004 US Presidential Election

What Bush wants people to think about Bush	What Bush wants people to think about Kerry
• Honorable military service history • Intelligent and graduate honors • Wants to keep taxes low • Man of God	• Kerry is stiff • Kerry is ultra-wealthy • His wife is rude • Lied about his war service

What Kerry wants people to think about Bush	What Kerry wants people to think about Kerry
• AWOL from his service • Bush is an idiot • Bush is ultra-religious • Bush can't tackle tough issues	• Decorated war hero • Decorated war hero!! • Married to a powerful woman • Wants low taxes for the poor

Patriot." It is, for example, an overstatement to think that Kerry seriously wanted to call President Bush "an idiot." Nevertheless, the matrix does make clear the important argument over the two candidates' military service.

In this matrix, you can see the argumentation over the candidates' respective military service, an important issue for a campaign that was taking place during two wars in Afghanistan and Iraq. The Bush campaign wanted voters to believe that their candidate had served honorably in the Air National Guard during the Vietnam War (although he had never been in actual combat). At the same time, the Bush campaign wanted to convey the message that Kerry had lied about his war service and to cast doubt on whether he deserved the medals he received for valor in combat. Kerry, by contrast, wanted voters to know that he was a decorated war hero for his service in Vietnam and that, meanwhile, Bush's family connections had allowed him to avoid direct service in Vietnam and, worse, that Bush had not really fulfilled his active-duty commitments in the Guard. The alert reader may object that this illustration and the one to follow both appear to violate the guideline that a public relations drive can only communicate three ideas simultaneously. But if we scrutinize these ideas closely, we will see how they are really all of a piece.

So much for strategic scheming: What happened in the campaign? During the Democratic National Convention that nominated Kerry, veterans who had served in Vietnam with the senator appeared frequently in the television coverage. When Kerry took the podium to accept the nomination, he began by giving a military salute accompanying his first words, "I'm John Kerry and I'm reporting for duty!" The speech that followed contained numerous references to his service and criticism of Bush's conduct of the wars in Iraq and Afghanistan. Kerry was joined on the podium by a group of men who had served with him on US Navy "Swift Boats" along the Mekong River in Vietnam. Thus, the opening shot of the campaign addressed the messages found in the four boxes of the grid, and in the process the Kerry campaign brought the issue of military service to the fore. But, as Karl Rove, Bush's chief strategist, argued, "Never go after someone's strength: go after what he thinks is his strength, but what is, in reality, a weakness."[10]

Unfortunately for Kerry, the arguments over military service did not end there. Soon after the convention, a group supporting but unaffiliated with the Bush campaign called "Swift Boat Veterans for Truth" launched a series of four television advertisements alleging that Kerry had overstated his combat valor and did not deserve the medals he had been awarded. In addition, upon his return from service, Kerry had led an organization called Vietnam Veterans Against the War and had testified before Congress against the war and had, furthermore, reportedly tossed his medals over a fence at the US Capitol. While there was good reason to doubt the evidence cited in the attack as to whether Kerry deserved his medals and had overstated his combat experience, there is no doubt that the members of the Swift Boat group felt aggrieved by Kerry's public statements upon his return from that most controversial American war. Evidently, the Kerry campaign did not take the Swift Boat commercials seriously enough to immediately rebut them and, as a result, the charges they made became more firmly fixed in the voters' mind than merited by actual evidence.

Based on this anecdote, many political managers have come to believe a cardinal rule of political communications strategy, namely that many voters will come to believe a charge or attack that is not vigorously refuted, no matter how spurious or thin the evidence. The

Table 5.2 Leesburg Grid of Messages by Proponents and Opponents of Charter Schools

What proponents want people to think about charter schools	What proponents want people to think about public schools
• Flexibility • Proven curriculum • Better for children with special needs • Smaller classes • One-on-one instruction	• Public schools (PS) are bureaucratic • Subpar curriculum • Standardized curriculum and testing • Mired by teachers' unions • Crumbling facilities
What opponents want people to think about charter schools	**What opponents want people to think about public schools**
• Takes funding away from PS • Heavy workload for teachers • Require parents to volunteer • Great variation in quality	• No cost • Community and neighborhood student body • Greater diversity of student population • Stronger job protections for teachers

folklore of the 2004 campaign would have us believe that the Swift Boat attack was the sole reason why John Kerry lost that race. Whether that's truly the case or not, campaign communications have become harsher as the competing candidates feel that every criticism must be countered loudly and vigorously.

Turning to an example drawn from a public policy fight, consider the example of strategizing over public communications by an organization supporting the charter school movement. In large part, advocacy for charter schools emerges from a critique of the quality of public schools.

Charter school proponents view public schools as overly bureaucratic, hindered by teachers' unions and local school boards, and delivering inferior education. As an alternative, these proponents are quite optimistic about the advantages of charter schools, citing their flexibility, their ability to adapt their curriculum, their capacity to serve children with special needs, and smaller class size. For their opponents—that is, for advocates for public schools—there is one major argument against charter schools: they draw funding away from public schools. Instead, the public money allocated to charter schools should be better spent revitalizing public education.

Careful readers will see two arguments in the above grid: one over the nature of charter schools and another over the pros and cons of public education. In terms of the overall communications strategy, these two debates are inseparable. Yet they can also be joined as distinct disputes. A public communications campaign launched by an organization supporting charter schools will want to win both arguments in the public mind. They will argue that it's worth taking money away from moribund public schools to finance a better education for children. Meanwhile they will press ahead with arguments that public schools have been captured by teachers' unions, making them unresponsive to parents. Readers attuned to political nuance will quickly spot an unspoken subtext here. Charter schools have implications for social and economic diversity of their student bodies, especially if they include schools initiated by religious institutions. The neighborhood-based diversity of public schools brings with it another argument focused on social values well beyond curricular issues.

Advocating Policy versus Values. In terms of content, communications that are linked to preexisting values held by the audience tend to be more powerful than messages relating to ideology or public policies. In large part, this idea derives from the principle that messages should be tailored to what the audience is prepared to hear. Take, for example, an argument advocating a given public policy concerning the national debt. For that to have a noticeable impact, members of the audience must recognize that the policy area is important, that it relates to their lives, and that they agree with the proposed policy direction. Given the complexities that relate to the national debt—including policy issues such as taxation, monetary policy, government spending, and so forth—one can foresee considerable difficulty in getting citizens engaged in an argument over the debt. In short, effective messaging demands a complicated calculus involving, at a minimum, substantial information about members of the audience and highly segmented targeting. Messages based on the more universal values as expressed in Maslow's hierarchy of needs[11] are often more effective in shaping the audience's thinking than are appeals based on public policy. So, for example, tying the national debt to individual needs such as food, shelter, and security is likely to make the policy more meaningful to citizens. Without this dimension, a complex and abstract policy proposal is unlikely to corral voters' attention and motivate their behavior. Twenty years into the 21st century, the COVID-19 pandemic provided a stark lesson in the efficacy of messages based on values. Public health officials talked about the issues raised by the pandemic such as lockdowns, school closures, vaccinations, social distancing, and mask mandates. Meanwhile, resisters rallied around the value of "personal freedom." Despite considerable evidence that vaccination would sharply limit death from the disease, many citizens refused to be vaccinated in the name of their freedom. Even with all the data, all the technical information, the public health officials were unable to reach a certain segment of the population. Values often outgun policy issues.

Julia Galef has probed deeply into why new information is so often ignored when it does not conform to the recipient's preexisting biases.[12] Her observations are correct as the examples over public health document. But for our purposes, note that political managers are often trying to tie their messages closely to the preconceptions they know their audiences share. They know that the way in which they frame issues will have an enormous influence on the effectiveness of their communications. It makes a difference, for example, whether the tax levied on personal wealth at the time of death is presented as an "inheritance tax," an "estate tax," or as a "death tax." When political manager Frank Luntz took on this issue, a majority of American favored eliminating the tax on estates and slightly more supported abolishing the inheritance tax. Meanwhile, fully 70 percent supported eliminating the "estate tax."[13] To be clear, we are talking about the same tax called by different names. Working with the leadership of the Republican Party, he was able to transform the public conversation into an argument over the "death tax." In 2001, Congress voted to reduce the tax gradually over 10 years and eliminate it totally in 2011. Though the Democrats subsequently moved to restore an estate tax at a lower level, the point remains that the frame in which an issue is presented to the public will shape whether communications have the intended effect.

A Changing Model of Communication Channels

In much of the world, politicians communicate with citizens through three different channels of media: means that are owned by politicians, channels that carry messages in the form of paid advertisements, and communications that are earned through contact with the news media organizations. To these, we will add a fourth channel, which encompasses the evolving technology of "social networking." Although it might be considered as a means owned by the originator or politician, the model of interaction is so different that we suggest it constitutes a separate category. The four channels yield a nice acronym (in honor of the currency of Mexico): PESO for paid, earned, social, and owned.[14]

The precise form that each of these means of communication exhibit evolved considerably over the course of the 19th and 20th centuries. Local newspapers were joined by local radio stations that were gradually aggregated into national networks. Then, television networks evolved only to be supplemented by cable systems. Each new medium joined and increased the panoply of communications media. The invention of Internet communications suggests that these accelerating changes will persist into the future. While most of this change has been commercially driven, political communications have piggybacked on these developments. Given that these media are structured as one-to-many communications, they are perfectly suited to the arenas of politics where the essential tasks are fulfilled by mobilizing vast numbers of supporters.

Owned media includes the many different means through which politicians achieve *direct* communications with voters. Those who would become political leaders have moved well beyond in-person speeches to groups of supporters as their primary means of developing political support. In modern democratic systems, party organizations enlist cadres of campaign volunteers who, in turn, could engage directly with voters. Early political managers used pamphlets, posters, and yard signs and then added the mass mailing of letters, postcards, and brochures that are often grouped under the general term "direct mail." Together these channels emerged by the last half of the 20th century as a system for delivering political messages. With the advent of digital media, direct mail and text messaging became available as new channels for reaching voters directly. In each of these cases, owned media have two distinguishing characteristics: they are not mediated by other actors and, accordingly, politicians exercise near complete control over the content, timing, and delivery of the messages conveyed to targeted audiences. This is especially true in the United States where the First Amendment to the Constitution creates broad protections for politicians seeking office. The reader should note that we are not commenting here on the relative effectiveness of owned media, merely on their capacity to reach appropriate audiences. In fact, voters award relatively less credibility to messages that they perceive to be so heavily under the control of politicians.

Paid Media. Over time, the available means of reaching voters evolved into privately held commercial media that necessitated a different strategy of political communication. So-called paid media refers, of course, to those numerous conduits that are owned by others but can be rented by political managers to meet their communications needs. In short, paid media refers to what we all know as advertising. Normally the political communicators contract with a vendor to purchase the ability to reach a desired audience, whether that means commuters driving past a billboard or viewers watching a sitcom. In most cases, these media can be described as "inadvertent" meaning that the audience has been constituted for some other purpose and the political communication piggybacks on the opportunity to reach a designated audience. For example, as noted above, in the latter half of the 19th century, newspapers migrated from subscription-based distribution to mass circulation based on commercial advertisements and a relatively inexpensive consumer price. Political communicators could reach out to the broader audience of the newspapers' customers. Currently, commercials placed on television and radio are the most obvious examples in the field of political communications. The entertainment programming offered by stations and networks serves to gather large audiences that can then be reached by politicians for a price. A complicated fabric of laws regulates the conditions under which political programming or announcements are permitted, both during the election and the governing stages of politics. In many nations, such stipulations are vastly more restrictive than in the United

States where government regulators have reduced restrictions on the privately owned broadcast media.

Earned Media. At the time of the American Revolution late in the 18th century, most newspapers were based on a subscription model built upon partisan leanings. According to Horace Greeley, by 1851 almost every town in the United States with a population of over 20,000 had two newspapers, one for each political party.[15] In essence, the parties owned those media. But as the 19th century unfolded, the business model of subscriptions began to break down as high-speed printing made possible the penny press that relied primarily upon commercial advertising targeted to mass audiences. Newspaper ownership passed over to commercial enterprises that sought to attain the widest possible readership. In the process, partisanship in the content of the news product weakened, both in the selection of what to cover and in the actual reporting. To be sure, a degree of partisan coloring of news content remained, but on the whole newspapers—and then radio and television broadcasting—took on a more objective approach to news reporting. These developments in turn forced political managers to develop strategies of communicating through both paid media and through influencing the work of journalists or so-called earned media.[16]

In a stream of constant technological innovation, the mix of news media evolved again when cable television opened the medium up to an explosion of new channels.[17] CNN became the first 24-hour news channel and those that followed took on an increasingly partisan slant to their content. While this development brought the media mix back to the partisan mix of the 19th century, the more important characteristic is that these outlets were owned by commercial corporations and, therefore, had to be courted by politicians rather than controlled by them. As such, they fall into the earned media category.

In many ways, the pursuit of favorable news coverage as a means of building political support is more interesting and complicated than either of the above two models of communication. In many nations, newspapers adopt a political posture that shapes their coverage of politics, making it easier—or harder as the case may be—for a politician of a given stripe to receive favorable coverage through that vehicle.

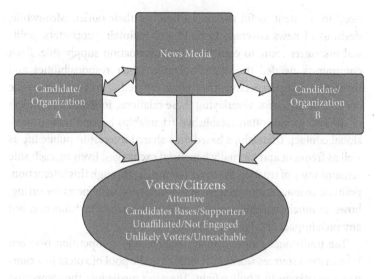

Figure 5.1 Traditional Model of Competing Sources of Information to Voters

In other countries, newspapers have evolved toward "objective" reporting, meaning that the news coverage is supposedly free of bias toward any partisan viewpoint. That trend meant that earned media has provided an extremely powerful vehicle of political communication, because voters generally accord greater credibility to news reporting that they deem as providing objective coverage.[18] This advantage in political messaging, however, is somewhat offset by the fact that the messages generated by political managers must pass through a journalistic process, which can alter the meaning and, thereby, lessen the effectiveness of the communication. As a result, political managers develop careful strategies designed to influence the work of journalists to maximize the chances that news coverage will reflect their preferred messages.[19]

In the United States during much of the 20th century, the relationship between political managers and journalists evolved into a synergistic antagonism. In terms of the exchange of information, reporters fell onto the demand side of the relationship, driven by their constant need for content to fill the "news hole" of their outlet. Meanwhile, desirous of news coverage to build and maintain supporters, political managers came to constitute the information supply side. Each community needed the other, but given their responsibilities and divergences of perspective, they often differed as to the appropriate content of the news. Overlaying these relations, individual members of the two groups often established friendships beyond their professional contact, friendships based on a shared interest in public life as well as frequent and mutually beneficial exchanges. Even so, each side remains wary of trusting the other too much. Through this interaction, political managers do exercise some influence over news reporting, however much journalists might resist recognizing that influence. But any such impact falls far short of control.

The traditional model displays a three-way competition between information sources working to influence the pool of voters in a campaign or citizens in a policy fight. The news media join the competing campaigns or policy organizations in their efforts to "educate" voters according to their perceived vision of the consequences of the election. In the process, members of either audience became exposed to differing points of view and can decide for themselves what is true and valid for them. As emphasized earlier in this chapter, the citizens or voters are not an undifferentiated mass. While certainly many are essentially disengaged from politics, some of them are heavily engaged in political discussions and activity and will pay a great deal of attention to political information. Others are already committed to one side or the other of the dispute and are likely to be attentive to messages emanating from that source and to news coverage about their favored choice. Still others within the general population are almost totally uninterested in politics. They are highly unlikely to participate in the election or be drawn into the policy debate.

Social Media. With the proliferation of media outlets in the United States early in the 21st century, driven first by cable television and then by the arrival of online communications, the neat dyadic relationship between political managers and journalists became transformed. The development of online communications stimulated the proliferation of communities constructed by social networks, markedly changing the nature of communications including those for building political

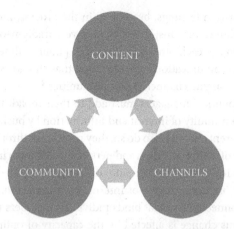

Figure 5.2 Emerging Model of Voter Communications

support. Literally scores of commercial enterprises endeavored to build audiences of registered users and especially "active monthly users." As the time of this writing, Facebook, YouTube, Google+, Twitter, Instagram, and TikTok have proven to be the most popular and well established in the United States.[20] In China, Qzone, Tencent Weibo and Sina Weibo lead the list, each with over 500 million registered users. But, as the history of rapid growth followed by significant decline of similar online services like AOL, Yahoo, and MySpace indicates, new competitors may well emerge to challenge the dominance of the contemporary communications behemoths.

A principal characteristic of social media—the fact that they were not structured as one-to-many vehicles—brought forth a significant evolution in the process for building and maintaining political support through communications media. Given the vastly expanded capacity for many-to-many communications, it's not surprising that another model of the communications process would soon emerge.

In the first place, the two communities began to merge; many of those who had established careers on the politician's side found employment in news organizations. Meanwhile, as the mass audience fragmented driven by a surge in the number of news organizations, several prominent news corporations moved to build an audience based on partisan leanings, becoming, in the process, more like political communicators. Instead of the above paradigm of two sides attempting to use each other to address the public, a different model of political communications emerged, one that should be called the "three C's"—content, channels, and communities.[21]

Effective political managers must add to their toolkit the tactic of creating a community of interest and information by pushing content through different channels. To do so, they must work through a never-ending cycle of communication and persuasion as shown in Figure 5.2 A "community," however, is quite different from an "audience." Community implies a degree of internal communications and self-conscious connectedness that binds individual members together. In large part, this change is affected by the capacity of online communications to allow multiple voices to participate in the conversation. Not only can members of the community address each other, they can speak back and interact with the politician in a way that they never could with broadcast media. The political communicator of today does not dominate the discourse of a community in the way that the mass media facilitated an ability to address and speak down to an audience. Instead, a politician is only one voice—albeit a louder voice—in the stream of a conversation, even when the community is composed of his or her supporters. As Peter Singer observed, "... in the age of social media ... the audience is both a target and participant in it."[22]

While a political manager may be the initiator of a conversation, the group may capture the dialogue and lead it in directions he or she never anticipated. An early and most visible instance of this difference occurred in September 2008 in the middle of Barack Obama's first campaign for US president. As a sitting senator, Obama was faced with a dilemma in the form of a Senate bill that could possibly have divided his supporters no matter which way he voted. Enacted during the Bush administration in the aftermath of the terrorist attack on the Pentagon and World Trade Center, the Foreign Intelligence Surveillance Act (FISA) came up for renewal during the summer of 2008, including a provision that granted telecommunications providers immunity from lawsuits if they disclosed information on their customers to the government in the name of national security. When Senator Obama announced that he would vote to reauthorize FISA, the civil liberties community, which had been strongly behind his candidacy, became terribly upset. Many in this community had become vocal and active supporters of Obama and frequent participants in his social network "My.BarackObama.com." To the surprise of the Obama campaign, these supporters began to agitate through this channel, petitioning the senator to reverse his decision. In other words, here was an instance in which the communications channel provided by a politician was used by some members of "his audience" to organize pressure upon that candidate. Under the banner, "Senator Obama Please Vote NO on Telecom Immunity—Get FISA Right," the group quickly became among the largest public groups organized on My.BarackObama.com. The pressure threatened to grow into a firestorm, so much so that the candidate felt compelled to issue a statement in response in an attempt to quell the discontent, arguing "this was not an easy call for me." For our purposes here, it's less important how he ultimately voted, and more significant that a community of supporters formed using the very mechanism that Obama had built to attract and maintain political support.

As we can see in this example, building a community can be a double-edged sword for political leaders. In past eras, the constituency ideal of political representation suggested that political leaders would bring to the halls of power the values and preferences of a relatively passive citizenry. A community built through modern social media, however, posits a great deal more engagement and power in the interconnected network of communications that a community generates. Friends and contacts can be tremendous motivators of action. Likeminded individuals, often of similar demographics, can encourage and support each other, irrespective of geography. Shared information and networked connections also empower a community and, at times, allow it to capture and constrain a political leader.

This evolution in the model of communications places new demands on the political manager. The conversation becomes continuous rather than periodic. In large part this occurs because the whole business strategies of the companies that convey social media are built around maintaining the attention of their audiences. Their "pursuit of eyeballs" allows communities of interest to form. No longer do these communications occur mainly at the political manager's pleasure and initiation. Members of the community participate in the ongoing conversation often on an equal basis. They also expect that the politician will listen to their participants and respond to them.

These services essentially allow individuals to create their unique, self-serving communities of friends, family, contacts or people or organizations they would like to know, learn about, follow, or communicate with. But that's less than half the story as to how these services have changed the processes of political communication. To maintain and grow a personal network, individuals must participate actively in outreach, sharing comments, observations, pictures, and short videos. Being active on a social network also means responding to the incoming messages from one's contacts, commenting, adding your reactions, "liking" on Facebook, "retweeting" on Twitter and so forth. In other words, while social networking may have vastly expanded the number of people with whom individuals can remain in constant contact, the burdens of being a diligent and attentive participant increase for both citizen and would-be officeholder alike.

Politically, social networking holds out for political managers the possibility of energizing whole networks of individuals. Just as people are more likely to socialize with individuals who are very much like them, so political communicators can hope to mobilize peer contacts to their cause. The potential of social networking in political mobilization rests on an assumption that the closer a communicator is to the intended audience, the more influential he or she is likely to be. By persuading a few individuals within a network structure to become their supporters, politicians aspire to leverage their contacts into a much larger support base. For example, in the 2012 election for US president, the Obama campaign asked supporters to give them access to their inventory of Facebook contacts. Then when their door-knocking volunteers located a reluctant or undecided voter, the headquarters could try to locate Facebook friends who might agree to reach out to that potential voter.

The presidential campaign of Donald J. Trump in 2016 relied upon the use of social media to an even greater degree. Each day, the candidate himself took to his Twitter account to reach out to a growing number of followers that reached more than 13 million by Election Day. Beyond the effect these messages had upon his supporters, this approach generated a continuing stream of controversy that fed the

24-hour cable news channels with content they could cover. Less visible was the campaign's use of Facebook. A hired consulting firm, Cambridge Analytica, was able to acquire, through legal but dubious means, the Facebook accounts for over 87 million American voters. That database allowed the campaign to communicate directly with a large group of potential supporters.[23] However, it appears that the Trump campaign did not adopt the "Three C's" model of creating a community through these social media. Instead, they treated these vehicles of communication as just another one-to-many conduit.

It's a commonplace observation that the mix of media available for political communication is ever changing. As new technical capacities meet the needs of individuals and groups of citizens, new media come into use. The first two decades of the 21st century were incubators of tremendous change in the tactical capacity for reaching voters. The number and capacities of various platforms increased markedly. Social networking not only allowed greater precision in targeting; it also has allowed acquaintances to share their views. Text messaging was increasingly mobilized to send urgent messages to supporters. Podcasting became popular, allowing citizens greater voluntary access to complex ideas and lengthy messages. As inboxes filled up with junk, email began to fade in effectiveness. Robocalls became so prolific that many people just stopped answering their landlines or dropped them altogether. At the same time, "apps" for communication such as WhatsApp emerged to replace email, if only temporarily. Competitors to Facebook began to crowd the social networking space. In other words, each innovation gave political managers enhanced possibilities for building political support, but ceaseless churn in the array of media channels is inevitable. This constantly changing world presents tactical challenges for political managers, but it does not alter the fundamental dynamics at the level of strategy in communications.

Conclusion

Thus far, we have considered three different ways of conceptualizing strategy in politics. First, we took note of the strategic parallels between war and politics, and we considered how the military defines strategy.

Next, we took up the most commonly used concept of strategy, that of strategic planning. Finally, in this chapter, we examined how the processes of communication—a critically essential aspect of political support building—need to be considered on a strategic rather than tactical level. These approaches, however, direct our attention to the things we might do to enhance our political power: the use of our resources, our possible options, and our actions. As such, they focus upon the strategies we need to undertake to advance toward our political objects. At the same time, these three approaches to strategy downplay the importance of considering what the competitor or opponent might do. That is the essential corrective of the fourth way of conceptualizing strategy, which we turn to in the next chapter.

The Essence of Political Communications

1. Political managers need to concentrate their attention on two crucial factors in communicating on a strategic level: the audiences to be reached and the messages that need to be delivered. How to undertake these communications is important but tactical and therefore secondary.
2. Communications media have evolved continuously during the conduct of democracy and will continue to grow and change in the future. The fact that newer forms of technological capacity will evolve will not change the fundamental strategic dynamics of political communications.
3. Effective communications demand that political managers adopt three strategic guidelines: simplicity, repetition, and responsiveness. The latter has become particularly important as social media accentuates the need for creating an ongoing community of supporters.
4. Whether political managers need to undertake either or both of the two fundamental tasks of political communications—to persuade or to mobilize—the mix of available media will offer owned media, paid media, earned media, and social media. All four must be employed in an effective communications strategy.

6
Managing Strategic Interaction

> The most fundamental element common to all strategy, and the root polarity in Clausewitz's thinking, is the clash of antagonistic, purposeful, and intelligent wills between opponents.[1]
>
> —Tiha von Ghyczy, Bolko von Oetinger, and Christopher Bassford

Consider this common occurrence. Two strangers approach each other from opposite directions on a sidewalk. At about the same time, each realizes that they are on a collision course. One diverts to his left while the other has moved to her right. Despite these efforts, they are still going to run into each other. Quickly observing the actions of the other, they both simultaneously correct their direction in order to avoid the looming collision. The result is that the two wind up doing a dance on the sidewalk, each reacting to the actions of the other. In the process, they are exhibiting the nature of uncontrolled interaction between two calculating actors.

In a similar dynamic, two friends, wanting to cross a busy four-lane street, are estimating the gaps in a rather constant flow of traffic. One of them steps off the curb to cross, while the other hangs back. The person who has started to cross senses the hesitancy of her friend and, changing her mind, jumps back onto the curb. Meanwhile, the friend standing on the curb sees her friend start off and, though uncertain as to whether the gap in traffic is large enough to cross, thinks "Uh oh, it's time to go." Each reacting to the other's actions, the two keep hopping on and off the curb. A single person in this situation may be better able to master this situation because there is but one mind at work.

Let's make this scenario a bit more dangerous. As one person steps off the sidewalk into the street, a rider on a bicycle bears down on him; they are headed for a nasty accident. The pedestrian stops and starts, trying to get out of the way, while the bicyclist weaves from one side to the other, uncertain as to whether to pass in front or behind the pedestrian. Someone better think fast to avoid a potentially fatal collision. Worse yet, suppose two pedestrians confront the bicycle rider. Because of their interactions, they may not present a coordinated response that would avoid a disaster. Again, one mind may be more effective than two.

Each of these scenarios presents us with the dynamics of uncontrolled interaction. They also lead us to ask a strategic question: "How does one gain control of this interaction?" Without some management, these situations could lead to disaster. How should one of these participants break into their interaction so as to avoid a rapidly developing catastrophe? The problem is really not one of intent; none of those involved wishes for there to be a harmful collision. Rather the issue is a lack of predictability of how the other party will behave. Recognizing this, the pedestrian confronting the bicyclist can simply stop and stand still, communicating to the other that the decision is his/hers as to how to avoid the collision. That would be a strategic decision. The pedestrians trying to cross the street together might vest the power to decide when to cross in front of one of the two friends. One of the strangers on the sidewalk might simply say, "After you." Or, after making eye contact, one could signal with her eyes how she intends to move.[2] Without knowing it, these individuals are engaged in a rudimentary display of strategy.

These examples may seem a long way from strategy in politics, but it was exactly the same decision-making that may have prevented the destruction of the world in October 1962. When the United States discovered that the Soviet Union was installing nuclear missiles in Cuba, President Kennedy instinctively understood the dangers of uncontrolled interaction between the United States and the USSR. He stood on the brink of a nuclear exchange that would have, in all likelihood, unfolded if he had accepted the advice of his senior military officers to order an invasion or air strike. President Kennedy sought to give predictability to the US actions while putting the onus for action onto the Soviet premier, Nikita Khrushchev. By ordering a "quarantine" of Cuba and threatening to stop any Soviet ships that tried to reach the island, Kennedy found a solution just like the pedestrian confronting the speeding bicyclist. To control the dynamic interaction, Kennedy in effect communicated to Khrushchev, "I will not act unless you do; your move." He thereby avoided a collision that neither nation would have survived. Controlling the interaction is the essence of strategy.

Human interaction often occurs dynamically, meaning that the eventual outcomes are the product of the actions of both actors and may not be intended by either. Each party is attempting to influence the other, each is acting to achieve its ends, and each is reacting to the acts of the other. Together their actions create a fluid situation, a spiral of ever-changing circumstances. Whether we are talking about two or more individuals, two or more organizations, or two or more nations, their reciprocal interactions may spin out of the control of the engaged parties. This dynamic is similar to engagements in warfare. As Karl von Clausewitz observed battles—and indeed wars—consist of the interaction of two willful, intelligent forces, each endeavoring to impose its will upon the other. So too politics. Though they conduct their conflicts within defined rules of civil conduct, political actors are, like warriors, engaged in trying to achieve their purposes in the face of intelligent, striving opposition. Dynamic interaction also characterizes political engagements.

In this context, the fundamental nature of strategy is to exert control over the joint interaction between you and another, to bend that spiral of action and reaction to your own purposes. As earlier chapters have expounded, the challenging environment of political engagement demands higher-order, long-range thinking, careful planning, and strategic communications. But it also requires a fluid ability to react quickly to changing circumstances, to cope with uncertainty, and to think creatively and faster than one's opponent. Clausewitz described the mindset of a successful military commander in much the same terms, particularly the required courage of decision in the face of uncertainty and the mental flexibility required for opportunistic insight.

Sun Tzu and *The Art of War*

The parallels between the logic of military conflict and political management suggest there is much to be learned from an ancient Chinese scholar, Sun Tzu, the unsurpassed authority on the dynamics of war.[3] Lee Atwater, a major political consultant in the late 20th century, once described Sun Tzu's book *The Art of War* as "the best book ever written about politics." That may overstate the case, but there are certainly a number of useful lessons that we can draw from this body of writings, despite the fact that they were produced 2,500 years ago in a very different culture and focused on state survival through warfare rather than democratic decision-making. Here I will emphasize four central themes from Sun Tzu's work: the necessity of preparedness, the importance of outthinking your rival, the value of deception, and the role of intelligence.

Preparedness. First, Sun Tzu emphasized that battles were often won before the first sword was even drawn. To him, preparedness meant a great deal more than simply developing the tactics necessary for victory. His advice dealt with a whole range of considerations such as the relationship between the king and the military commander, the structure of the army, the army's physical state and morale, the ground over which it would move and fight, and so on. Sun Tzu also knew that strategy involves thinking before acting:

> The general who wins a battle makes many calculations in his temple ere the battle is fought. The general who loses a battle makes but few calculations beforehand. Thus do many calculations lead to victory, and few calculations to defeat: how much more no calculation at all! It is by attention to this point that I can foresee who is likely to win or lose.

Sun Tzu went on to argue that the height of strategy is to win without having to fight, because skillful maneuvering made the enemy concede the war without violence. "Hence to fight and conquer in all your battles is not supreme excellence; supreme excellence consists in breaking the enemy's resistance without fighting."

For Sun Tzu, preparedness included the mental state of the general and sovereign. There is a story—perhaps apocryphal—written about him by Sima Qian a Chinese historian who lived about 350 years after Sun Tzu. Asked by the king of the state of Wu to demonstrate his prowess by making a trained army out of 180 concubines, Sun Tzu first appointed the king's favorite women as the commanders of two companies. When the women failed twice to execute a simple command, Sun Tzu had the two commanders beheaded, even over the vehement protests of the king. After that demonstration of his seriousness, Sun Tzu had little trouble getting the women to follow his orders. Here, as in many instances emerging out of *The Art of War*, the lessons taught occur on multiple plains. On one level, the story illustrates the demonstration effect that stern punishment can have on compliance. But, at another level, Sun Tzu was also teaching the king to comprehend the rigors, demands, sacrifice, and temperament necessary to fight a war. "War is cruel," he was demonstrating, "are you sure you have the stomach for it?"

Outthinking Your Rival. Second, Sun Tzu understood that strategy requires an ability to project yourself into the mind of the opposition, to comprehend the interactive situation as he or she sees it, and to intuit how she or he will act. In part, this means careful observing the enemy, his actions, his options, and his skill. Thus, Sun Tzu wrote, "[R]efrain from intercepting an enemy whose banners are in perfect order . . . refrain from attacking an army drawn up in calm and confident array. . . . this is the art of studying circumstances." Observing the outward signs of preparedness in the enemy should be a clue as to how the battle will unfold.

Sun Tzu also meant this guidance to probe to a deeper level of the enemy's readiness, down to his psychological state. One needs to understand the opponent's emotional state, his motivations, level of confidence, fears, mental alertness, and the like. In contemporary terms, we would say that a strategist needs to "psych out" his competitors. Sun Tzu's general advice is phrased in the following concrete examples:

> Do not interfere with an army that is returning home because a man whose heart is set upon returning home will fight to the death against

any attempt to bar his way, and is therefore too dangerous as an opponent to be tackled.

When you surround an army, leave an outlet free. This does not mean that the enemy is allowed to escape. The object is to make him believe that there is a road to safety, and thus prevent his fighting with the courage of despair. For you should not press a desperate foe too hard.

The lesson that Sun Tzu teaches us is that conflicts can be won or lost in the thinking or beliefs of the opponent. As much as steel on steel counts, so too does the mental warfare that shapes the beliefs, morale, and actions of the combatants. Today, we should go further to state explicitly that strategic opportunity can be discovered in the mind of the opponent. Win that battle and the physical contest will follow. Pop culture would label this aspect of human interaction as engaging in "head games" or "gamesmanship." For example, having learned this general lesson, when ordered by President George W. Bush to invade Iraq in 2003, the American military first launched a massive air campaign that they dubbed "Shock and Awe." Their objective certainly was to degrade Saddam Husain's military capacity; that's the steel-on-steel dimension. But, by its overwhelming intensity, the bombing campaign was equally designed to undercut the morale of the Iraqi military. Again, strategic opportunity lies in the mind of the opponent.

As one can imagine, there are numerous examples in history in which military commanders have not taken Sun Tzu's words to heart, much to their detriment. One explicit example occurred on Friday the 25th of October in 1415 on the fields of Agincourt, France. There are differing accounts of the battle between the English army led by Henry V and a much larger French force under Charles D'Albret, the constable of France, including one of Shakespeare's most well-known plays, *Henry V*. But one thing that they agree upon is that a much larger French force was blocking the English escape and their way home. Evidently, D'Albret had not read Sun Tzu. The French also underestimated the power of the English longbows that at close range could penetrate armor. D'Albret also ignored the marshy ground over which his men-at-arms would have to march in full armor to engage the English. By the time the French arrived at the English lines, they were exhausted and besieged by the English archers. In the event, the English fought, in Sun Tzu's words, with "the courage of despair" and turned a battle in which they were outnumbered by at least three to one into a rout. Numerous errors of judgment by the French contributed to the English victory, but prominent among them was their failure to consider the psychology of the opponent they were facing. As we noted above in Chapter 3, Napoleon Bonaparte understood that the moral was three times more important than the physical.

Thus, an interactive construct of strategy demands that one think carefully about the perceptions and likely moves of the opponent. That means you must develop the capacity to perceive the changing state of affairs from your competitor's point of view and that projection must also include how your opponent sees you. What does he believe you will do next? How does he think you will react to the reciprocal conflict? The result creates a confrontation in which two willful competitors face each other, each trying to outthink and outmaneuver the other. The calculations each makes can go on for several contingent steps: "If he thinks I'm going to do A, then I should choose option X. But what if he thinks that through and second guesses me? Then I should go for Y. But what if he thinks that I'll go for Y? Then, . . ."

The Value of Deception. Because of the reciprocal effort to comprehend the opponent's thinking, Sun Tzu's third principle is the importance of deceiving the enemy. The most often quoted example from *The Art of War* reads as follows:

> All warfare is based on deception. Hence, when able to attack, we must seem unable; when using our forces, we must seem inactive; when we are near, we must make the enemy believe we are far away; when far away, we must make him believe we are near. Hold out baits to entice the enemy. Feign disorder, and crush him.

This lesson could apply to politics as well. In complex political situations, the grasping for control over an evolving back and forth may often necessitate concealing your own objectives and planned moves. In policy fights during governance or in election contests, one needs to constantly bear in mind that the opponent wishes to diagnose your objectives, motivations, beliefs, and likely actions and to use those understandings to shape the competition to his benefit. Sun Tzu emphasized again and again the need to be crafty, even deceptive, in order to increase the opponent's uncertainty and keep him off balance. The more predictable you are to the opponent, the more likely you are to be bested. Elsewhere, he observed, "That general is skillful in attack whose opponent does not know what to defend, and he is skillful in defense whose opponent does not know what to attack."

Consider this example of the use of deception drawn from American campaign politics. By law, television stations are required to make public in advance the purchases of political advertising. For the station to actually run a commercial, the campaign must do three things: reserve the time slot of its choosing, deposit the money in advance, and transmit to the station the ad that the campaign wishes to broadcast. If any of these steps is missing, the ad won't run. Upon occasion, crafty political managers have reserved the time slots but failed to deliver the funding. Still, the station is obligated to reveal the reservation of ad time, which means that the campaign's opponent may act upon the deception. The supposed ads may even be named in such a way—"Attack #1," "Attack #2"—as to make the opponent think that a major assault is forthcoming. The objective is to cause the opponent to plunk down money earlier than planned in defending against an attack that never comes.

In much of public life, however, political managers must apply this dictum with caution, navigating a subtle line. Remember that both Machiavelli and Sun Tzu were analyzing situations involving conflict between sovereign entities and hence survival of the state. A danger exists here on two levels for political managers. Personal reputations are critically important in developing the trust necessary to work in concert with other players. Politics is a social phenomenon: very little can be accomplished by one person acting alone. Alliances are essential. One must be careful not to become perceived as too manipulative by those around you. Deceptiveness can equate to untrustworthiness. Even those on the same team may be alarmed by the ruthlessness with which one treats the opponents. In the competitive community formed by the struggle for political power, reputations are often used as a political weapon. Players seen as too crafty by other political managers may find their effectiveness curtained.[4] Even so, it's important to develop a name for yourself as an aggressive, valiant, and effective fighter for your team. There's a balance of appropriate judgment to be established here. Keep in mind that Lord Palmerton's dictum can apply on an individual level: "We have no permanent allies, we have no permanent enemies, we only have permanent interests."

Your concern that a reputation for deviousness can limit your political career exists on the level of public opinion as well. Public life is about building public support. Except in obscure situations usually involving career advancement, the combatants are rarely isolated from public opinion. It is not as though political warriors are two lone combatants on an empty field prepared to fight to the death. Political fights are carried out in public with citizens and voters constantly judging the players. What the public thinks of the individual players matters. Once a reputation becomes solidified in the public mind it becomes very difficult to alter. The fact that there are some prominent counterexamples—both Richard Nixon and Bill Clinton were elected to the US presidency after their opponents successfully affixed to their public image the monikers "Tricky Dickie" and "Slick Willie"—does not change the fact that one needs to carefully guard his or her public reputation.[5]

Be aware that your efforts to husband a reputation of integrity can be compromised by skirmishes given the vitriol of politics. Political leaders, corporations, and interest groups have gone beyond positive public relations campaigns and increasingly resorted to carefully calculated effort to damage the reputations of their rivals. One major example was surfaced by the *New York Times* in reporting upon Facebook's efforts to defend itself against charges that it had not been sufficiently vigilant in guarding against Russian efforts to tilt the 2016 American elections in favor of Donald Trump.[6] The company hired political consultants to guide journalists to negative information about Google and Twitter, two of Facebook's rivals. Among other efforts, they also commissioned investigations into the financier George Soros, a liberal icon and frequent critic of Facebook. Thus, reputation management can include efforts to tarnish your political opponents as well as to enhance your own standing within the political community.

Intelligence. Sun Tzu's fourth lesson is the importance of information about your opponent's capacities and intensions. He advocates employing spies to find out what the enemy is up to, a practice that may be acceptable when national survival is involved but is generally deemed to be outside the bounds of fair play in a domestic, civil polity. Nevertheless, controlling the interaction depends upon one's ability to predict the competitor's actions, and intelligence facilitates those predictions. As Sun Tzu wrote, "What enables the wise sovereign and the good general to strike and conquer, and achieve things beyond the reach of ordinary men, is foreknowledge." Undoubtedly some low-level spying does exist in democratic politics in the United States and elsewhere. The broader point is certainly valid: one should endeavor to learn as much as possible about the opponent's intentions, options, strengths, and weaknesses. Staying within the limits of acceptable behavior, political managers would also be wise to gather as much information as possible about the larger strategic environment within which policy and political conflict will occur. Certainly, this should include intelligence beyond opposition research, such as data and perspective on the critical policy conflicts of the moment as well as information necessary to backstop a rapid response team. If undertaken at all, this research should be accomplished with the understanding that the means by which one gathers information can become dysfunctional. The appropriate balance calls for judgment on the part of political managers. One helpful injunction common among American political operatives reads as follows: "If you don't want to see your actions reported on the front page of the *Washington Post* or the *New York Times*, don't do them."

Each of these lessons—preparedness, gamesmanship, deception, and intelligence—apply equally well to civil politics, within the limits of propriety. Taken together, they are all of a piece, reinforcing each other and preparing political managers for the competitive interaction of oppositional politics. Moreover, because they are all analytical skills, they speak directly to the strategic dimension of political collaboration and conflict.

A Few Lessons from Game Theory

Economists and political scientists have advanced the principles of game theory to understand interactions between two rivals.[7] While the arguments and propositions of game theory can become quite complex and mathematical, here we need only to adopt its basic precepts to understand the logic of competition between two or more parties. If strategy is conceived as the effort to control human interactions, then game theory is relevant to understandings of political striving. Before we turn to that, it is useful to observe that the language of game theory has infiltrated political management. When someone says uses the phrase "zero-sum game" or observes, "It's like the prisoner dilemma," they are using terms straight out of game theory. Similarly, when someone is urged to "think outside the box," she is being encouraged to consider an alternative not contemplated in a payoff matrix, which looks like a box.

In the bicycle and Cuban missile scenarios described above, game theory yields the understanding that one actor transformed their interactions by changing the rules of exchange. Instead of a situation in which both players were acting simultaneously and in ignorance of their counterpart's actions, their interactions became sequential. One actor was in effect communicating, "I've made my move, now you react." The other actor was forced to accept responsibility for the outcome of their joint decisions. If that person perceived the probable outcome as catastrophic, he or she would likely take steps to avoid that result. When strategy is viewed as control over interactions among competitors, then paradoxically there are times when one can control a situation by forcing the other actor to choose between disaster and a rational decision.

Thus, the order of play can be manipulated to one's advantage. The Constitution of the United States, for example, dictates that, formally, the Congress passes legislation that the president can then sign or veto. But, presidents do not always like that sequence, preferring instead to jump the gun and announce their intention to veto a bill if Congress passes it with certain provisions. Game theory provides a means of analyzing these competitive interactions.

Consider the following situation and seriously try to envision yourself engaged in an exercise frequently employed in executive training. You and another individual are seated facing each other. You are handed an envelope with $25 in it, and told that you may offer any amount of that $25 to the other individual. If he or she accepts that division, you pay out what you promised and you get to keep the rest. If she or he turns you down, both of you walk away with nothing. You are in an exercise called "the ultimatum game." This is not a bargaining circumstance; it is a take-it-or leave-it situation. You can make one offer and the other person can either accept or reject your ultimatum. What should your reasoning be?

You could offer $1 and keep $24. That would be the best outcome for you, but only if the other person accepted that division. Will he? Possibly. After all, one dollar is better for him than no dollars, which is the only alternative. But how likely is it that he will accept such a one-sided division, especially if there are observers watching and evaluating the interaction? Is he likely to feel disrespected and consequently turn your $1 offer down?

You could consider an alternative: suppose you offer to give him $24, keeping only $1 for yourself? The probability of his accepting that division is likely to be 100 percent. At least you're nearly certain to walk off with $1. But you can do a lot better. You're likely to consider what is the least that you can offer and still have a fairly high probability he will agree to accept? Would he accept $8? Or $10?

As the alert reader will have quickly perceived, we are driven back to the wisdom of Sun Tzu in emphasizing the importance of intelligence. What do we know about our counterpart? Is he impoverished? Is she highly social? Is he worried about how he is perceived by others? Does she exhibit an outsized self-appreciation? Is she regarded as a leader or follower? How has he behaved in your prior encounters? Is he ruthless or benevolent? All of these and other considerations will influence the probability that he will accept a given offer. All of these calculations should factor into the decision you make as to how to divide the $25. Value and probability of acceptance are interlocked.

When abstracted to the social level—that is ignoring the particulars of this individual opponent—there is another calculation at work. If this exercise is conducted in a classroom setting, there is a degree of comradeship among those likely to be more or less similarly situated. Such a community will accentuate the value of "fairness." In short, as one considers proposing a near equal division of the $25—say $11 or $12—the probability that your counterpart will accept your ultimatum approaches 100 percent. In the abstract, a middle-ground proposal is likely to yield you the most benefit. A proposed split that gives the opposition too little will have a low probability of acceptance, meaning zero for both of you. An offer of near the full $25 is very likely to be accepted, but the leftover value for you will be meager. Then too, there is the matter of your own reputation with this opponent and within the larger community. Leaving aside the short-term reactions of the group, do you want to be perceived as unduly lenient or aggressively hardnosed? Perhaps, a better idea would be to stick close to an equal division, increasing the likelihood of acceptance and gaining a reputation for treating others "fairly."

Similar logic would apply to an encounter in a less abstract situation. Suppose, for example, you find yourself sitting across a table from a representative of an opponent's campaign, hoping to work out the details of a live debate on television. You'll need to estimate what he or she will accept and what will cause the other party to walk out. Of course, this situation is not quite the same as the ultimatum game in that you and your counterpart will have opportunities to make more than one suggestion. But, all of the same issues of guesswork informed by intelligence come into play. Even though you and your counterpart can go back and forth several times narrowing the differences, you'll never really know if you came close to the other's walkaway point.

The Prisoner's Dilemma

Now consider the infamous game known as the Prisoner's Dilemma. The payoff matrix for these two unfortunate fellows is presented in Table 6.1.

In the prisoner dilemma scenario, the two "players" must decide whether they want to confess their crime of bank robbery to the police or keep silent. The police inform the two alleged bank robbers that, depending upon the choice each player makes combined with that of

Table 6.1 Outcomes in a "Prisoner Dilemma" Game

	Player 1 Remains Silent	Player 1 Confesses
Player 2 Remains Silent	Player 1 gets 1 year in jail Player 2 gets 1 year in jail	Player 1 gets no jail time Player 2 gets 20 years in jail
Player 2 Confesses	Play 1 gets 20 years in jail Player 2 gets no jail time	Player gets 15 years in jail Player gets 15 years in jail

his fellow criminal, the individual may spend no time in jail or serve the rather lengthy sentence (20 years) for robbing the bank. If one of the thieves confesses and the other doesn't, the prosecutor will use the testimony of the confessor to convict his cohort. If both keep silent, the police admit that they do not have enough evidence to convict these criminals, but they can send them away for a year on gun charges. If both confess, the prosecutor won't need the other's testimony, but each will get a somewhat lighter sentence (15 years) for "acceptance of responsibility."

The problem with the prisoner dilemma is that, for most of us, we cannot really project ourselves into role playing this scenario. Consider, therefore, a similar game, and again visualize yourself as one of the two players. You and a competitor are each told you can choose Option A or Option B, resulting in a simple two-by-two table of outcomes. You will choose simultaneously, meaning that you will not know what the other person has chosen until after both are committed. And you two will be given different dollar rewards depending on how you each choose. The payoffs presented in Table 6.2 constitute a version of the "Prisoner Dilemma game," modified by proposing

Table 6.2 Payoffs in a "Prisoner Dilemma" Game

	Player 1 Chooses A	Player 1 Chooses B
Player 2 Chooses A	Player 1 = $10; Player 2 = $10	Player 1 = $25; Player 2 = $5
Player 2 Chooses B	Play 1 = $5; Player 2 = $25	Player 1 = $0; Player 2 = $0

a payoff matrix of positive rewards rather than negative years in jail. Rather than trying to imagine yourself in the position of a criminal deciding whether to "rat out" a partner in crime, think about receiving greater or lesser money depending upon the choices you and your opposition might make. A prisoner's dilemma game for money makes the dilemma more accessible to us.

As noted, the promised payoffs from Table 6.2 convert hypothetical years lost in jail into dollars gained. Nevertheless, the structure of the rewards still creates the same dilemma and contains an incentive for both parties to choose Option B.

As in the prior example of dividing up an envelope of money, each party is attempting to "psych" the other out. Each player must try to figure out what the opponent will choose and, to do so, each needs to consider whether that opponent is likely to be cooperative or self-oriented. If they are allowed to talk to each other, the dimension of trust becomes relevant. Participants often agree to accept an equal reward by both choosing A. But, of course, the more convinced each becomes that his or her competitor will in fact choose A, the stronger becomes the incentive to break that promise and choose B. The choice becomes imbued with overtones of fairness, duplicity, trust, manipulation, and reputation.

The reader may object that the prisoner dilemma is little different from the ultimatum game proposed above. In terms of money being distributed between two players, that is true. But it does make a difference that here, in the prisoner's dilemma, decisions of the two players are simultaneous. Both players are active; both are free to choose how they will move. In order to prosper, each must bring essentially the same mentality to their decision. They are both trying to estimate how their counterpart will move and make their own choice contingent upon their conjecture. The ultimatum game awards the initiative to the player with the envelope; in the prisoner's dilemma both hold the initiative. Of course, the array of rewards can give an advantage to one player, so they are not equal. Assume for the moment that Player 1 would receive, not the $25 as in Table 6.2, but instead $250 for choosing B. In considering his move, Player 2 would certainly have to weigh the strength of that incentive in Player 1's calculations.

When playing with real money, the two participants will sometimes figure out that they can "game the system" by agreeing that one will choose A and the other B, and then later they can split the $30 evenly. So doing, however, takes the dilemma out of the game and, in the process, vitiates the logic of competition. But, not entirely, for what they are really doing is turning the tables on the "game master" who tried to put them into a prisoner's dilemma in the first place. By agreeing to cooperate rather than compete, they are playing a different game, an example of literally thinking outside the box. Out of bounds from the point of view of the game master, but commendable nonetheless. If the dollar rewards are coming from his own pocket, the game master would prefer that the players actually compete against each other and wind up with both choosing B in hopes of capturing the $25 for themselves. That outcome, of course, minimizes his lost. If the reader has indeed been able to project herself into this little game and can imagine trying to resolve this dilemma in competition with an opponent, then she can begin to see how crucial it is to be able to put herself into the mind of her rival. As we insist, that is the essential task of strategy when looked at from this interactive perspective.

When Donald J. Trump, Jr., was elected to the American presidency, he ran on the theme that he would shake up Washington and "drain the swamp." Upon taking office he set about doing just that in ways that were never contemplated by his supporters, detractors, or opponents. Many of his decisions broke long-standing norms, actions way outside the box of expected presidential conduct. In one example that is hard to tell whether or not he was serious, Trump asked his military advisers, "If we have nuclear weapons, why can't we use them?"[8] He had unacceptably nasty things to say about a couple whose son had been killed in Afghanistan, and he attacked a senator widely regarded as a war hero for his long imprisonment during the Vietnam War. He chose individuals to run his departments that he knew could never be confirmed by the Senate, so he filled those seats as temporary appointments. In these and numerous other ways, Trump continually surprised journalists, observers, and politicians as to how far he was willing to reach outside the norms established by precedent. As a result, in a demonstration of pure strategy—but at the cost of true leadership—Trump's efforts to shake up Washington produced the most polarizing regime in over

150 years.[9] Yet, it's fair to say he dominated American and Washington politics to a greater extent than most of his predecessors, even while producing relatively little change.

Here, we need not delve deeply into the mathematics and logic of game theory for there is an excellent book, *The Art of Strategy*,[10] written by two economists, Avinash Dixit and Barry Nalebuff. Beyond their detailed analysis of game theory, they—like Sun Tzu's *The Art of War*—propose some broad understandings that are applicable to political management. First of all, they suggest that when confronted by an interactive competition, one should "reason ahead and think backward." Good advice for a number of situations. Instead of thinking, "What should I do next," it is often helpful to start from the full range of possible outcomes and, having deciphered the best of those for you, work backward in a logical chain of interaction to conclude how you should act now.

Interaction with another "player" can be mapped out as a tree-like diagram. At the simplest level, the diagram could help one think clearly about the whole set of actions the opponent might make and lead backward to consideration of acts that would narrow his choices to those most favorable to you. A two-step model like this would, however, vastly understate the complexity of most human dynamics. In most situations we might expect the tree structure of a logical chain of back-and-forth interactions to occur in multiple levels. The situation may be likened to two chess players trying to project the game four or more moves ahead. But, given that the two players have the same information about the state of the board and that both the players' goals and the rules of movement are fixed and known, chess—as complicated as it is—is still a simplified replica of human competition.

Dixit and Nalebuff progress from their advice about backward reasoning to discuss the difficulty of knowing for certain the mindset of the opponent. They reason as follows:

> To really look forward and reason backward, you have to predict what the other players will actually do, not what you would have done in their shoes. The problem is that when you try to put yourself in the other player's shoes, it is hard if not impossible to leave your own shoes behind. You know too much about what you are planning

to do ... [You] have to know what they know and not know what they don't know. Your objectives have to be their objectives, not what you wish they had as an objective.[11]

Inability to predict the coming moves of your opponent is a major, if not the major, source of uncertainty in a strategic situation. Dixit and Nalebuff are correct that prediction with near certainty is impossible, but there are several ways in which one can rationally proceed in these circumstances.

Predicting the Opponent's Moves

Our first piece of advice on predicting others' actions emerges from the approach to battlefield planning by the military. Military strategists prepare for war by assessing everything that the opponent is capable of undertaking and then preparing a counter for each and every possible enemy action. They develop a comprehensive plan to deal with whatever the enemy throws at them. But that is not enough, for they do not want to be purely reactive, waiting for the opponent to move first, and then working to counter his actions. They want to implement plans on their own initiative. Certainly, much of the assessment of the opponent's capabilities will be useful in planning their own proactive moves.

We need to go a step further in our thinking. If we are trying to predict how the enemy will behave, we should also do so based on probability. Having anticipated all that he *could* do, we now narrow that to an assessment of what he *is likely* to do. Thus, readers should learn the maxim, "Plan on the basis of possibility; implement on the basis of probability."

Of course, this advice—implement based on probability—merely throws us back to the dilemma of how can we predict the probability of the opponent's choosing among his alternative moves. The first direct approach derives from Dixit and Nalebuff's thinking: namely, trying to put yourself into the mind of the other person. While accepting their counsel, it still should be possible to make some guesses as to what the competitor will do by considering how you would react in the same situation as your opponent finds himself. This technique is often called a "theory of mind" prediction.[12] Since one can never be sure what is taking place in the mind of another human being, we assume—that is, we theorize—that others around us have minds of their own that are mostly similar to ours. At its core, theory of mind requires that one understand the objectives, desires, beliefs, options, and perceptions of the world even while making allowances for the fact that these may be different from our own.[13] A principal supposition of this type of projection is that the "others" be rational. We certainly are; why would they not be likewise? In reality, however, you will need to be cautious because neither of those assumptions has proven to be valid in every case. That is, our opponent will not always behave rationally. Nor will we. Nevertheless, by careful observation of the behavior of others, we may discover the extent to which—narrow or wide—their behavior deviates from the rational ideal that we believe to characterize our own.[14] We might invest the resources to create what the Central Intelligence Agency calls a "pattern of life" or a detailed portrait of how a given person or a group of individuals has behaved in similar circumstances.[15] In many instances, this second procedure should be intuitive but inconclusive, which leads to the question, are there other ways of predicting how others will interact with us?

A more robust procedure for projecting the likely moves of opponents derives from one of the understandings of game theory, called a "dominant strategy." Presenting this interaction will require a dive into the details of a "payoff matrix" that will undoubtedly seem to the reader to be far removed from democratic politics. But game theory does provide a means to understand the logic of competition. Consider the dollar payoffs represented in Table 6.3 below.

Table 6.3 is shown in the formal fashion preferred by game theorists in which convention dictates that the numbers in the *upper right* of each cell constitute the payoffs to the column player or "C." The numbers in the *lower left* of each cell represent the rewards that would be achieved by the row player "R" if the two wound up in that cell. Note that Column can choose from among five options, while Row has only four choices. In other words, if Column chooses option 4 and Row chooses R1, then Column would receive $8.00 and Row's return would be $7.00. Though each player has preferences as to the preferred

136   ARENAS OF STRATEGY

Table 6.3 Payoffs Where One Player Has a Dominant Choice

	C1	C2	C3	C4	C5
R1	+$5 +$4	+$7 +$2	+$4 +$4	+$8 +$7	+$17 +$5
R2	+$9 +$6	+$8 +$8	+$5 +$5	+$13 +$8	+$10 +$3
R3	+$3 +$10	+$9 +$9	+$3 +$8	+$8 +$12	+$7 +$7
R4	+$6 +$6	+$7 +$5	+$4 +$3	+$6 +$10	+$5 +$4

outcome, neither can alone determine in which of the 20 cells they will wind up. That result is jointly determined by their separate actions. They are, moreover, going to choose simultaneously without knowledge of the other's choice. But, not knowing does not preclude speculating.

To "solve" this game, one might adopt the viewpoint of the column player, who starts by pretending that the game involves sequential decision-making, not simultaneous. He or she might reason, "If I knew that Row would choose R1, what would I then choose? Clearly, I should choose C5 because 17 dollars is a lot better for me than any of the other possible payoffs. But, wait. What if Row choses R2? Then, I should choose C4 because 13 dollars is certainly better for me than $11, $9, $8 or $5." Following this reasoning to its logical conclusion, Column discovers that if R chooses R3 or R4, then C2 would be the best response. In other words, Column has no obvious choice and would very much like to predict what Row's choice will be. So what happens if Column tries to see the situation from Row's point of view?

As it turns out, the matrix provides a different result when looked at from the point of view of the row player. If Row goes through a similar analysis projecting a response to each possible choice that Column might make, he or she will soon discover that in every case choosing R3 provides her with the highest payoff. Of course, there are clear differences for Row from a high of $12 to a low of $7, depending on

Column's choice. Nonetheless, Row's choice is clear, a fact that makes Column's rational choice clear as well. Assuming that Column takes the time to analyze the situation from Row's viewpoint, she should choose C2 and they should wind up in the cell R3, C2. For Row, this situation is one in which he has a dominant strategy although the current author prefers the term "dominant choice," reserving the term "strategy" for the thinking that lies behind choices rather than the choices themselves.

Stepping back from these details for a moment, some readers may complain that this matrix of payoffs to be so contrived as to be irrelevant to the world of political actors. Thought of more generally, however, we can predict that, if there is one thing that our opponent can do which will maximize his outcomes for all choices we might make, then he has a dominant strategy. Whether he goes through the above formal analysis or not, he is most likely to intuit and implement this dominant choice. In other words, one way to predict how our opponent might behave is to consider whether he has a dominant choice.

The administration of President Bill Clinton provides an example. As he was plotting his first presidential campaign and, later, while he was in office, Clinton adopted policies that would move the perception of the Democratic Party toward the center of the political spectrum.[16] He believed that, after 12 years of Republican presidents, positioning his political appeal around the same arguments that had dominated the political dialogue for 40 years would be a losing proposition. The forces on the left side of the party were constantly trying to pull him toward their vision, especially during the healthcare fight early in his presidency. On a whole series of issues, Clinton opted for a dominant strategy of taking issues away from the Republicans. According to his consultant, Dick Morris, he settled on three "signature issues" that would define him as a different kind of Democrat: crime, the federal deficit, and welfare reform.[17] On these three policy fights, Clinton was able to propose centrist alternatives but still present policy solutions that would weaken the political appeal of Republican conservatives. He was re-elected rather handily and, despite becoming mired in a sex scandal and being impeached by the Republican-dominated House of Representatives, he finished his two terms with comfortable public approval ratings.

The table below, Table 6.4, suggests some additional advice for us in its structure of payoffs. At first blush, this reward matrix may look identical to that presented back in Table 6.3. And, so it is for the column player. But, if you will look closely, you'll discover that the payoffs for Row have been changed so that she no longer has a dominant strategy.

Suppose that the row player happens to know a bit about Column's personality. She has concluded that Column is not particularly analytical and, instead, tends to be both impulsive and self-absorbed. Such an opponent might be attracted to the largest payoff, meaning the Column would be likely to choose C5 hoping to reap $17. That would mean that Row should opt for R4, which would provide her with a bigger payoff than her other choices, so that together the two players would wind up in R4, C5. Note that, in strict game theoretic terms, however, this result is unstable, because it is not optimum from Column's point of view. Column might suddenly analyze the situation and predict that Row could be thinking that he—Column—would go for the big prize in C5 and would, accordingly, choose R4. In that case, Column would improve his return by switching his choice to either C1 or C4.

Conversely, Column might be the kind of person who is cautious and highly risk adverse. Such a mindset might lead him to try to maximize the *minimum* payoff she would receive. She might opt for what game theorists call a "maxi-min strategy." Such a player would scrutinize each choice, C1 through C5, to see which one would provide her with the largest minimum guaranteed return. Think of this person as

Table 6.4 Payoffs without a Dominant Choice

	C1	C2	C3	C4	C5
R1	+$5 / +$4	+$7 / +$8	+$4 / +$8	+$8 / +$7	+$17 / +$5
R2	+$9 / +$10	+$8 / +$4	+$5 / +$5	+$13 / +$8	+$10 / +$3
R3	+$3 / +$6	+$9 / +$7	+$3 / +$5	+$8 / +$12	+$7 / +$4
R4	+$6 / +$6	+$7 / +$5	+$4 / +$3	+$6 / +$10	+$5 / +$7

constantly focused on the least attractive outcome for herself and then choosing the best of those worsts. "How can I guarantee for myself the best of the worst outcomes?," she might ask herself. If Column chose C1, for example, she might receive only three dollars; if he chose C2, she might get five dollars. The maxi-min mindset would dictate that Column should choose C4, knowing that at a minimum she would receive seven dollars, more than the minimum return from any other choice. Here again, given the payoff matrix in Table 6.3, a wise row player, in light of careful thought about his opponent, would make his choice contingent upon his prediction of how Column would choose. Row wants to know whether Column tends to be "risk adverse" or a "highflier."

Moving on from these simplistic measures of value inherent in game theory payoffs, another attempt at predicting one's opponents moves emerges out of an understanding of what actions have brought our opponent success in the past. Success has a way of locking in behavior. For example, in *The Making of Campaign Strategy*, Marjorie Randon Hershey[18] found that when candidates for US Congress won, they were likely to replicate the same strategy in their re-election campaigns. But if they lost and then ran again, they were likely to change their strategy substantially. Similarly, in *Presidential Character* political scientist James David Barber[19] argued that presidential actions were heavily influenced by their first independent success. It makes intuitive sense that success in one's past would affect how that individual would behave subsequently. So, this thought suggests to us that we examine the actions that have benefited our rivals in past circumstances, because they are likely to be repeated now in a conflict with us. In 1976, when Albert Gore first ran for the US House in Tennessee, he distanced himself from his father who had been a well-liked senator before him. He asked his father to not campaign for him, wanting to be his own man. Twenty-four years later, as the Democratic candidate for president, he repeated that strategic choice by confining President Bill Clinton to the sidelines. At the time, Clinton remained quite popular with Democratic voters even after having been impeached because of a sex scandal. He might have helped Gore, his vice president for eight years, win in several states that were extraordinarily close. A narrow electoral college loss might have been reversed.[20]

Consider, for example, the case of Donald Trump who came into political power from a career as a self-promoting real estate developer. Trump pictured himself as an extremely successful transactional negotiator, perhaps the best ever, a fact that colored his first years in office in two ways.[21] First, Trump was especially attuned to exchanges that involved money, but less able to understand the nuanced and intangible values associated with identity, ideology, vision, and the like. Second, since President Trump pictured himself as the world's best negotiator, that meant that, by definition, any deal that had been negotiated by his predecessors could be improved upon. So long-standing treaties and institutional arrangements that had served the United States well were all subject to cancellation or at least renegotiation. Sure enough, when he ran for re-election in 2020 his campaign was nearly a carbon copy of his surprising victory in 2016.

One last thought emerges from game theory that relates to influencing your opponent's thinking. In the 1960s, the United States and the Soviet Union placed a great deal of trust on the notion of deterrence. Basically, the strategy relies on threats of retaliation that are designed to deter an opponent from taking a given course of action. The two nations each built up stockpiles of nuclear warheads and missiles so massive that their enemy understood that a first strike would fail to suppress a substantial retaliation. For each, the probably of a successful attack would be perceived as low and the costs substantial. If one launched an attack, both would be destroyed. For deterrence to be successful, however, the opposing side must believe that the provoked response will be painful, and that the opponent has the capability and the will to carry out the retaliation.

In other words, deterrence refers to another strategy in which one party endeavors to influence the thinking of its opponent. It's rightly called a "head game." In political life, there are circumstances in which a political manager could threaten an opponent to deter her from an action that would be harmful to his interests. Doug Bailey, a highly successful Republican consultant, once stated that he knew of an election contest in which the opposition research of both campaigns had turned up very damaging information. In the negotiations leading up to a candidate debate, the two sides agreed not to bring the damning material to light if the other side also kept its findings secret.[22]

Remaining Unpredictable

The interactive approach also dictates that strategy must be conceived of as a two-way street. In addition to the difficulty of predicting how the opponent will act—putting yourself into your opponent's shoes as Dixit and Nalebuff would have it—political managers must also consider how they should act so as to throw the opponent off balance. That is, in order to predict the actions of one's opponent, not only does one have to endeavor to see the situation from the opponent's perspective, one has also to calibrate the effect of one's own moves upon the opponent's thinking and reactions. All this takes place even while the opponent is making the same calculations as to how you are thinking and what are your likely moves. For you to be a successful strategist, you must simultaneously predict what your opponent will do while endeavoring to be unpredictable to that opponent. Projection and surprise are flip sides of each other.

Essentially we are addressing the inverse of predictability that we have just been considering. The argument begins with the proposition that in an interactive conflict, your opponent will be trying to predict how you will act and will be calculating his best move to counter yours. In politics, competitors are not just seeking to maximize their returns; they are also endeavoring to win in the short run and, by increasing their power, they hope to win in the long run as well. Becoming predictable to your competitor is one sure way if not to lose entirely, then at least to achieve less than you could.

Bradley Tusk, a self-described political "fixer," recounts a prime example from when the ride-sharing company Uber was establishing itself in New York City.[23] The fight began in 2015 when Mayor Bill de Blasio, announced a proposed regulation that, in the name of reducing traffic congestion, would limit Uber's growth to 1 percent per year going forward. The mayor, as befits an ardent liberal, saw this fight as defending poor taxi drivers up against a big, multibillion-dollar company. Tusk was hired by Uber founder Travis Kalanick to stop this regulation from being approved by the 51-member city council, a body that was filled with de Blasio's supporters. Tusk realized that the best way to win lay in the surprising strategy of taking de Blasio on from the liberal perspective. "No one had ever thought they could question his progressive bona fides."[24] Tusk's job was to transform the fight into an aggressive move by de Blasio in support of the rich medallion taxi owners who had contributed handsomely to his campaign. He wanted to make de Blasio look "right wing, anti-immigrant, antiminority, and corrupt."[25] Uber funded television ads pointing out that medallion taxis were in short supply in the outer boroughs, that many Black residents often complained about being passed up by empty cabs, that young millennials loved the service Uber provided, and that Uber drivers came heavily from immigrant communities. Riders and drivers responded when they were summoned to demonstrate outside city hall against the proposal. Slowly Uber began to peel away de Blasio's votes in the city council. Finally, under growing public pressure of demonstrations and TV advertisements, city hall capitulated and pulled the bill. Uber's unpredictable strategy had won.

Edward Luttwak would endorse Tusk's move, suggesting that, because of expectations, one should avoid the easiest, most direct option. The harder, more difficult choice becomes preferable precisely because that is what the opponent least expects.[26] Dixit and Nalebuff provide us with a similar approach, namely the importance of mixing your moves.[27] By mixing your moves, you become less predictable to your opponent. In other words, they strongly suggest that one not always try the same approach in confronting an opponent. This reasoning also underlies the advice of Sun Tzu: "Do not repeat the tactics which have gained you one victory, but let your methods be regulated by the infinite variety of circumstances." To be sure, he is suggesting that each situation be analyzed anew but also that repeating successful tactics will make one predictable to one's opponent. For their part, Dixit and Nalebuff also point out that, if one has moves that are not particularly effective in comparison to others in your repertoire, then your opponent will expect you to rely upon your stronger moves. Therefore, one way to become less predictable is to work on improving the efficacy of your weaker moves.

The Essence of Interactive Strategic Dynamics

1. From the perspective of the dynamic interaction between two or more actors, strategy consists of the efforts one player exerts to control those interactions to his or her benefit. Accordingly, the core meaning of "strategy" should be reserved for situations of competitive interplay between two or more parties. In this sense, strategy prescribes the means for employing power to your benefit.
2. Winning the interactions between you and an opponent will require you to understand the mind of your opponent in two senses. First, you need to understand or at least predict how she or he will act and react. Strategic interaction places an equally important premium upon "head games"; you should seek to influence—positively or negatively—your opponent's perception of the interaction between you.
3. Conversely, adroit political managers seek constantly to keep secret their own motivations, information, options, and planned moves. Surprise allows one to maintain the initiative in interaction, forcing the competitor to react to one's actions. Cloaking one's possible moves may require a bit of deception that, despite the temptations of pursuing victory, must be kept within the bounds of civil conduct in politics.
4. A great fog of uncertainty will surround your predictions of what your opponent will do and how she or he will react to your moves. While game theory provides some suggestions of ways to reduce this ambiguity, inevitably your efforts to understand and predict your competitor's actions will be marked by doubt. Resolving to action despite uncertainty is an essential prescription.

Conclusion of Part II

We have now examined four different ways of thinking about strategy: a military approach, strategic planning, communications, and in this chapter an interactive conception. Strategy is all of these approaches. They are all necessary and intertwined and not meant to be hierarchical such that we should consider one as more important than the others.

The different models provide general statements by which strategy can be understood, but no practical advice as to formulating the actual choices political managers must make. In the next chapter, however, it is time to redress this shortcoming and consider the practical guidelines that should shape strategic behavior in the political realm.

7
Guidelines to Effective Strategy

What have we learned thus far? Power is the essential commodity for achieving one's goals through politics. Strategy can guide us to the most effective means for employing power. Military strategists reserve the term for fundamental decisions that hold significant and long-term implications for the conduct of battle. They describe a conflict between two opponents—two calculating and competing wills—who are actively seeking to overthrow the other. Strategic planning emphasizes the need to calculate deliberately and rationally the employment of available resources to achieve one's goals. A focus on the processes of communication suggests that political managers should concentrate first on the audience that they need to reach and then upon the messages to be delivered. Finally, political managers understand the importance of predicting and controlling their interactions with opponents while achieving, in their own actions, the unpredictability that randomness provides.

Through all of these perspectives, we have emphasized that political strategy must be "situational." This point is absolutely essential when it comes to formulating and acting upon a strategy. The complexity of political engagements means that the circumstances you confront will determine your strategy. You must consider the setting, the opponent(s), the formal and informal rules of the arena in which the confrontation takes place; your goals, resources, and options; the interests of other players; and, in politics, the reactions of bystanders who may be observant citizens and voters. Rules, laws, axioms, or principles that attempt to decree a strategy in a particular set of circumstances will only provide you with guidelines—not dictates—that can help you to decipher how to behave in a particular situation.[1]

The situational mandate of strategy means that there are no hard and fast rules that you can follow![2] Instead, you have to be content with some generalized guidelines of political management that will improve your chances of success. We have in mind such characteristics as a competence for planning; an ability to remain flexible and to allow your intuition to influence your actions; an attentiveness to the power dynamic of any interactions with others, whether colleague or opponent; a capacity to remain steadfastly focus on the long-term goals; an ability to separate strategy from tactics, plotting from acting; and a willingness to hold and use power when necessary to achieve your objective. These general predispositions will improve performance in situations requiring strategy.

The fact that there are no rules—no single formula—should be instructive for those working in politics. Why no ironclad rules? Simply because the "clash of competing wills" that defines political confrontations implies an interactive dynamic, one that the strategist seeks to control. Following a standard rulebook in these circumstances means that you might become predictable to your opponents, which can work to your disadvantage, especially if they have read the same rulebook. Sun Tzu argument for "formlessness" as a means to avoid becoming predictable serves as good advice to the strategist in both politics and warfare. Too much attention to how things worked in the past can be a disservice to innovation and flexibility in an emerging environment. Studying successful strategies used by others in the past can be enlightening, but you can almost never simply replicate them yourself. Thus, we cannot provide here a roster of stratagems that you can follow to achieve success in political disputes.

The complexity of political engagements also means that there will be different pathways to accomplishing your objectives. The trick is that you must act and react in a fast-changing world that is determined by the confluence of your action *and* those of your allies and opponents. But remember that the same is true for your opponent. Every action by one of you changes the situation for both of you. Adapting to the altered circumstances will require flexibility on your part. You will be compelled to act even in the face of a high degree of uncertainty. Here Clausewitz—understanding the necessity for action amid confusion—provides useful counsel. He found a solution in boldness and strength of will. Today, we might say one needs self-confidence, resolve, courage, and grit.[3]

Finally, it is important to keep in mind that strategy is a cerebral exercise. In developing a strategy, you should be thinking, not acting. Implementation of a strategy tends to become tactical in short order. In fact, a distinguishing feature between strategy and tactics is that actions are tactical, designed to execute a strategy developed through thoughtful contemplation. This means that, to be successful, one must create the circumstances in which one can think. Given a political environment in which allies, opponents, and the media are constantly in action and in which information is pouring in minute by minute, then being able to carve out time for deliberation is no easy task. Attention naturally drifts to the immediate actions and engagements.

Recall that campaigns tend to be temporary organizations. That characteristic often results in a certain fluidity of power within the organization. Everything revolves around the candidate. Facetime with the candidate can be the key to influence during the campaign and, possibly, employment after a victory. Why then did three seasoned political managers—James Carville, George Stephanopoulos, and Paul Begala—sequester themselves in a "war room"[4] in Little Rock, Arkansas, while letting other, less-influential staffers travel on the airplane with Bill Clinton during his 1992 campaign for president? They knew that traveling with the candidate, they would be being dragged down into tactical considerations such as memorizing who the pols would be at the next stop, or in which hotel would the campaign staff sleep, or which media interview requests should they accept. Plotting strategy from the campaign's headquarters, the three professionals were able to distance themselves from the tactical and give themselves time to think: that is, to strategize.

Political managers function in the world to make a difference and to achieve their ideals and goals. We cannot predict the situations they will face. Accordingly, we present here some general guidelines for formulating a strategy. They should help readers to learn the basics of thinking strategically. Then, aspiring political managers will be better prepared to innovate and execute as novel, concrete situations arise.

Factors That You Can Control

At the start of a political fight—to the extent one can decipher the beginning of another engagement from among the constant stream of unfolding events—one should pay attention first to those elements that one can control. This means one should start by considering one's own goals or objectives. Remember Sun Tzu's dictum: strategy starts by knowing yourself (and your opponents). As an initial step in formulating a strategy in any situation, one must be as specific as possible as to what one hopes to achieve. As we argued in Chapter 4, precisely defined goals provide the basis for strategy development. Political managers are very likely to discover that this can be one of the most difficult tasks in strategic thinking and one that is all too easy to gloss over. For example, it is not sufficient merely to say, "Our goal is to enact this piece of legislation." One must define precisely how much support from which types of constituencies will be needed for victory. "We will need 250,000 pieces of mail directed to these 38 legislators, emphasizing support for our proposed legislation and we want to achieve margins of at least 57% approval among their constituents, including wide agreement among females, religious conservatives, small business owners, and households with income over $75,000." Notice that this statement also implies a substantial amount of careful calculation as to which are the critical legislators the organization hopes to influence. Stated with that precision, our objective can be implemented, benchmarked, and monitored as progress is achieved. Carefully delineated and concrete goals allow you to assess whether you are succeeding in moving along a path toward success.

Simply put, the more effort put into defining your objective, the easier it will be to observe whether you are succeeding. A clearly defined objective will also lend precision to the strategy you will employ to achieve it. If, for example, one knows the constituencies that compose the winning coalition within the electorate, the strategic approach to those audiences and the tactical means of persuading them to your cause become a lot clearer. "To grow our support among married women with children, we are going to need to address several issues about education and family values and try to draw our opponent into an argument over tax deductions for childcare which he opposes."

Finally, precisely stated objectives will help you define the metrics necessary to measure progress toward the goal effectively. "If we make this number of phone calls and mail these brochures to these small businesses by this date, we should see support among this critical constituency rise above 60% two weeks before our supporters in Congress will put our legislation up for a vote."

As a next step, you should consider explicitly how important is winning to you? In doing so you may find yourself confronting some nasty moral and ethical questions. At the very least, you may wind up doing some productive thinking about benefits and costs. How far are you willing to take the pursuit of a given objective? What are you willing to risk and sacrifice for the sake of winning? Are the goals you set worth the resources you may have to expend? Will your long-term objectives be contravened by winning in the immediate context? Answers to these and similar questions are likely to be heavily influenced by the degree of polarization within the political community. You should be aware that strident differences may make one more willing to transcend the bounds of appropriate conduct. Inevitably, those who are in the arena in the struggle for power will confront ethical and even moral questions of where the line lies between desired purpose and justified actions. Machiavelli has been misinterpreted as saying the ends justify the means. What he did argue is that *some* ends justify *some* means. This interpretation, however, provides little guidance for the political manager wrestling with an ethical trade-off and trying to define his or her limits of appropriate action.

The author takes the position that political managers should think hard about whether their actions will do damage to the institutions of democracy. If they do, such actions should be considered as unethical and avoided. You should, however, remind yourself that power is essential to purpose. That is, you may well have to overcome a natural reluctance to exercising power over other people. There is no point in being squeamish about this; you need power in order to make a difference in this world. Political leadership necessitates communicating your values, goals, and vision. Nonetheless, you should recognize that the potentials of persuading others to see the world as you do and to act in concert with you are only effective to a limited degree. Ultimately you will have to use power. If that idea bothers you, seek to secure a position of authority and with it the power that comes from a designated position or formal role. Exhortation, persuasion, leadership by example, and authority are frequently more acceptable and effective than punishment by sanction, targeted rewards, or threat of force.

Factors You Cannot Control (but Possibly Can Influence)

After considering how you will employ those factors that you have the ability to manage, it will also be necessary to address those factors that you *cannot* control. You are sure to confront some major constraints within the present situation that are well beyond the capacity of one individual to change in the near future. We have in mind historical, societal, and economic determinants that evolve only slowly through the joint efforts of numerous individuals and institutions. The list includes worldwide economic shifts, technological advances, social conditions like endemic racism or sexism or a caste system, famine, large scale migrations, and so forth. Uncontrollable events like weather-related natural disasters, earthquakes, and volcanic eruptions can also shape the strategic environment in which you must act. Such events can become "givens," but how you react to them is within your influence. With careful thought, you will be able to generate a list of factors that you do not control directly but you *may* be able to influence, if only slightly.

To take the next step, political managers analyze their own situation and that of their opponent. In Chapter 4, we discussed the usefulness of a SWOT analysis, which provides a model for undertaking the necessary thinking within a systematic framework. In the process, you must analyze your assumptions, available resources, and options or choices for employing those resources. Recognizing the interactivity of political conflicts, moreover, you will need to give serious attention to the perspective of the others involved, whether they are allies, enemies, and/or bystanders. As much as possible, you want to be able to see the situation from their viewpoint.

This systematic effort to assess your objectives and then to understand the current situation should lead you to formulate a game plan to close the distance between your present situation and where you want to be. In this regard, a strategy can be thought of as the roadmap of how you plan to move from the current situation to the desired objective. You should pay particular attention to the likely evolution of events and the probable reactions of your opponent(s). That task will force you to be precise about what you know and what you are assuming. The greater the precision you are able to bring to your assumptions, the easier it will be to critically evaluate their accuracy. Second, as events unfold, if the assumptions you have made prove to be inaccurate, that fact can serve as a barometer to consider changing the strategy. Plans do not always achieve the desired result and, therefore, knowing when to change the plan is a critical skill based upon both judgment and experience. If the game plan is abandoned at the first sign of trouble, it is not really a plan. Instead, you are merely reacting to external events. But, if the facts change, then the strategy might have to be adapted. But, if the assumptions you made are in error, then your plan definitely needs to change. Monitoring the validity of your assumptions may be the surest way of deciding when it is time to modify the plan.

Suppose, for example, you are in a legislative battle over school funding. Whether you have explicitly written it down or not, you have been assuming that the governor will not take a stand until after the legislation reaches her desk. But all of a sudden, the governor criticizes the proposal you have been promoting. That could only mean a change in strategy, perhaps minor, possibly extensive. At a minimum, someone should find out why the governor unexpectedly intervened. How did it happen that your assumption was so wrong? There will also be a new "call list" of legislators. You'll have to readjust who gets lobbied first and you'll need to reassure those who have already committed to you. Quite possibly, doors will open to the offices of legislators who dislike the governor. You may have to take a different tack in dealing with the news media. And so on.

At this point you should already have started writing down a document that will guide your actions going forward. As a start, consider the possibilities of establishing the agenda of issues that will be decided during the political dispute you are entering, whether that dispute occurs as an election contest or a public policy battle. If you can frame the issues that will be addressed in a political engagement early enough, you may be able to achieve much of your goals before the fight really starts. In the example above, merely getting the issue of school funding onto the legislative agenda may mean that some policy change will be forthcoming. You may not get everything you desire, but the partial changes that do come about could be to your benefit.

In some instances, political struggles can be orchestrated around a question rather than about a policy outcome or a candidacy. Whether the conflict over abortion policy becomes positioned, for example, as a matter of the right to life versus a woman's right to control her own body will go a long way to determining the outcome. In other words, ask yourself what question do you want the members of a legislative body think they are addressing in a legislative proposal you are advancing? What question do you want voters to have in their minds as they consider what is at stake in an election? Even though this process may be derisively labeled as "spin," establishing the question at issue constitutes effective political management. In other words, you should carefully consider and endeavor to frame the central question that, when answered, will lead to your objective.

Another possibility is to seek to establish the decision rules or the arena in which a decision will be made. All political fights take place under some rules of conduct, and quite often the rules determine the outcome. For example, US presidents often seek "fast track" authority in order to conduct trade negotiations with other nations. Fast track means that when the measure has been negotiated and comes before Congress, the vote will be an up or down vote, meaning approval or rejection. Congress agrees in advance to give up its right to make changes in the deal, knowing that no other nation will want to reach a deal with the administration only to have Congress renegotiate terms more favorable to the United States. The fast-track rule pretty much guarantees congressional approval. Similarly, in some nations, the rules for contesting elections allow only approved candidates to contest elections. Again, the rules that manage the conflict will often determine the outcomes. This means that, as a practical matter, figuring out how to determine the choice of forum or institution within which your political fight will take place can be a strategic move of significant benefit to your side. For example, in the effort to secure more funding for schools discussed above, it might have been a better strategy to start with the governor's office instead of the legislature.

In thinking through your strategy, you might pause to consider whether it is worth your effort to take on a given political dispute. One way of thinking this through is to consider whether those factors that you cannot control weigh more significantly on the outcome than those that you can control or influence. If so, then perhaps the inherent risks in the whole undertaking are so great that the endeavor should be postponed or abandoned altogether. Consider this example. In American politics some 90 years after Roosevelt's New Deal programs were enacted, Social Security has become known as a "third rail" of public policy. Projecting into the future, a political manager might conclude that payments to recipients will soon far outstrip the positive balance built up over many years. Yet, politicians in both parties are reluctant to propose changes that would make the program solvent for years to come. It will take strong, courageous—some would say "suicidal"—leaders to address this festering problem, even while most observers recognize that something needs to be done and even while the problem grows worse with every year's delay. It is perhaps a pathology of democracies that in some cases public sentiment works to prevent politicians from taking on necessary policy change.

We should, nevertheless, remember that societies are often moved by a few committed individuals. As the great anthropologist Margaret Mead once remarked, "Never doubt that a small group of thoughtful, committed, citizens can change the world. Indeed, it is the only thing that ever has."[5] While a realistic assessment of the odds of significant change may prove daunting, history has shown time and again that dedicated and unrelenting activists can punch through those barriers and create significant change. This observation harkens back to the analysis of different strata of political engagement presented in Chapter 5. We argued there that much of the discussion and activism relevant to politics takes place within a thin layer of the population, while the bulk of the citizenry focuses its attentions elsewhere.

Remembering that politics and warfare are about both hard realities as well as perceptions of those realities, political managers should consider the psychological reactions of their opponents to their interactions. Questions about the determination, confidence, and moral of competitors are extraordinarily important to ponder. Remember that no less a strategic genius than Napoleon thought that these insubstantial factors were more important than the concrete elements of a conflict. In thinking strategically, competent political managers recognize that their opponent's beliefs, perceptions, and attitudes are fair game for influence.

Predicting Your Opponent's Moves

Strategic opportunity can be found in the mind of your opponent. In politics, as in warfare, there is a concrete, factual aspect to conflict. Each participant brings different tangible resources to a conflict. But we must also be prepared to deal with the psychological facets of strategic interaction that can be even more important. The targets one aims for in the thinking of the other side could be their assumptions about the situation or the future, their perceptions of the opposition *they* are likely to confront, the options they perceive for action, their morale or psyche and courage with which they face the conflict, and the initiatives they are able to exercise. If well executed, it may even be possible to make—or allow—the other side believe that they are making decisions on their own, decisions that are really in your interest.

A president, for example, might drop a hint in a meeting with members of Congress from the other party that a particular idea could be nursed into needed policy proposal. Then, by allowing them to turn the suggestion into a draft bill that he could support, he would let them capture the idea as their own and achieve a legislative success. As the well-worn saying in politics goes, "You can get a lot done in Washington, if you don't care who gets the credit."[6]

In democratic politics, one should always be aware of the need to manage the expectations of others, including those of your opponent(s) and those of critical observers whose attitudes may shape the environment in which the conflict unfolds. Examples from contemporary American politics abound. Debates between candidates for elective office are rarely clear-cut events in which one candidate concedes that the opponent's position on a policy matter is better than his own. Inevitably, which candidate has "won" a debate is a matter of ambiguous judgment, but one that journalists, those deemed "informed commentators," and indeed many voters are all too anxious to make. Accordingly, before the event, candidates and their staff are eager to downplay how well they will do in a debate so that a mediocre performance would seem unexpectedly strong. Likewise, in the drawn-out process of American presidential nominations, the significance of a candidate's performance in an early caucus or primary is subject to interpretations that are heavily influenced by prior expectations. There are numerous recorded instances in which one candidate over performed the generally accepted prognostications and was, therefore, perceived as having "won." The hard "facts" may be superseded by perceptions. Conversely, a candidate who had been expected to rack up a significant victory in a primary election but underachieved those expectations may be seen as a loser, even if she received the most votes. To state the lesson more boldly, political managers can work to establish in advance the expectations for their cause or for their opponents that will determine the perceptions of the actual outcomes.

Little in political fights can be more significant or more necessary than trying to predict how an opponent will act. Ultimately, political managers must accept the fact that prediction can be a perilous exercise. Given that a clever competitor will be doing his utmost to seize the initiative through surprise, predicting what he will do can be quite difficult. Despite these difficulties, however, there is every reason to fix your attention on the thinking and actions of your opponent. As argued in Chapter 6, projecting the opponent's move should always be an essential component of strategy. In fact, we could argue that it is *the* essential component.

Given the inherent problems of prediction, however, how should skillful warriors undertake to forecast the opponent's likely actions? Start by going through the same planning process we used to initiate our own strategy, this time from our opponent's perspective.

1. Understand the objectives that your opponent is likely to pursue and consider what is in his/her best interest.
2. Try to decipher the assumptions that the opponent is likely to make about the evolving conflict.

3. List the options that are available to your opponent. What is she capable of doing?
4. Think carefully about the payoffs for your competitor that are likely to be associated with each of the options available and assume that she will choose the option that promises the largest payoff.

All of this is to say that, in most—but not all—political engagements, we expect our opponents to behave rationally, at least as a starting premise. The logic of this process cannot promise a perfect result. We are never going to be able to put ourselves completely into the mind of our adversary. Remember also that the above schema assumes that your opponent will be rational and self-interested. That could be an erroneous calculation.

A different approach is to estimate, based on his or her past behavior, whether your opponent is likely to take risks or be very cautious. Some individuals tend to be risk adverse. While these are not likely to be the kind of people you will find running for elective office—a highly risky activity—nonetheless the risk adverse will be encountered among political managers working in all aspects of political life. Their behavior is easier to predict than that of the entrepreneurial risk takers. Consider, for example, what are the prominent solutions to a problem, what most people would choose to do, and what seems the obvious option for him/her to pursue. What does society or culture expect in this kind of situation? These are likely to be the preferred options for the risk adverse. For the risk takers, you can expect that they will be more attracted to the option that would bring them the highest reward, disregarding the probability that it will actually occur. In general, the more you know about the others involved in a political fight—opponents and allies—the better you can predict their behavior, which is another argument for carefully studying up on your competitors. In the long run, however, you will probably have to fall back on Carl von Clausewitz's dictum that, in battle, one must learn to live with and act in the face of uncertainty; it's inevitable. Clausewitz's counsel of readiness for action and boldness in execution applies equally well to political life.

Rational Decision-Making

Those who work in positions of significant political responsibility often describe their management tasks as akin to trying to drink from a fire hose. Whether one is serving in public office or standing for an election, the pace of incoming information often overwhelms the ability to engage in rational thinking and planning. A torrent of events creates new crises each day, all seemingly of major importance. Recall for the moment the argument voiced earlier in this chapter that strategy is cerebral and, as such, requires time to think. Too often that maxim goes by the board in response to the pressures of complex responsibilities and in the face of the interactions and conflict. Yet effective political managers must figure out how to stop exclusively reacting to the moves of their opponents and instead undertake proactive strategies. How can you seize the initiative? How can you take the time to engage in rational thinking?

In this environment, your planning and analysis should be focused first upon the allocation of the scarce resources available to you, including financial, human capital, communications, policy commitments, as well as your own time. All of these are limited assets requiring adroit management. But they are under your control. Where available resources like time and money are limited, they should be allocated according to some careful thinking. How can they be most effectively channeled toward the major goals?

In many circumstances, you may find it helpful to establish a priority assignment like the triage systems developed in field hospitals during the First World War. A triage nurse would evaluate each wounded soldier brought in for treatment, separating out those for whom medical help bore little chance of keeping the patient alive, those who could survive without receiving immediate treatment, and those for whom immediate treatment would make the difference between life and death. The limited attention of the hospital staff could then be focused on the latter group, despite the tragic and seemingly callous conduct toward the first group. If time then permitted, the doctors could then turn their attention to saving—if they could—those in the first group that had survived.

An analogous logic applies in politics. In a legislative fight, some representatives may not be worth lobbying, so hostile are they to our proposal. Others may not need much attention because they are fully committed to our objectives. That leaves a middle group of legislators that might be persuadable to our cause. Rationally, that where the bulk of our attention and persuasive efforts should go. In earlier chapters, we discussed how the logic of triage can also help in zeroing in on the group of voters who could make the difference between winning and losing an election campaign.

Finally, drawing wisdom from military strategy, you should strategize on the basis of your opponent's capability—what can they do—but tactically execute your strategy based on probability—what they are most likely to do. Here strategy and tactics may diverge. Strategy prepares one for all that an opponent is capable of, while tactics determines how you will actually engage depending upon predictions of what the opponent will do. For example, when the US military landed in Iraq in 2003, they had assessed Saddam Hussein's forces and capabilities and prepared contingency plans to counter all the Iraqi military might do. Thus prepared, when they actually engaged, they did so on the basis of what they thought he would actually do. As we have argued above, prediction of the opponent's action is not always foolproof. Based on their erroneous assumption that the Iraqis had the so-called weapons of mass destruction including chemical weapons, the US forces carried with them the necessary equipment to defend against a chemical attack that never materialized.

The idea of contingency planning, which maintains a firm hold in the military, should be adapted into political life. Take, for example, the planning involved in launching a presidential campaign. Candidates and their advisers should carefully assess their strengths and weaknesses in the array of multiple primaries and caucuses during the nomination fight. Critical at this stage will be their predictions of which states will be emphasized by the other candidates and which the news media will adjudge to be critical for each candidate. Even though these calculations will undoubtedly evolve as the primary season unfolds, political managers should estimate separately what their competitors could do versus what they are most likely to do.

Guidelines for the Engagement

One tried and true strategy for gaining power is to get yourself into the middle position from which you can exercise pivotal influence. The justice who occupies the middle ground in decisions of the Supreme Court enhances his or her influence within the court. Arguments to the court are frequently targeted toward that one individual because the contending lawyers recognize that her vote can determine the outcome. Similarly, in a closely divided legislature, those members who constitute the middle position on the issues being debated are likely to be catered to by executive branch officials, and by party leadership, their colleagues, and interest groups. In so doing, these middle-ground actors may find themselves under intense pressure, pulled in both directions. But their reward is the power to dictate the result and to use that leverage to modify the legislation to their liking.

Another important guideline of strategy in politics is to always seek to maintain the initiative. If at all possible, do not allow yourself to be put on the defensive reacting constantly to the advances of your opponent. Instead, seek to constantly change the circumstances that confront your opponent so that he/she will be forced to react to you, rather than being able to advance his/her own strategy. Keeping the opponent off balance works in your favor.

You might adapt the OODA Loop described in Chapter 3: a decision cycle of observing the enemy, orienting yourself to the situation, deciding how to react, and then acting immediately. Your goal would be to process through this decision loop faster than your opponent. In the process, you would change the situation he/she confronts faster than he/she can react, thereby maintaining the initiative. In politics contingency planning is valuable, but even more valuable is the ability to react rapidly and make quick decisions on the basis of changing conditions. Thus, in the waning years of the 20th century, both national political parties, most campaigns, and many interest groups, developed a rapid response capability to take the initiative against breaking news or attacks from their opponents. In order to be ready for unexpected developments, these political managers created databases with the positions, statements, and policies of their candidate or cause and those of their competitors. Research staff were then primed to respond quickly with information and positions casting their issue or candidate in a favorable light as well as facts that could discredit their opponents. With the growth of 24-hour news programming on cable television and the arrival of digital communications early in the 21st century, the news cycle shortened from a daily event to an hour-by-hour stream. No longer could political managers leisurely formulate their reactions to breaking events and actions of their competition. Falling behind risks yielding the initiative to others.

Another means of maintaining the initiative is to recognize that the complexity of politics and policy often allows political managers the latitude they need to become unpredictable. Given that a recognized advantage can be achieved by understanding in advance what your competitors will do, conversely being unpredictable keeps your opponents off guard, uncertain, and likely in a reactive posture. There is, however, a fine line in which the dictates of strategy—despite its advantages—conflicts directly with the necessity for consistency and constancy in political leadership. Thus, you may encounter a trade-off here between strategy and leadership, a fact that we will consider more directly in the final chapter. Establishing in the abstract where that line falls is likely to be impossible; it must be judged in each circumstance.

In 2020, near the end of his term as president, Donald J. Trump provided a telling example of how strategic unpredictability can contradict strategic leadership. Less than a month before the inauguration of Trump's successor, Congress passed a major relief package in response to the COVID-19 pandemic. Trump's own Treasury secretary had participated actively in the extremely difficult negotiations that produced legislation that could muster enough support to pass both House and Senate. At the eleventh hour in this long, drawn-out political battle, the president surprised all—and displeased most—of Washington by announcing that he had significant disagreements with the bill. If Trump thought he could extract concessions by refusing to say whether he would sign or veto this legislation, he was mistaken. Even after four years as president, Trump didn't really understand the process by which Congress produces legislation. It was simply too late for Congress to revise the legislation in ways that Trump would approve. The choice was either the existing bill or no effort to mitigate the social and economic dislocations of the pandemic. After several days of complete confusion, Trump had to sign the bill even though none of his demands were met. In the process, he provided a stunning example of inept leadership. The major political newsletter of the day summed up this fiasco as follows: "What a bizarre, embarrassing episode for the president. He opposed a bill his administration negotiated. He had no discernible strategy and no hand to play—and it showed. He folded, and got nothing besides a few days of attention and chaos."[7]

When under attack and on the defensive, consider whether it is possible to turn the attack to your own advantage by confronting the opponent's charge directly. For example, in 1960, the Democratic candidate, John F. Kennedy, was invited to address a large gathering of Protestant ministers in Houston. Could it have been a trap? Of course, but instead of refusing the invitation and thereby creating a storm of criticism, he turned the invitation into an opportunity to address head-on the issue of his Catholicism. His frank recognition that many voters were uncertain about his beliefs and his assurances that he would not be dictated to by the Vatican, to say nothing of his articulate manner, served to reassure many in the electorate. The election turned out to be very close indeed, so he probably would not have won if he had not taken up this challenge. A similar example can be found in Barack Obama's speech on the divide over race in America during the 2008 campaign. Of course, to perform this political judo skillfully and successfully requires intelligence and careful reflection on the likely reactions of opponents.

The 20th century's Cold War brought to the fore the idea of deterrence as a principle of strategic conflict. Both sides in the conflict—the Soviet Union versus the three nuclear-armed nations of the West—understood that provocative acts could initiate an upward spiral of violence that could eventually lead to mutual annihilation. Accordingly, policy makers were extremely cautious in their dealings with the other side, particularly after the adventurism of Nikita Khrushchev in placing missiles in Cuba brought the world to the brink of nuclear war. One should not overlook the possibility of employing deterrence as a strategy to prevent your opponent from undertaking a course detrimental to your interests. The author knows of instances in which two competing campaigns each have knowledge damaging to the other side and together they strike a semiformal—and perhaps unspoken—agreement not to use that information in attacking the other.[8] Perhaps deterrence only works under some conditions. There must be recognition on both sides that they are engaged in some sort of conflict, and each must know of the capacity of the other to impose significant damage upon them. The potential damage must be greater than the benefits possibly achieved by initiating some new aspect of the conflict. Deterrence works best, moreover, when each side believes that disastrous response of his/her opponent is inevitable, especially if each side has little capacity to control their opponent's actions.

The idea of using deterrence as a strategy to influence your opposition suggests that political managers should be careful about stating explicitly what they will *not* do in response to the actions of another. President Richard Nixon argued that a political leader gives away too much freedom of action by announcing what he won't do in a particular situation. Nixon argued that it was better to keep the other side guessing. At first blush, this advice might seem to contradict the fact that to be effective a deterrence threat must seem to be inevitable. But there is an important strategic and psychological difference between threatening an enemy with how you will respond to his actions versus to alerting him as to what you will *not* do. Taking some options off the table should be reserved for those instances in which peace negotiations are possible and productive.

It will not be surprising to many readers that most people working in politics actually hate to lose a battle. If they are on the losing side of a skirmish, they are strongly motivated to rationalize the loss by thinking that the process itself was unfairly stacked against them. Remember from the above counsel that it is often possible to win by shaping the rules under which the competition will take place. If there is a downside to this maneuvering, it may come about in that it allows the losers to blame the process rather than their ideas or actions. They will work to weaken your victory symbolically by complaining about the process by which they were defeated; they will find it easier to carp about the process than to flat out admit to a loss. Be prepared to guard against this likely effort to defraud and devalue your achievement.

From Strategy to Tactics

If strategy is a cerebral process, tactics are about doing. One level is calculation and plotting; the other is action. The line between the two concepts may not always be crystal clear—especially in the heat of battle—because many of the same principles apply to both levels. We can think of several examples. First, as you detail the assumptions upon which your strategy is based as well as the tactics you will employ, the more precise and quantifiable your thinking, the easier it will be to monitor performance and progress as you carry out the plan. A second principle governing the conception of a strategy and the execution of a tactic is that—at both levels—political managers should focus on factors that they can influence. In other words, you should seek to manage that which you can actually manage. Political managers should not put too much energy into trying to influence factors that they cannot control. Third, just like the assumptions you make in formulating a strategy, those dynamics that are beyond your control should be monitored closely for developments that will affect your actions or success. Finally, in strategy and in tactical actions, you should keep your plans and actions obscured from the opponent(s) view. Strive to be unpredictable. And, be aware that surprise is more likely to be achieved at the tactical level than at the level of goals and objectives.

In his monumental work on strategy, Lawrence Freedman places great emphasis on the importance and dynamics of formulating coalitions as a means of gaining power.[9] Given that power is often plural, political managers must depend on other people either as allies or as subordinates. While combining forces with other actors can accumulate influence, however, coalitions also extract a cost and entail a weakness. That is, while Freedman is certainly correct on the level of strategy, on a tactical level you will find that creating and holding coalitions together present some challenging management tasks. No coalition is going to be completely homogeneous. The interests and objectives of its component members will certainly overlap somewhat. Otherwise, there would be no coalition. But differences will also be present. More importantly, those opposing the coalition will naturally seek to identify the "hinge points" that bind the elements of the coalition together and, if possible, raise issues that will drive the components apart. So, if you form a coalition, analyze what will weaken the coalition and expect that your opponent will do just that, directing his forces at those points of weakness. In addition, consider and guard against those events or factors that would drive a wedge between you and your allies.

Coalitions bring more people into the arena of conflict, a fact that can have some other detrimental consequences. As a general rule, the larger the number of people involved in a decision and its implementation, the longer it will take to plan and execute a resulting strategy and the greater likelihood your strategy will leak to the opposition. Mobilizing numerous individuals into concerted action can take significant planning and time to accomplish.

As the reader surely knows by now, the main point of this writing is the assertion that strategic thinking in politics is crucial. So far, so good. But we must also acknowledge the abundant evidence that thinking by itself is not enough to make change happen. Consider, for example, the development of communism during the beginning of the 20th century, before it was largely rejected by most of the world. Karl Marx had developed a theory—a strategy really—of class warfare,[10] but it took a man of action—Vladimir Lenin—to bring that strategy to implementation.[11] In short, execution is critical to the success of a strategy.

Karl von Clausewitz brings to our attention two concepts that hinder the accomplishment of even the most carefully conceived strategy: "the fog of war" and "friction." The former describes the rampant uncertainty, the confusion, the doubt, and the insecurities that are likely to engulf the warrior amid a conflict. For the general or admiral in battle, ascertaining what is happening, what the enemy is up to, or even how one's own forces are performing will likely achieve only a muddled impression. "Friction" meanwhile refers to those many little things that can go wrong. On the large scale of the battle, they can accumulate to cause big problems in implementation. For example, a crucial military unit makes a wrong turn or arrives at its assigned place late, throwing off the effectiveness of other planned actions that were contingent upon its participation. Thus, for the political manager, making sure that tactics are appropriately implemented at the operational level can be critical to success.

Ensuring effective implementation may require a specifically designated individual in charge of execution, for it requires a different mindset from the strategist, and, indeed, can be disruptive of the process of creating strategy. For example, modern campaigns and increasingly those successful political organizations will hire a "chief strategist" in addition to a campaign manager. The former is charged with conceptualizing such issues as how the conflict will evolve, what its opponents are likely to do, how public attention and thinking will evolve, how journalists will cover the conflict, and so forth. Meanwhile, the political manager is charged with running the organization, making trade-offs between possible efforts, and implementing the strategy of the institution. With respect and talent, there can be harmony between these twin roles, but certainly there will be tensions to manage as well.

Timing as a Critical Factor

There is no such thing as the right strategy at the wrong time; timing is an integral component of a strategy. There are several ways in which political managers should consider and calculate carefully the timing of their actions, for timing alone may be a critical determinant of success. Inadequate attention to the element of time will probably portend failure. With diligent deliberation over the timing of actions, a political manager can create surprise and seize the initiative. If, for example, your power, or resources, or capacity for control are growing stronger, it may be wise to delay in taking on a political engagement. Conversely, if your resources are declining, you may have to engage as soon as possible. Timing your actions can also be a critical means of creating a sense of momentum. Spacing your actions so the interval between them keeps shortening will convey the impression of gathering steam.

Timing may well determine your success in another way. If it is at all possible, for example, take on only one opponent, one battle, at a time. Just as a two-front war often poses a sharply escalated challenge for military leaders, so does diffusing your concentration on more than one competitor in politics. If at all possible, do not disperse your attention. Stay focused on one battle, one opponent at a time. Conversely, if possible, try to make your opponent defend himself/herself on two fronts simultaneously. For example, attacking a proposed piece of legislation on two sharply different grounds may cause the proponents to respond in a diffuse and ineffective manner. Different elements of a coalition opposing legislation can launch simultaneous attacks that appear to be unrelated but are secretly coordinated. Here again, by forcing your opponents to deal with two attacks, you may also create an opportunity to seize the initiative in your interactions.

Note, however, there may be situations in which bringing another player into the fight might serve your purposes. For example, in election campaigns, there have been instances in which one candidate has enticed a second opponent from the other party to enter the fray. Whether by behind-the-scenes encouragement and covert help or by overt attacks designed to goad a potential opponent into action, the desired effect is to split the opposing vote in two. While this move might make victory easier for the conspiring candidate, it should be undertaken cautiously. Too much involvement in encouraging opposition usually results in a storm of criticism from journalists and may be self-defeating. Similarly, in legislative politics, advancing a substitute proposal that is weaker than the legislation you oppose often provides a means of diffusing the unity of your opponent's coalition.

Finally, if it happens that your opponent is in the process of inflicting harm on himself/herself, this is the time to say nothing and do nothing. You do not want to interrupt the process of self-destruction. You do not want to divert the attention of journalists from your opponent's problems.

Winning from a Weaker Position

Political managers often find themselves in an unenviable position of having a political dispute thrust upon them when they are in a poor position to enter battle. There is not much that can be done in these circumstances, but perhaps the following advice will prove helpful.

Start by considering explicitly whether you have to fight at all. If you are at an extreme disadvantage, the best course may be to let this battle pass you by. Some of this calculation should be related to the factor of timing discussed above. If you think that you will be in a stronger position at some point in the future, then perhaps a strategic retreat is the better option at this moment. You cannot count on winning every battle and, in some instances, delay may give you the opportunity to prepare one of the approaches below.

If you cannot delay a fight that you have a high probability of losing, then at least before you engage, endeavor to develop a "Plan B." That is, if possible, you will need to try more than one approach to contesting this issue. If all attempts fail, it cannot hurt for you to have prepared for a loss by having considered in advance your available options if you lose this battle.

Much of the above advice on engaging in a political struggle should be magnified when you are in the weaker position. Plan to focus your attack at the opponent's weakest point. Perhaps concentrating all your pressure on one element of the opponent's position will inflict enough pain to make him/her back off. Work harder to maintain the initiative in the evolving argumentation. Constantly changing the terrain on which you and the stronger opponent are engaged can keep a larger, less-nimble opponent off balance. Deception also becomes more important in this circumstance since you cannot win without surprise or making your opponent commit resources needlessly. Finally, when you are at a disadvantage, it becomes all the more essential to emphasize execution. Implementation has to be perfect in order to maximize your effectiveness. Committing fewer mistakes than your opponent may be the only way to survive, much less to win.

Beyond the above ideas, which admittedly are not particularly reassuring, there is one classic strategy for contesting against a superior foe: form an alliance with another stronger player. Forming a coalition may be, as Lawrence Freedman argues, the best way to enhance one's political (and military) power.[12] Bringing another participant into the dispute serves to change the game. Obviously, there will be costs to you. A coalition partner will have slightly different objectives, meaning that you will have to give up on pursuing in this fight some of your goals. The stronger player is likely to insist on maximizing his wants and only giving secondary attention to your needs. Hopefully, you can hold onto your core objectives. There is another, more serious cost to consider: having invited a bigger player into the game, however, you may not be able to convince him/her to leave after you have escaped defeat. When a weak nation invites a stronger military to fight its wars, the stronger nation may decide to stay. Assistance turns into conquest. So too in business: a friendly loan can turn into a yoke. So too in politics. So, be mindful.

As a final thought about fighting a losing battle, you may have to recall the words of Henry John Temple that have come down to us as Lord Palmerston's dictum: "We have no eternal allies and no perpetual enemies." That is, try to remember that in the complexity of modern politics and policy fights, yesterday's enemy may be tomorrow's ally. This is especially true in conflicts over public policy. Your opponent on one piece of legislation may simultaneously be your ally on another bill. At some point in the future, your group may join forces in a coalition with that same opponent. Thus, the fluidity of power relationships in democratic politics can constitute a severe constrain on your strategic options. If possible, do not let the competitive relationship become so vituperative that you have created a perpetual enemy.

Caution: How to Lose Power

In a democratic system, you will lose power by undercutting your own integrity. Your reputation for fairness and honesty is critical in building a constituency of willing supporters. But destroying a reputation for integrity is a lot easier than creating one. The easiest way to lose power is by abusing your authority. All authority is bounded by formal and informal rules as to its scope. Transcending those boundaries will weaken the trust that is a central and essential element in maintaining that power. Abusing that trust undercuts the legitimacy of what authority you do have and will ultimately require you to resort to force. The more you have to turn to force, the more resentments and resistances will grow, causing a cycle of revolt and ever-increasing authoritarianism on your part. In the end, civil politics will be destroyed.

Political power is at least one-half perception. The remainder comes about in actual application. The psychological dimension of your reputation as being powerful is critical to your being able to exercise power. Do not overlook the fact that your opponents could be working hard to tarnish your reputation using sophisticated public relations technique consultants.[13] As crazy as it sounds, if you are actually forced to exercise power, that fact alone can become a demonstration of weakness. Employing power as in using force implies that others resisted your perceptual power enough to mount a challenge.[14] Power is precious; exercise it adroitly. Unless carefully managed, a public loss or defeat will allow others to feel freer to challenge you. Thus, power loss can create a downward spiral. Before you get into a fight you might lose, employ all the above guidelines to consider whether you must take on that battle.

Instructive examples have been provided by the first year in office for both President Bill Clinton and President Joe Biden. Both launched ambitious plans for major social policy initiatives. Clinton tried to completely reform the American healthcare system, while Biden proposed a large—and expensive—package of social reforms under the rubric "Build Back Better." In both cases they could not find the last few votes in the Senate to push their legislation through to completion. Neither were able to deliver on their major campaign promises. As a result, the influence of their administrations was significantly weakened, and the personal popularity of both presidents plummeted.

Conversely, victory, particularly against a foe perceived as more powerful, can serve to enhance your power by setting in motion an upward spiral. Having won, avoid the temptation to punish the defeated. Allow yourself to at least consider whether being magnanimous in victory will avoid resentment among the losers and instead serve to cement your power.

Finally, knowing how to preserve a balance in your competitive instincts based on propriety can be crucial to long-run success. An overly aggressive strategy may succeed in the short run, but it can build up resentment and resistance and can create hardened enemies. Again, I hope you will remember the wise counsel of John Emerich Edward Dalberg-Acton, Lord Acton's dictum: "Power corrupts, and absolute power corrupts absolutely."

The Essence of Effective Strategy

1. There are no ironclad laws that prescribe strategic judgment because (a) strategy is situational, and (b) following a predetermined set of rules makes one predictable to the opponent and therefore more vulnerable.
2. In the fluid, reciprocal dynamic of political combat, seizing and maintaining the initiative in that interaction is paramount. Seek to make the challenger react to your actions by changing the situation he/she confronts. Always keep in mind the natural tendency to focus on your own actions and not on the likely acts of your opponent. Yielding to that tendency increases the likelihood of defeat.
3. Understand that perceptual realities are just that, realities. To be sure, they are most often rooted in the concrete, actual facts of an environment, but perceptions can have real political potency even when they are demonstrably false.
4. Timing can be a critical factor determining the success or failure of a strategy. The timing of a strategy needs to be explicitly considered as a separate issue for decision.
5. The lust for power and victory can overwhelm political managers and must be guarded against vigorously. Power should be instrumental for achieving purpose, not as an end unto itself. Assess your own actions against the standard of whether they will serve to weaken democratic institutions and principles. If so, discard those actions as impermissible.

PART III
PLACING STRATEGY IN PERSPECTIVE

8
Strategy and Negotiations in Politics

Up to this point we have concentrated exclusively upon exploring the concept of strategy and the need for strategic thinking. We have argued that four different conceptions of strategy create power for those working in politics. Such a single-minded approach is justified because the concept of strategy in public life has been poorly understood, and the practical use of strategy in politics has suffered. Readers should not assume, however, that only strategy will allow them to accomplish their political goals. We should acknowledge that, in their essence, strategies of political management embody a self-centered pursuit of objectives by an individual, group, organization, or interest. Politics is the vehicle through which collective action creates the future, so it is natural that participants will pursue their vision through competition, often hard fought. This book would be incomplete, however, if the reader were left with the impression that civil politics can move us toward a better future only through focused pursuit of self-interest. In fact, the arena of policy determination does not have to be a seething milieu of Hobbesian competition and conflict. The future that we seek will also be determined by collective action, in some instances overlaid by individual assertiveness, but in other instances by joint, cooperative action.

In their quest for a future in line with their vision and values, political managers can also succeed by employing the techniques of negotiation to complement those described here as "strategy." However, negotiations will require you to adopt a different mindset. Like strategy, negotiation presupposes two or more actors, each with a separate inventory of desires, goals, and purposes. Yet, the orientation toward other parties must include a sense that these differences are not irreconcilable. Those engaged in a negotiation must assume that they are not engaged in a competitive, winner-takes-all or zero-sum situation. This difference calls for alternative terminology. Following the

Strategy in Politics. F. Christopher Arterton, Oxford University Press. © Oxford University Press 2023.
DOI: 10.1093/oso/9780197644836.003.0008

lead of James Freund, I prefer the term "counterpart" to refer to the other parties in a negotiation.[1] That label connotes respect, equivalent status, and a working relationship, much more so than the labels used in strategy such as competitor, adversary, opponent, foe, and enemy.

The approach to the other party in negotiations requires that warriors leave behind much of their military mentality. For a platoon leader who must enter a hamlet populated by civilians who may be hostile or friendly, skills at negotiations would definitely be helpful. Imposing one's will through overwhelming force is quite likely to produce resistance. It may even encourage clandestine help to the enemy. Negotiation rather than guns may offer a more successful approach.

In addition, when and if the two sides to an armed conflict agree to peace negotiations, the military generally steps aside, and political leadership takes over the bargaining with the enemy. The latter may have sharper negotiation skills because those interactions are quite common in political life, especially during the policymaking process. Recall for a moment that we view politics as a means of solving social problems that otherwise could fester into armed conflict. We have flipped Clausewitz's insight that war is an extension of politics into the domain of violence. Ultimately, if complete conquest is impossible or unwise, the final solution to warfare will come about through negotiations. It follows that political managers need to acquire the skills of a negotiator to be maximally effective.

This analysis should not, however, be taken so far as to suggest that strategy is absent from negotiations. In fact, many elements of strategy come into negotiations, including the importance of understanding and predicting the dynamics of two individuals or teams confronting one another. Participants should also take time to plan for the negotiations, going through all the same steps we emphasized above. In addition, as in strategy, effective communications can be extremely important to the outcome of a bargaining session. But to be successful, political managers need to accord both respect for and reciprocity with those on the other side of the bargaining table. An attitude that views bargaining exchanges as characterized by a clash of competing wills is certain to generate hostility and likely to produce suboptimal results.

Entering a negotiation requires that the political manager understand that the interests of the parties will often conflict in some parts but not in everything. Instead, there may be some goals that are entirely compatible. Consider, for example, contract negotiations between a political manager and an environmental interest group. One participant wants to earn a living while helping advance causes she believes in; the other wants solid strategic advice as to how they should navigate the policymaking machinery. They are likely to have conflicting desires as to the price to be paid, and there may well be differences on other terms such as start date, length of employment, ancillary benefits like health insurance, and the like. There are also questions that relate to the working relations between the two: issues such as the consultant's range of authority, ability to hire other staff, the basic outline of the kind of tactics that can be employed. Nevertheless, overall, both parties hope to find a point at which both the political manager and the interest organization are satisfied, at least minimally.

In other words, like strategy, negotiations involve interpersonal interactions in which the outcomes are determined by the decisions and actions of two or more parties. But the attitude with which each party approaches that interaction is not one of all-consuming self-interest and triumph. Rather, understanding that the other party controls resources that they desire, both parties seek to maximize their own benefits while sufficiently satisfying the desires of their counterpart. How sufficiently will be heavily influenced by whether the resulting transaction is to be a singular event or will, hopefully, establish a working relationship over time. As we shall see, in a "one-off" exchange, the parties can be more single-minded in pursuing their interests.

In politics, the policymaking process relies heavily upon negotiations. Finding a solution to a perceived social problem will require satisfying, at least minimally, most of the interested actors. If a proposed outcome is overwhelmingly beneficial to one party and rather distasteful to the others, the anticipated solution will not long endure. The other parties will work to stall implementation and may take the issue to the executive agencies or the courts to seek modification. Authentic negotiations during the policy adoption process are more likely to produce solutions that the major interests will accept. If the interest groups present at the bargaining table are genuine representatives their constituencies, the adopted policy has a greater chance of being accepted by segments of the citizenry. Policies that fail this test do not survive for long. Think, for example, of the American experience with a prohibition of alcohol as a failed public policy.

A final point about attitude needs to be made before we discuss some of the basic dynamics of negotiations. As in the chapters on strategy, there are two related ways in which this book could approach negotiations, either as an analyst or an adviser. First, we could stand outside the interpersonal relationship and analyze how the participants should behave in order to achieve a successful result. The analyst works to understand how maximal success can be achieved through negotiations. An adviser, however, would seek to educate would-be political managers directly as to how they should behave so as to maximize their outcomes through negotiations. These approaches are so intertwined that at times it is difficult to tell where analysis leaves off and advice begins. Take, for example, the above discussion of attitude toward the other actor. *Analysis:* negotiations over public policies are more likely to succeed when the participants view the other parties as counterparts. In fact, the process of marking up a complex policy into a bill that the legislature can pass can be described as colleagues trying to craft language that a majority can accept. A strong push of self-interest by either side will likely antagonize and create resistance. *Advice:* keep firmly in mind that not everyone engaged in a negotiation perceives the opposing party as an equal or somebody to treat fairly. Instead, the other party may see the situation as fundamentally calling for strategy, an orientation to maximize their benefit at your expense.[2]

Political managers should keep in mind that there certainly are situations in which one or more of the parties to a negotiation really does not wish to reach an accord. They view the present situation as more to their liking than any possible negotiated outcome. Another possibility often occurs in international peace negotiations in which one of the parties believes it is gaining in strength. They may drag out the back and forth waiting for their situation on the battlefield to improve and with it their strength at the bargaining table. Under these circumstances, they may enter into interactions that formally look like negotiations, but their actions are a smokescreen designed to delay and obscure their real intent. They may engage in tactics such as introducing ideas, which may sound principled, but which in reality are "poison pills" designed to torpedo the negotiations.

Basic Dynamics: MAD, ZOPA, and BATNA

Beyond the attitudes with which the two parties approach each other, we want to consider some fundamental aspects of negotiations. Let's start with a simple example. The chosen illustration does not emerge from the arena of politics or the battlefield. Instead, let's think about a private transaction involving a used car, where the principal—and sometimes the only—bargaining point relates to price. While negotiations in the arenas of politics and public policy most often involve a great many more factors than cost, we can, nonetheless, illustrate important basic dynamics built around the desire of one individual to sell his old car and the interest of another to purchase a used car. The seller, we are told, is in the process of buying a new car and has received an offer from the dealer of $3,500 as a trade-in value of the car in question. Both seller and potential buyer have access to information services that provide a range at which the car in question might be valued in a private sale. The seller consulted a directory that listed a value of $4,500 up to $6,000, depending upon the condition of the car including mileage, repair history, minor damage, etc. Thinking his car is in pretty good condition, the seller has placed an ad in a local website offering to sell the car at "$6000 obo" (that is, "or best offer"). The buyer, meanwhile, checked a different online directory as the seller and found a somewhat lower range of values, between $4,000 and $5,500. The Buyer has contacted the Seller, they have met, and the Buyer has seen the car. Now the negotiations start.

Each of the participants has in mind a dollar range within which they would be willing to make a deal. For the seller, the range is $3,500 up to $6,000. Of course, the seller would strongly prefer something near the top of this range. Seller knows that if the car is not sold privately, he can always use it as a trade-in with the dealership. He cannot help but think that every dollar above the trade-in value is a dollar less paid for the new car. Meanwhile, the buyer has saved $7,000 in the bank earmarked for the purchase of a car, but would like a price near the bottom of her range, around $4,000. Upon examining and driving the car in question, she recognizes that this car is in very good condition, so she would be willing to pay more, but not anything like the $6,000 price tag as the asking price.

An experienced negotiator would certainly introduce other aspects of this deal, like access to repair records, a qualified inspection, the delivery date, a necessary cleaning, possibly new tires, and so forth. But, for the sake of simplicity, let's assume that only the price is at stake. If no new factors intrude on this interaction, the two are likely to agree on a selling price somewhere between $4,000 and $6,000. Where exactly they come down to within these limits will depend upon the skill of each negotiator and the degree to which each is enthusiastic about completing the deal. It may also be determined by whether or not the two participants like each other.

For our purposes now, it really does not matter what price these two hypothetical actors finally settle upon. Rather we introduce this scenario because it is useful in illustrating four basic concepts in negotiation. First of all, each party should have established—prior to their meeting—a price beyond which they would not want to reach an agreement. Economists refer to this point as either the "reservation price" or the "reserve price" meaning the minimally attractive proposition one would accept. Negotiators also frequently call this a "walkaway point." Here, I denote this concept as a MAD—the minimally acceptable deal. For a memory hook, I suggest, "Don't get mad; at least get your MAD."

In the example above, the seller is likely to conceive of his MAD as close to the bottom of the range of value he found on the used car evaluation website, somewhere above the trade-in value, probably around $4,000. That would at least give him $500 over a trade-in. For buyer, the MAD is likely to be $6,000, the top of the valuation service she consulted and near the total of her savings. Of course, neither of the two negotiators hopes to wind up at or near his/her MAD. Each would like to receive greater value from the negotiations: the buyer would really like to pay $3,000 and the seller would be extremely happy with a price of $7,000. The fact that these two price points are outside of the other's MAD, however, makes them highly unlikely.

Effective negotiators need to define their MAD before entering negotiations and hold onto it in the process of the give-and-take discussion. Remember that, in the confrontation of the moment, one can get carried away and lose track of a carefully calculated decision point.[3] Suppose, for example, the buyer really falls in love with a particular car that has the color, the interior, the sound system, and all the options she really wants, including heated seats! If she hasn't firmly established in her own mind $6,000 as the highest she will pay, she may get so involved in the ambiance of the negotiations that she will be persuaded to a deal beyond her MAD. After all, she does have the capacity to pay $7,000.

A second concept derived from the above example can be referred to as the "zone of possible agreement" or ZOPA,[4] which is the range between the two MADs. For our two bargainers, there is a zone between $4,000 and $6,000 within which the two can find a price point acceptable to both. Again, a memory hook may be helpful: "No ZOPA; no deal." In other words, if both participants have calculated and stick to their MADs that jointly do not produce a ZOPA, then they can bargain and cajole for hours but they are not going to find an outcome both can accept. To cite another example, if a job applicant has calculated his living expenses and concluded that he needs a salary of at least $50,000 to meet his expenses, but the employer who wants to hire him can only pay $40,000, they have no ZOPA and will not be able to reach a deal successfully. Before this chapter concludes, we will provide some hints as to how the participants in a negotiation can ferret out whether or not they have a zone of possible agreement.

The third concept illustrated by our example comes from the work of Roger Fisher and his colleagues at the Harvard Negotiation Project.[5] Negotiators should consider explicitly what options they have if the negotiations fail. They need to calculate and bear in mind their "Best Alternative to a Negotiated Agreement," or BATNA. Basically, the BATNA is a "Plan B," if the negotiator cannot reach an acceptable deal. In the case of the two negotiating the sale of a used car, the seller has a clear BATNA: he can always trade his car in to the dealer for $3,500. The buyer's BATNA is not so clear-cut; she will need to keep looking for a car to buy, one that minimally satisfies her needs and can be bought for under $7,000. In either case, unless they know their BATNAs, they may be more enthusiastic about a pending deal than they should be, particularly if their BATNA—if they thought about it carefully—turns out to be not such a bad outcome.

Having computed one's BATNA, the savvy negotiator will, upon additional thought, discover that the greater the positive distance between the deal on the table and his BATNA, the more enthusiasm one will have for concluding a deal. If our seller is considering a selling price of $5,000 in a vacuum, he may not be terribly excited. But if he realizes that the offer is $1,500 above trading the car to the dealer—that is, above his BATNA—he may become a lot more pleased. A price of $5,500 would be that much more satisfactory. If, however, there is little difference between the BATNA and the deal being discussed, the temptation may grow for him to wait for another potential buyer. For example, if the buyer is offering our seller only $4,500 and also wants a list of non-price options like a thorough cleaning, a new coat of wax, and an immediate turnover, the seller may conclude that the deal is now more trouble than it's worth, even though it's above his BATNA.

We need to make a final point about BATNA. As a negotiator, you should try to become cognizant of your counterpart's BATNA. Often, a simple question early in the conversation will elicit information that could provide a powerful argument later in the negotiation. You will have the option to recall for your counterpart that the deal under discussion is a lot better than his BATNA. An innocent sounding, "What's your alternative?," may elicit a wealth of leverage. But, if your probing questions do not yield a clear picture of the other's BATNA, then, as in strategy, you will need to try to put yourself in your counterpart's shoes. Viewing the negotiations from this perspective, try to estimate his or her BATNA.

While we can learn a great deal about the dynamics of negotiations from these relatively simple car sales, in the domain of politics, negotiations are going to be significantly more complex than these examples suggest. For one thing, negotiations in public life are likely to involve more than a simple transaction of money in return for a good or service. But even if the parties are only trying to work toward an exchange of value, other, complicating factors will come into play.

Furthermore, transform this bargaining into a situation in which an interest group wants to hire a political consultant. Each of the basic concepts—MAD, ZOPA, and BATNA—would apply. If the negotiations are only about salary and assuming that both parties have thought carefully about that issue, the political manager would have a minimum she could accept and the interest group leader would have a maximum he could pay.[6] Hopefully, there would be some point between those two salaries that would be acceptable to both. Each would be thinking about what their fallback plan would be if they were unable to strike a deal. In other words, the analytics of the hiring negotiations in politics is straightforward. However, there will be many more issues involved. The consultant and the organization's CEO will likely also negotiate such issues as the start date, or how many other clients will occupy the consultant's attention, or how long the interest group expects their claim on the political manager's time will last.

Consider, instead, a negotiation between two opposing campaigns over the terms of an upcoming televised debate. Before the bargaining even started, a competent political manager would have engaged her candidate in a detailed conversation about how much the campaign needed to debate the opponent. That is, they should discuss the likely risks and the possible rewards. Deciphering a BATNA—essentially that would mean assessing the costs of not debating—could be a more complex, subtle calculation. Instead of cash or salary, the contentious issues could concern items such as the optimal schedule, a choice of moderators, topics to be debated, the use of notes or props, the length of statements, the ability to react to the opponent's statements, the use of podiums, and on and on. Each campaign would have made assumptions about each of these tactical elements, trying to project advantages to their side. For example, an older candidate might press for shorter debates seated around a table with a senior journalist as moderator. One campaign might conclude that a particular subject matter would be to its advantage. Of course, one of the campaigns could become so insistent on some of their demands that they would rise to the level of a MAD.

The complex details of many of the above elements preclude splitting the difference as in a salary figure or a used car price. In this event, negotiators often resort to arranging trade-offs between items that are close to being their MAD's. The choice could come down to pairing the selection of a moderator that one side detests for longer opening statements that the other side abhors. In this negotiation, both political managers should be aware that the other side will be maneuvering to make some items seem much more objectionable to them than is truly the case. As in strategy, uncertainty will prevail: one may never know the true value of a bargaining chip to one's counterpart. That other side will be anxious to keep confidential the fact that some issue is highly important to them. They would be concerned that if you learned this was critical to them, you would drive a harder bargain in return for a small concession on their key issue. However, if either side has an issue that is so important to them as to be a "deal breaker," they should state that at the very beginning of the bargaining. Deal breakers introduced late in the negotiations will not be credible.

Basic Dynamics: "One Offs" versus Enduring Relationships

There is another, important contrast between the above scenario of a used car sale versus negotiations common in the work of political managers. It is critical to distinguish between negotiations that are "one off" and those that are part of a continuing interaction. Political managers need to ask themselves, Is this negotiation the end of a relationship or the beginning? In the transaction over a used car, the buyer and seller will make their deal or not, and then they will, most likely, walk away and never see each other again. This means that, within the bounds of their negotiations, they can be tougher in pushing their positions, especially if there is little difference between their BATNAs and the deal emerging in the negotiation. They are not trying to build a working relationship for the future. While certainly they want to consummate a deal, they also want the best deal that they can convince the other side to give them.

Not all negotiations are like that. In public life, negotiations are more likely to be efforts to initiate a longer term and continuing relationship. Political managers turn to negotiations to build a supporting and enduring coalition that will further their goals. Where that is the case, then too forceful an approach in negotiating the terms of an alliance—as in pushing aggressively for one's position—can cause resentment and encourage the other party to seek ways of avoiding the commitments they made under pressure. Political managers should consider negotiations that create a coalition of parties as especially important for they provide a means by which their power can grow. As Lawrence Freedman points out, rational actors are likely to build coalitions to improve their chances of winning.[7]

Moreover, given that the circle of participants in policymaking is relatively finite, negotiations in the public sphere are rarely one-time occurrences after which the two parties will separate completely. Political managers brought together by one policy fight are likely to be mutually engaged in other policy areas. Bargainers should bear in mind that the effects of either principled negotiation or a combative style will carry over to other engagements down the road.[8] Negotiations successfully conducted in one arena are likely to have a healthy effect on other theaters. In the short term, bargaining, when conducted prudentially, can build a long-term successful relationship.

For this kind of problem, effective negotiators cannot push their counterparts to the wall, using every negotiating advantage to its full effect. Instead, political managers should utilize negotiations to craft public policies that can achieve the requisite public support and that will not embitter the other side through overly hard-nosed bargaining. Given that democratic systems offer multiple pathways for influencing public policy, overly aggressive behavior at the negotiating table may drive one's counterpart into seeking redress in other venues such as the courts, administrative agencies, local and state governments, elections, or referenda.

The essence of compromise in a car sale is that one party moves closer to the position of his counterpart, hoping that the other party will respond by conceding part of the remaining distance between them. Through back and forth, they get closer and closer to a price they can both accept. But, in politics, negotiations are likely to be multidimensional, which raises the possibility of a different form of compromise. As noted above, each party decides to swallow an objectional provision in return for stipulation that they really want. Both negotiators decide on a trade-off agreeing to a negative in order to achieve a greater positive. We will never know, for example, if President Obama could have gotten some Republican votes for his healthcare reform in 2009 if he had agreed to accept malpractice legal reform as part of a package. He might well have lost the votes of some of his own partisans but produced a bipartisan compromise that would not have been so bitterly contentious for the remaining seven years of his presidency. In public life, complex policy disputes are more likely to be resolved when political managers are willing to accept trade-offs in addition to trying to narrow the differences on every dimension at issue.

The Impact of Constituencies

Negotiations in public life cannot be adequately understood without recognition of the importance of constituencies. In a simple transaction over a car, the buyer and seller are acting in their own interests. They are unfettered in deciding what is in their best interests. Public officeholders, however, have a formal constituency that they represent.[9] If they want to be re-elected, they must pay great attention to the desires of at least a majority of those who vote in the geographical area they represent.[10] Many officeholders will also have a broader group of committed supporters constructed around given policy positions or personal attributes. These informal constituencies may well be free of geographical boundaries and quite often are engaged during the process of political fundraising. Whatever their composition, constituencies are simultaneously a source of political power and, in negotiations, a constraint. Public leaders cannot move too far beyond the interests and desires of their established constituencies without weakening their own political power. To a certain extent, supporters can be replaceable as the nature of public issues evolves and casts public disputes in a new light. But leaders who too often change their positions will ultimately lose their constituents. As a result, the flexibility with which political managers can bargain in the domain of politics will necessarily be constrained by their loyalty to their constituencies. As they prepare for negotiations in the public realm, political managers should understand the reality that their counterparts are also bound by the constraints of their constituencies. Such knowledge should feed into the calculations of the MADs and BATNAs on either side.

One example of constituency constraints occurred in June of 1972. Elected delegates to the Democratic Platform Committee of the various candidates running for the Democratic presidential nomination met in a Washington hotel to draft the party's platform. The leading candidate, Senator George McGovern, had a commanding lead in delegates and, therefore, the greatest influence over the platform language. But McGovern did not yet have a lock on the nomination that he would eventually secure in the national convention in Miami early in July. Among the candidates represented in negotiations over the wording of the platform was the anti-busing governor of Alabama, George C. Wallace. Representatives of each campaign gathered to draft the platform for the committee's approval.[11] When the plank addressing forced school busing came up, the committee agreed to pass over language suggested by staff and complete the rest of the document before returning to that contentious point between liberal McGovern and conservative Wallace. When the negotiators returned to the plank on busing, collective wordsmithing over several drafts produced language that the delegate for Wallace thought the governor *might* accept: "Transportation of students is another tool to accomplish desegregation." A long call to the governor down in Montgomery produced a "thanks-but-no-thanks" answer. The proposed language on school busing was itself only moderately acceptable and much of the rest of the platform was just too liberal for Wallace to accept. In effect, these negotiations were really over whether Wallace would publicly endorse and support McGovern once he secured the nomination. It was a valiant effort by the McGovern campaign to entice Wallace, but the effort was probably doomed from the start by Wallace's constituency. In Alabama and nationally in his presidential campaigns, Wallace had built a constituency particularly around school busing that limited his ability to accept the platform language that undercut his strong anti-busing position.

The Dynamics of Leverage

Differences among parties arise not only in their objectives but also in the resources that they bring to the bargaining table.[12] Leverage in negotiations provides an analogous concept to power in strategy. But leverage is influence, not power. "Leverage" does not describe an authoritative relationship, nor one in which one participant can force a deal on the others. Their relationship is reciprocal, each having different resources of influence they bring to the back and forth.

How should we conceptualize the advantages and weaknesses that negotiators hold or can introduce into the negotiations? James Freund, a law professor and professional negotiator, discusses four different factors that shape the degrees of leverage that negotiators bring to their interactions with their counterparts: need, desire, competition, and time.[13] To these, we will add a fifth: sunk costs.

The first two factors—need and desire—are similar concepts that vary by the degree of perceived urgency. Both serve to increase the distance between the negotiator's BATNA and MAD. The value of a given deal is enhanced by the bargainer's wishes. At the same time, any alternative may seem less attractive. Need and desire, therefore, reduce the influence of a bargainer who inadvertently reveals her wants to her counterpart. If someone simply must do a deal due to outside factors that generate a real need, he has reduced capacity to push for an outcome wholly to his satisfaction. Suppose, for example, that a person has been unemployed for a substantial period and has run through both government benefits and life savings. That person really needs to find employment and may have to take a job that otherwise would be a major step backward in his career. The diminished leverage gives him little choice.

Desire will diminish leverage in much the same way. If a buyer has decided that she wants a particular type of car, her ability to strike a beneficial deal may be reduced. Given that desire can be resisted where need cannot, however, it produces a less intense impact on leverage. When need or desire is present and strong, however, that party's BATNA may be a poor substitute for a negotiated agreement. In fact, as suggested above, the greater the conceptual distance between the value to a negotiator of a possible agreement and that person's BATNA, the weaker the leverage she or he will have in the negotiations.

The effects of need and desire upon leverage are especially true if the counterpart detects their presence, a fact that creates a subtle tension in the communications surrounding a negotiation. Skilled negotiators will ask probing questions that may allow them to diagnose the level of need or desire of their counterparts. The question "Why do you want to sell/buy this product?" may sound like an innocent-enough conversation starter, but if one listens carefully, the answer may reveal clues as to the other party's urgency in reaching an agreement. At the same time, negotiators who understand the consequences of giving away the importance they place on attaining a deal will be at pains to guard information that reduces their leverage. While there is no obligation to undercut one's own position by revealing a felt need or desire, one should also be extremely careful to stay on the correct side of truth. Lying and dishonesty, if discovered during the negotiations or afterward, will completely wipe away the trust that is essential to reaching an agreement in the first place or keeping to the deal once in place.

Competition is a third factor that will reduce bargaining leverage. We speak of a "sellers' market" when there are substantially more people wishing to buy houses than there are houses to sell. Within the bounds of their need or desire as well as their financial capacity, buyers will compete, thereby driving up the cost of desirable homes. Here again, because perceptions can shape reality, one may seek to influence the counterpart's assessments. Informing a car salesman that you have fallen in love with a particular model is a sure way to weaken your bargaining power. Instead, while keeping to the truth, a wily car buyer should express admiration for the models sold by other dealers, giving the impression that they are equally attractive to the car being bargained over. In other words, it is sometimes to your advantage to introduce competition to the other side of a negotiation, making your counterpart aware that you have alternatives should he not make you an attractive offer. If that is true, moreover, there may be times when it is in your interests to remove from the negotiations a third party that is competing with you. Brandenburger and Nalebuff note numerous situations in which, during an acquisition fight, the target company will endeavor to encourage competitive bids, as well as instances in which a suitor will pay a potential competitor *not* to submit an alternative bid.[14]

Time deadlines constitute the fourth factor influencing comparative leverage. If either party has a deadline by which the deal must be completed, that party has corresponding less power in the negotiation. And the loss of leverage becomes more potent if the counterpart becomes aware of the time deadline. Having learned of your time deadline, your counterpart might be tempted to delay reaching an agreement until the deadline is immediately upon you. As a deadline approaches, the need for settling an agreement goes up and your leverage declines.

The factor of time can shape negotiations in another way: empirically speaking, most agreements are reached in the final hour. To some extent, this is because when the parties agree, the negotiations are over. But it's also true that, as deadlines loom, the parties tend to offer compromises, especially if the outcome under discussion is superior to their alternatives. In union contract talks between employers and unions, for example, one or both parties may establish an arbitrary deadline, solely for the purpose of forcing closure to the bargaining. Union leadership can try to ratchet up the pressure on management by securing a vote by membership to strike if an agreement is not achieved by midnight on a given day. If the final hour looms and an agreement seems near but not yet achieved, the parties can always agree to stop the clock for the few additional hours necessary to conclude a deal.

Time deadlines play an important role in the politics of legislatures. In many states, the legislature has calendar prescribed by law or the state constitution. The result is a logjam of potential legislation as the deadline nears. The desire on the part of legislators to enact the necessary bills may decrease the scrutiny they give to a complex piece of legislation. In the American Congress, there's a syndrome best described as "if we can't pass this legislation by X date, it's time to move on to other matters." The party leadership may set an artificial deadline to pressure their fellow lawmakers into agreeing to a vote. Of course there will also be those pushing for delay, knowing that delay will enhance their power to kill the bill entirely.

To these ideas of James Freund, we add a fifth that he mentions only in passing: the influence of sunk costs.[15] Here is an illustration drawn from the world of hiring in a university setting. The normal process of bringing on a colleague to an academic department involves complicated internal negotiations and convoluted considerations. The existing faculty decides to fill a perceived hole in the department's intellectual capital. A committee is appointed; advertisements are sent out; the committee reviews the submitted applications and selects a limited number of applicants to invite for interviews. Each of the finalists will spend a day at the department, meeting individually with collectively with faculty, students, and presenting the ritual "job talk" discussing the applicant's research. Having received input from all these sectors, the committee ranks those who have been interviewed and takes its recommendation to the full department for its approval. If the department vote is near unanimous in its approval, the departmental chair then presents the appointment to the university's central administration.

If all goes well with that clearance, the chair is then empowered to make the winning candidate a job offer. At that point, the naive applicant may not fully recognize that all this complicated process amounts to very significant opportunity costs for the department. No department chair wants to go through that whole recruitment process again or to have to deliver the department's second-choice candidate or to have it clear to the outside world that the department has suffered a "failed search." The adroit applicant will intuitively understand that at this moment his or her bargaining leverage is at a maximum. Hiding her absolute delight at receiving the offer, she should seize this opportunity to maximize in her favor the circumstances of the appointment: teaching load, salary, committee assignments, research leave, and so forth. The lesson is clear and generalizable. Make use of leverage when you have it! Though the example may be a bit extreme in terms of sunk costs to the department, there are analogous dynamics in decisions made in the political arena. As a parliamentary committee moves along in shaping a piece of legislation, for example, the members put in time considering, debating, and rejecting ideas. In the process, they are accumulating costs that commit them to an ever-narrowing range of options. Savvy political managers learn quickly that they must enter the process early enough to influence the debates that gradually accumulate commitments to some ideas and others not. As the negotiations evolve, some ideas will be eliminated by the mounting sunk costs. Moreover, to the extent that one party puts a substantial effort into a negotiation, that effort will entail sunk costs that will weaken that party's leverage if the other party becomes aware of it.

Employing Leverage

The factors that lead to leverage—need, desire, competition, time constraints, and sunk costs—subtly shape the conversation and relationship between the parties. All are matters of comparative balancing tests. For example, both parties will have some level of desire, if only because their BATNAs are comparatively worse. Except in very rare circumstances, prospects of competition will exist for both sides. In their efforts to comprehend the nuances of their relative leverage, both experienced negotiators will be simultaneously asking probing questions while trying to cloak those factors that would weaken their own position. These communications can be dispositive of the outcome precisely because the dynamics of leverage are highly contingent upon the negotiators' mutual perceptions. A proverbial "brave face" may communicate a stronger position than the true facts would warrant.

There are dangers in the back and forth between the parties. A line can be crossed that—if discovered—can ruin the negotiation. It cannot be repeated often enough that projecting confidence and protecting information that would diminish leverage, negotiators must scrupulously avoid lying. Lying will destroy the trust upon which all successful negotiations are grounded. The question "Why did you leave your last job?" posed to an applicant who was actually fired, will certainly provoke an awkward moment during a job interview. But, facing up to the question directly may be the only alternative to misleading a future employer. To be sure, the truth may sink the prospects of getting hired but, if subsequently discovered, lying may also wreck the applicant's subsequent evaluations and can result in another firing even long afterward.

Consider another example emerging from a legislative committee hearing. Suppose that the chair turns to the leader of the minority party and says, "What does your side want and what will you accept?" In effect, she is asking for her counterpart to reveal their party's MAD on the piece of legislation before the committee. The question is fraught with danger for the minority members of the legislature. In the process of answering, the minority leader might inadvertently divulge severe disagreements within his party, a cleavage that will make that party's leaders unable to develop a cohesive policy response. Alternatively, the ranking member might disclose his party's strategy for contesting the next election. In addition, behind the public reasons for supporting or opposing the legislation in question, there could be a deeper, true agenda. It is also possible that he doesn't know what provisions his party will eventually accept. Regardless of the concerns that shape the minority party's position on the legislation, the ranking member has to come up with some answer. He is likely to talk expansively about what his side wants, but never give an indication of what minimum it will accept. If he goes too far, presenting his maximal wants as though they are minimal demands, he may well be painting his party into a corner. Lying or misleading the chair is likely to destroy any trust between the two parties and make cooperative legislation impossible. Of course, the chair knows that she's not likely to get a completely candid answer to her question. But she will be listening carefully so as to assess the vehemence with which the ranking member delivers his answer. She may have even framed the question so bluntly to put the ranking member in an uncomfortable position and just to see what information he might divulge.

Those entering a negotiation should be sensitive to another subtlety in their deployment of leverage. During negotiations that are intended to initiate an enduring relationship, experienced political managers should undertake a substantial and consequential calculation as to how aggressively they should employ their leverage. In general, they can be tougher in circumstances in which the interaction is a "one off." As noted above, buying a car has a different dynamic than negotiating a public policy, not just in complexity and interests to be satisfied, but also in how the participants should treat each other. Consider, instead the dynamics of negotiating a deal that will establish an ongoing, working relationship or that involves fashioning a policy intended to mitigate a social problem through governance. Aggressive bargaining and employment of maximum leverage may result in a settlement on terms very favorable to one of the parties. But the word "settlement" could be misleading in this instance because a deal that leans too far toward the interests of one party is likely to become unsettled as those who feel aggrieved by the process seek alternatives. Pushed into a corner by unequal leverage and forced to accept a result less favorable than they were seeking at the bargaining table, wounded counterparts might turn in the future to other partners or deliberately underperform on the terms of the agreement or seek redress in other arenas. For this reason, Vice President Walter Mondale once famously adopted the terminology of academic grading to observe that, in politics, B + solutions may be preferable.[16] If an agreement is an A + for one party, it is likely to be a D- for others, and they will continue to seek ways to overturn the agreement, including actions such as mobilizing heretofore uninvolved stakeholders, sabotaging implementation, or seeking redress through the courts.

Much of the above reasoning should serve as an indictment of legislative leadership that takes advantage of a slim majority to ram through legislation that is abhorrent to the minority. Tables do turn and when that minority party wins enough seats to capture the majority, they will certainly try to repeal the repugnant policy.

An additional caution about aggressive employment of leverage will stand the reader in good stead. As a general rule, the number of people engaged in political life on a regular basis is normally a very thin slice of society. Many citizens will take no part in the politics of their country; many others will be minimally engaged. Political managers should recognize that a small number will be attentive to and informed about the ongoing debate over political issues, but even so, they will actively participate only periodically, usually during times when elections are being held. The latter group may be activated through interest group organizations that seek to keep them informed about a range of policy deliberations. Those that we can characterize as continuously active politically or even professionally engaged will inevitably constitute a small subset of the whole. The point for negotiations is that given the level of information that this segment possesses and given their active quest for power and influence in public life, there may not actually be any such thing as a "one-off" in politics. As belligerence creates resistance, forcing a "deal" on others may be within one's capacity but at the cost of creating resentment and future enemies. And, because the circle of participants is relatively small, one may easily acquire a reputation of overly aggressive self-interest even among those with whom one has never met or bested in a negotiation. They may never want to deal with you at all or, at some future point, they may come to a negotiating table spoiling for a fight.

Perhaps the best advice about how to benefit from favorable leverage comes from James Freund, who suggests that one should not comment directly upon one's power. Doing so will only be perceived as threatening and will, most likely, antagonize one's counterpart. Instead, one should use an indirect approach, conveying an awareness of the strength of one's position through the confidence with which one addresses the other party and enters the bargaining. Coupled with an occasional casual and indirect reference to a particular aspect of leverage, a posture of self-assurance will continually but subtly transmit one's advantages. Indirect allusions and contingent statements that refer to leverage but do not state it explicitly will often get your point across.

Information in the Negotiating Process

In the conduct of negotiations, there's truth to the phrase, "Information is power," but it is certainly not the whole truth. All of the above factors that give comparatively more or less clout to the negotiators are influenced by the information possessed by both sides. This aphorism becomes especially applicable when we consider that actual leverage may not be as important as each side's perception of their respective negotiating power.

When it comes to bargaining in the arena of politics, one should assume that participants on all sides will have prepared thoroughly for the negotiation. While these preparations will involve internal decisions about such important factors as objectives, minimally acceptable demands, and BATNAs, a great deal of external information gathering is necessary as well. In most situations, intelligence should be gathered to allow predictions about the substance of the negotiation, aspects such as facts and data, interests of the parties, recent history of the dispute, possible policy alternatives, and political support behind each approach. Then too, one should endeavor to assess the other players, their likely concerns and goals, their allies and support groups, their past positions on closely allied issues, their bargaining style, and all the attributes that combine to form their personality. Much of this information will be readily available, as the counterpart political manager will have publicly communicated with her constituencies and with other groups of supporters and allies. Tracking her efforts to build support and represent constituencies should give you an idea of her approach to the negotiations.

Before the parties arrive at the negotiation table, you should have systematically gathered and analyzed whatever knowledge is available of your counterpart's likely position. All of these understandings will supply negotiators with the sagacity and strength they will need when they sit down to bargain. But, once they are actually at the table, a new dynamic is at hand, meaning that the interaction between the counterparts may overtake all the preparations. Surprise may come in the discovery that one's counterpart has different facts, different understandings, or different interests than forecast. Beyond those, the negotiators will also be concerned with ascertaining how the other perceives the balance of power between them. Direct questioning may provide some answers. More likely, scalpel-like probes for information may be cloaked by casual, innocuous questions. Whatever her approach, the experienced negotiator will be anxious to acquire an understanding that will allow her to assess the comparative degrees of leverage, including the perceptions of leverage by her counterpart. In particular, she will be alert to evidence of weaknesses in the position of her counterparts. In short, the friendly banter between participants before getting down to business is never entirely innocent.

All the while that an experienced negotiator is probing for knowledge of the other side's strengths, she will be simultaneously seeking to obscure information that could damage her own position; factors such as a critical, looming deadline or a strong need for what the other side can offer, or a comparatively poor alternative. The alert reader will, no doubt, have noted that there is difficult line to draw between misleading one's counterpart by not disclosing damaging information, on the one hand, and outright lying, on the other. Once again, ultimately negotiations are grounded on trust, and nothing destroys trust faster than a discovered lie. We repeat the strongest injunction in conducting negotiations: "Don't lie!" At the same time, a negotiator should be under no obligation to reveal facts that would undercut her bargaining weight, unless she is asked a direct question that cannot be sidestepped. It may ease this dilemma a bit to note that the factors that create leverage all have to do with *why* one is negotiating, not with the material substance over which the parties are negotiating. A lie, a material misrepresentation in the latter is the stuff that produces lawsuits when what is promised is not delivered. Thus, within the bounds of the injunction against trust-destroying lying, we can grant a bit more latitude when it comes to an information exchange about why one wants to do a deal. Full disclosure comes with a risk, namely an invitation to be taken advantage of.

In *Getting to Yes*, Roger Fisher and William Ury devote chapter 2 to the need to separate the people from the problem.[17] Their counsel may be both wise and useful, but it can be carried too far. Consider another aphorism much in use in political life and relevant to this discussion: "It's not personal; it's just business!" Don't believe it! It's always personal and will be taken that way. Touchy egos all too frequently combine with the struggle for political power and policy influence to personalize even the smallest slight. In public life, negotiations should emphasize information exchange, representing your constituencies interests, understanding your counterpart's needs, giving one's honorable word, compromise, achieving agreement, creating effective coalitions, and building enduring relationships. They should not be the occasion for manipulation and power plays.

To summarize, like strategy, negotiations take place as an interactive relationship between two or more actors who have different objects. But, in strategy one views the other party as an enemy to be bested by whatever means as long as one stays both within the law and within the bounds of peaceful conduct of a civil, democratic polity. In contrast, a negotiation puts one in the position of dealing with a respected "other" who controls values that one wants. A spirit of reciprocity and compromise constitute the mental framework that negotiators should bring to their interactions. In the long run, political managers may well discover that they can achieve more by negotiating with their political adversaries than by applying the crafty, manipulative guile of interactive strategy or all the political muscle at their command, an approach that may trigger resistance and revenge.

The Essence of Negotiations in Public Life

1. During negotiations in political life, one is presented with opportunity rather than opposition. The other party should be treated as a "counterpart," not an enemy, even recognizing that they will have interests that conflict with yours. Your approach should be to ferret out those areas where you can agree.
2. Before entering a negotiation, you should always calculate your minimum acceptable demand (MAD), consider your best alternative to a negotiated agreement (BATNA), and diagnose whether there exists a zone of possible agreement (ZOPA).
3. Need, desire, competition, time deadlines, and sunk costs all work to diminish the parties' influence or leverage over the final outcome. They are all simultaneously both factual and perceptual, reality and belief.
4. Political managers should constantly keep in mind that negotiations are based on trust and nothing destroys trust faster or more completely than a discovered lie. Within the bounds of this injunction, one should endeavor to protect information that reveals weakened leverage, all the while probing to discover the factors of leverage affecting the counterpart.
5. While some negotiations may be transitory transactions, negotiations in the political realm should more commonly produce coalitions and enduring relationships. At the bargaining table, political managers should act so as to achieve at least some minimal benefit for all parties.

9
Political Leadership

Of all the many situations in which leadership is essential for collective action, leadership in political life may well be the most complicated and demanding.[1] Given the level and variety of responsibilities, the diversity of constituencies represented, the frequent emergence of unintended consequences of public policies, the continual presence of competitors, and the often-caustic scrutiny by both political opponents and the news media, the tasks of public leadership can seem overwhelming. It's not surprising that the skills required of leaders in the public arena are manifold; diverse; and, at times, contradictory. Political leaders must excel at communications and persuasion, at negotiation and coalition building, at both directives and responsiveness, at strategy and compromise. They must exhort and plead, cajole, seduce, and command. In the face of rampant uncertainly, they must project an aura of self-confidence and articulate a set of values that they believe should govern an indeterminate future.

For our purposes, I take a broad view of who counts as a leader in the realm of politics. Whether or not you hold a formal position or political office, if you are using the skills of political management in an effort to mobilize the power necessary to shape the future of a public arena, then you are acting as a political leader. Much like individuals involved in strategy or in negotiations, political leaders and their constituents or supporters are engaged in an interactive relationship in which each side endeavors to influence the other. But, to put it bluntly, the precepts of leadership serve to erect robust guardrails on the exercise of strategy. As we shall argue below, political leaders cannot be the ruthless manipulators that strategy at its most extreme might countenance.

There are fundamental differences in the relationship between leaders and their followers, found primarily in the motivations of the participants. To capture this range symbolically, I use different terms for the participant other than the leader or political manager: "competitor" in the case of strategy; "counterpart" in negotiations; and "constituent" in leadership.[2] The relationship of leaders to their constituents is not egalitarian, but certainly leans that way in spirit, if only because it frequently involves an exchange of rewards either material or psychological. As we shall see, the tasks of leadership are quite different from the tactics of either strategy or negotiation.

Political leaders need to demonstrate and balance two dimensions of influence: inspirational traits and realpolitik adroitness.

The fundamental and principal undertakings of leadership are those of creating and communicating a vision of an ideal future for a group, collectivity, corporation, organization, or nation. Political leaders need to take "the vision thing" very seriously.[3] Whether through their words or by their example, whether they are whole-hearted believers or hypocrites, whether they do their work as charismatic exemplars or demagogues or as hermitic pamphleteers, whether they incite violence or promote compassion, whether they unify or divide, whether they coerce obedience in their followers or inspire them to self-generated achievements, leaders create followers by generating ideas as to how things *ought* to be. Thus, the tactics by which leaders effectively raise followers and through them exercise influence are not dominating and manipulative as in strategy; nor bargaining and transactional as in negotiation; but rather persuasive, inspirational, and relational. Leaders create bonds of comradeship based on sustained contact that creates shared purpose and trust.

I do not mean to suggest that effective leadership is antithetical to strategy or negotiations. In fact, to be effective, leaders need to be skilled negotiators. They also must think strategically and employ stratagems, even in their most competitive, manipulative form. Particularly in the management of politics, leaders are not idealists, divorced from the requirements of exercising power or the necessity of outthinking their opponents. Instead, they understand the ways of power; they recognize that sometimes deceit is necessary; they are shrewd in planning their future moves; and they are crafty in assessing the strengths, needs, and capabilities of others. For successful political leaders, the ways of strategy and negotiations become the tactical means of moving supporters toward their vision.

The "art" of leadership comes about in maintaining a delicate balance between these two traits. Preserving this equilibrium is no easy task. Political leaders encounter a continuous flow of events that must be managed. A victory or defeat merely changes the situation confronted and demands strategic thinking anew. In a never-ending loop, a revised set of challenges requires a different inventory of strategies and tactics. You will need new strategies both because the situation has changed and because your opponents will have learned some of your moves.

Writing in the 16th century, Niccolò Machiavelli had little appreciation for the possibilities of popular sovereignty or the potency of democracy.[4] Much as he lauded the virtues of the Roman Republic, he understood the importance of a strong ruler in nurturing the survival of a small city state surrounded by numerous enemies. As a result, Machiavelli's writings undervalued the capacity of leadership to unite citizens voluntarily behind a common set of values. Hopefully, over the intervening 500 years, we have learned a great deal about the capacities of persuasive leadership and democratic institutions. Given the tools of printing press and mass media, leaders are capable of articulating a set of ideals that can attract and maintain political support even within a very numerous citizenry. Unfortunately, political leadership can be a two-edged sword. History has given us much experience with both leadership that can unify a populous behind ideas that manifest the best instincts of a community and with demagogues who inspire brutal mass movements that ultimately destroy societies and the people within them.

How Should We Assess Leadership?

The contrast between leadership that produces general improvements versus that which generates suffering and destruction raises a question: Should we measure leadership solely by its effects? On the one hand, we feel a natural tug to ascribe leadership to an individual with whom we agree as to the values she articulates and the vision she espouses. On the other hand, at times we wish to attribute leadership to individuals who clearly made a difference from what would have happened in their absence, regardless of how we feel about their accomplishments. Yet, most observers would perceive a substantial difference between say the societal influences of two prominent examples: Adolph Hitler and Nelson Mandela. One unified many, if not most, Germans behind a vision that ultimately brought suffering and death to millions. The other took a society that was careening toward turbulence, racial hatred, ethnic retribution, and violence, and through his ideals and example, produced a polity that could move on with minimal vengeance for past suppression and brutality. There's another fact that distinguishes these two. Once in power, Hitler used coercive force to control his supporters and eliminate his opponents, whereas Mandela relied upon personal example and verbal persuasion to move his nation. Clearly there are important differences between these two examples, but should we consider them both as leaders?

Much as we may laud and admire the Nelson Mandelas of our world, many readers will want to argue that Hitler was a leader even though the vision he articulated was abhorrent. They argue that if someone has supporters and followers, we must automatically ascribe leadership to that individual. In essence, this approach is tantamount to rating all visions as equally valid and paying attention only to the effects of leadership, not to the directions in which society is moved. Instead, in a highly partisan world, we might downplay the validity of a given political manager's leadership simply because we hold it to a different partisan perspective. If we reject the vision or purpose she seeks to advance, should we refer to her as a leader? We can all think of politicians who advance policy preferences with which we disagree, even while acknowledging that their views fall within the legitimate bounds of appropriate civil discussion. In these cases, we recognize that we should not exclude them from the roster of "leaders" simply because we disagree with their advocacy of policies we consider wrongheaded.

The differences between these arguments may amount to a distinction between the denotation and connotation of the word *leadership*. Speaking concretely, we use the word to denote the effectiveness of an individual in generating supporters and shaping the evolving future. On one level, we recognize that Adolf Hitler was a leader, as repugnant as were his policies and his effects on the world. But we also want a brighter overtone to the word; we want it to refer to more than a limited meaning of impact. Our "leaders" should bring us change for the better or protect the things we value just as they are.

Even if this is a meaningful dispute, we can live with the ambiguity of both levels of meaning. The discussion does, however, point to the prominent role that ideas play in democratic politics. Leadership emerges from vision. For all the importance placed in this volume upon thinking and acting strategically, our future is also forcefully shaped by the competing visions enunciated by our would-be leaders. In democracies, ideas are integral to the creation of the political power that followers generate and the capacity for change they facilitate.

Leadership can be for good or for ill. This premise needs to be stated emphatically. It is too easy to argue that since the victors write history, accordingly, wherever our leaders take us will be adjudged positively in retrospect. Rather, we should be mindful that leadership can create great mischief for societies. Evil leadership can foster centuries of human pain. However much we would like to rely upon a pure impact measurement of leadership, the content of the leader's vision is inevitably important.

In a seminal book on leadership in the political arena, John W. Gardner gives us six characteristics of effective leaders.[5] To paraphrase: (1) they think long-term; (2) they grasp the big picture; (3) they reach and influence constituencies beyond the limits of their formal boundaries; (4) they have multiple skills to deal with the conflicting requirements of multiple constituencies; (5) they emphasize intangibles of values and vision; and (6) they work toward regeneration and renewal of the values of their community. These ideas dovetail completely with the scope of this book. The first two of these characteristics align perfectly with the military's conception of strategy and the next two are components of effective negotiation skills. But as the final two talents suggest, leaders also use different approaches to influencing supporters, approaches that motivate and inspire, which create and communicate a vision that directs the attention and energy of their followers toward accomplishing collective goals.

James McGregor Burns, a foremost scholar of leadership in politics, takes the view that it is important to judge leaders by the value of their views, not just by the impacts they generate. He argues, "Leaders must offer moral leadership":

They can express the values that hold society together. Most important, they can conceive and articulate goals that lift people out of their petty preoccupations, carry them above the conflicts that tear society apart, and unite them in the pursuit of objectives worthy of their best efforts.

To make the tasks of leadership more specific, Burns offers us a useful distinction between "transactional leadership" and what he refers to as "transformational." The former concept derives from negotiations, introduced here to explain the relationship between political leaders and their supporters. That is, the transactional model focuses upon the exchange of benefits. Leaders supply their followers with material and psychic benefits; followers provide political support in the form of concrete acts like voting, petitioning, protesting, and other means of demonstrating the popularity of the leader's vision and policies. In the days of strong urban party machines in the United States, for example, party leaders would famously distribute turkeys to their loyal voters during the Thanksgiving celebrations. Such symbolic rewards for loyal party membership were often augmented by stronger incentives such as municipal jobs or lower property assessments or greater police protection or more frequent trash collection or any number of goods and services that could be invented by political parties or the governments they controlled. A sense of belonging to a community with shared interests could establish a degree of psychic value that leaders can generate for their followers. In return, followers supply the voting power to keep the politician in office and they generate public opinion support for the individual leader and the policies she enunciates. Ardent supporters also make financial contributions large or small that increase the leader's access to power and freedom of action.

Burns believes that this transactional exchange constitutes a too-narrow, limited definition of robust leadership. Leaders should inspire and transform their followers, appealing to widely and deeply held values, such as justice, liberty, and brotherhood. By satisfying the human needs lower on the value hierarchy,[6] leaders allow these higher motivations to arise and elevate the conscience of men and women.[7] At times, this task of envisioning and persuading followers to adopt a particular vision of a better world will necessitate choosing between inconsistent values. Burns argues:

> The essence of leadership in any polity is the recognition of real need, the uncovering and exploiting of contradictions among values and between values and practice, the realigning of value, the reorganization of institutions where necessary, and the governance of change. Essentially, the leader's task is consciousness-raising.[8]

Quite often, the frustrations of leaders evolve from contradictions encountered in balancing desired outcomes against the process required to implement them. Where power is essential to forcing change, transformational leadership also demands responsiveness. Both the popular understanding of leadership and the definitional arguments of scholars distinguish between collective, inspirational persuasion as opposed to the use of manipulation or coercive force. The ability to motivate a constituency to act simply because they accept and wish to pursue the leader's vision is a transforming act of far greater consequence than can be achieved by intimidation, oppression, trickery, or even bargaining. Where Machiavelli famously opined that it's better to be feared than loved, Burns would argue it better to be both loved and feared, in that order.

As Gardner reminds us, in accomplishing their basic task, leaders influence constituencies beyond the limits of their formal boundaries. Gardner is suggesting that leaders influence more than the formal constituency that an elected officeholder officially represents. Leaders do not necessarily have to exercise formal authority or hold a formal office to be highly influential. Certainly, occupying a public office imbued with resources and powers can contribute to one's ability to communicate a vision. But many of the most profound leaders held no public office at all. Mahatma Gandhi and Martin Luther King are two notable examples in public life.

William A. Cohen, a retired Major General in the US Air Force Reserves, has made this same point in reverse, arguing that true leadership is more than mere authority.[9] Examining successful military leaders, he contends that the ability to issue orders is simply too limited of a construction of the essence of leadership. Instead, by personal example, by integrity, by persuasive ability, leaders inspire followers to willingly do their utmost. Inspiration is more powerful than command. This line of thought about effective military leadership descends from a quote attributed to Xenophon, a fourth-century BC Greek historian and philosopher, "Willing obedience beats forced obedience every time."[10]

Cohen's perspective is echoed time and again through a substantial amount of published writing on leadership in the military. Barking orders may be necessary in emergency situations, but effective leadership means a relationship of mutual trust and respect up and down the chain of command. According to the US Army's Field Manual 22-100, "Leadership is influencing people—by providing purpose, direction, and motivation—while operating to accomplish the mission and improving the organization.... there's more to influencing than simply passing along orders. The example you set is just as important as the words you speak."[11] The Manual goes on to describe the skills needed at three levels of leadership: direct, organizational, and strategic. The first refers to leaders of small groups, the second to larger systems and processes, and the third to national and societal perspectives.

Robert Kelly has advanced a complementary notion in his book, *The Power of Followership*.[12] Noting that most of the actual work of change is performed by followers, not leaders, Kelley seeks to de-emphasize the single-minded attention on leaders. The secret to change, he suggests, is found in creating followers who will lead themselves. In other words, rather than dictating and controlling, leaders should seek to empower their followers. Kelley argues that we should appreciate the role of effective followers as a source of much achievement. Leaders do that by enabling their supporters; by endowing them with the power to act; and by inspiring them toward a shared, collective purpose.

To sum up the above discussion, leadership can be a powerful stimulus to beneficial change and growth in a society as well as, conversely, an impulse toward a dictatorial narrowing of the scope of freedom allowed in a polity. It is a double-edged sword. Unless our conception includes some personal judgment about the direction of the leader's vision, we cannot establish a difference between the directions in which political leaders might wish to move. If we are engaged in politics in order to shape the future according to a particular vision, it makes a difference how we adjudge who to follow and who to emulate. At the same time, within a democratic polity with its emphasis on pluralism, diversity and free speech, we should not go so far as to condemn as non-leaders those with whom we disagree over legitimate policy differences. Instead, the appropriate stance should be something akin to, "I don't agree with his views on this matter, but I recognize the legitimacy and effectiveness of his leadership." This position raises the question of whether, within the bounds of democratic leadership, there is a boundary that defines the scope of legitimate political leadership. In other words, while recognizing the leadership capacity of individuals with whom we disagree—even vehemently—it still may be valid to make some judgments about the content of their vision and action.

Leadership in Democratic Politics

Political managers—leaders in a democratic system—have an affirmative set of obligations that supersede their goal of implementing their vision. That is, vision and purpose—so essential to leadership—need to be circumscribed by the value of preserving the strength of democratic institutions. A "winning-at-all-costs" attitude can undercut the legitimacy of political leadership if it leads to behavior that transcend the norms of democratic politics. As the preeminent political theorist, Robert A. Dahl, has repeatedly pointed out, democratic institutions are only a product of the values and norms that support them, norms that can be weakened by the actions of political managers.[13] Consider, for example, actions such as using the government's prosecutorial authority to go after one's political opponents. Or, what if the leader imposes a rewritten constitution that guarantees a predetermined result such as securing re-election? Such actions emasculate democratic institutions. In so doing, we argue that they fall outside the scope of legitimate leadership in a democracy. Thus, in order to understand the limits of leadership in a democracy, we need to delve into the values of democratic politics that undergird the institutions through which political competition proceeds.

This is not to say that democratic institutional structures must be immutably locked in stone. In fact, a good deal of continual change takes place gradually as the forces moving in society put differing pressures upon institutions. So adaptation to these changes is necessary but must be contained within the values that support democratic systems. For example, the US Senate languished in relative unimportance for much of the first 150 years of governance under the US Constitution. Then in the 20th century, after the enactment of the 17th Amendment to the Constitution providing for direct election of senators, the institution gained in visibility, respect, and influence.[14] The main point to be drawn is that institutional change took place over many years, with much debate, and with due regard for democratic values and politics.

During the latter three decades of the 20th century, the two major political parties in the United States took different approaches to constituting their national conventions. The Democrats appointed a series of commissions empowered to set the rules for the next convention including those for selecting convention delegates.[15] Unfortunately, the aspiring presidential candidates could not resist the temptation to shape the rules in ways that would advantage their candidacies. As a result, rather than creating procedures widely accepted as "fair," these commissions themselves became swept up in the contending politics. Far better, in the author's opinion, was the approach of the Republicans. As part of the business of one national convention, they finalize the rules for the *next* convention. This action meant that the rules are set before the outcome of the November election is known and, therefore, before the contending candidates have stepped forward. In this way, the rules and procedures by which presidential candidates are nominated are less susceptible to manipulation by those candidates. The broader lesson here is that recognizing that institutions do have to evolve, it is better to reform them slowly so that, as much as possible, changes are divorced from the politics of the moment.

What then are the principles of democratic practice that should not be violated by political managers?[16]

1. **An Informed and Engaged Citizenry.** Leadership, as conceived here, refers to a relationship or a pattern of interactions built on shared purpose and reciprocal trust between a political manager and potential supporters. Not surprisingly, the first set of obligations that political leaders should take on relate to that nexus between themselves and citizens. Leaders seek to influence their followers, but at the same time,

they also endeavor to be responsive to the needs and desires of their constituencies.

In a functioning democracy, the political system should encourage citizen participation in political decision-making. If we have learned anything from years of experience with democratic systems, however, it is that there are limits upon the degree to which citizens actually want to be directly engaged in politics. It is quite normal that democracies will exhibit a broad range of citizen engagement from political managers who are involved full time, down to activists who engage only part of their time, down to citizens who are attentive to and involved in political discourse and acts of individual participation, down to those who usually take part in voting but little else, and finally, down to citizens who are completely separated from political life. The percentage of the populous that falls in each of these levels will vary, heavily influenced by cultural traditions; population demographics; economic prosperity and stability; political history; the political disputes of the moment; and, of course, the nature and rules of political institutions. The percentages that characterize these levels of engagement may also change over time, rising and falling as events shape the issues of contemporary politics and impact the interests of different demographic groups. These differences across the range of citizen engagement in politics are natural and healthy. But this reality means that the boundaries between these levels must be permeable. A healthy democracy allows citizens to move easily up and down the scale of political activity.

Political leadership is centrally occupied by these dynamics. Some political managers will aggressively seek to expand the pool of active participants, wanting to enlist them as supporters within their power base. Others may be tempted to leave things as they are or even endeavor to discourage citizens from becoming actively involved in politics. The harsh truth is that an election can be won by expanding the number of supporters and getting them to the polls on Election Day or by discouraging the opponent's supporters from voting or by erecting roadblocks to their participation. The first strategy represents the exercise of democratic leadership; the latter two constitute a deliberate weakening of democratic institutions. Those who wish to encourage greater levels of participation will normally find that task to be a challenge, particularly in those many democracies that exhibit high levels of citizen cynicism. But as a statement of political ethics, political managers should not endeavor to restrict the flow of information to citizens or limit their ability to become involved in the processes of public choice.

2. **Advocacy and Responsiveness.** Leadership involves advocacy. On the one hand, we want political leaders to be passionate promoters of their vision of a better future. Educating citizens as to the perspective and worth of that envisioned future is essential to political mobilization and to leadership itself. On the other hand, intense commitments are very likely to warp judgments as to objective facts, so at the extreme, leadership can devolve into misleading the public. When this advocacy becomes knowingly and deliberately deceptive, the political manager has crossed the line into leadership that weakens democracy.[17] Where the line between persuasion and falsehoods fall in any given instance is a matter that individual political managers should worry about. Intentionally misleading the public falls outside the bounds of legitimate leadership.

Advocacy should be paired with responsiveness. We want political managers to be decisive yet responsive. At the same time as we endeavor to create an informed citizenry, we also seek to encourage an engaged citizenry, meaning that a strong value of democracy lies in stimulating direct citizen participation in public affairs. One way of conceiving of this value is to observe that ultimately, sovereignty should lie with the citizenry. Democratic political leaders should reinforce this illusive objective by their own actions and by creating strong institutions that provide channels for citizen control. Anything less undercuts the tenets of democracy. To achieve this goal, democracies allow freedom of thought and expression by all citizens without fear of governmental, political, or community pressure or coercion. In addition, whether individually or collectively, citizens of a democracy must be able to petition government officials and agencies for redress of their grievances without fear of arrest and prosecution. A democratic polity allows and even inspires its citizens to organize themselves into groups for collective action and speech—including peaceful protests and demonstrations—without fear of arrest or prosecution. Finally, governmental decisions, actions, and policies must be broadly transparent so that interested citizens can understand, appreciate, abide by, and ultimately influence those policies. Though most democratic polities will exhibit a wide range of citizen engagement, the point here is that the institutions and acts of political leaders should make relevant information available, even if few citizens take advantage of the opportunity. To the old adage, "You can lead a horse to water, but you cannot make him drink," we add, "Yes, but you can keep the trough full!"

As noted above, the relationship between leaders and citizens is manifold, interactive, and extremely complex in part because many aspects of engagement by average citizens demand support from would-be political leaders. That is, even in a well-established and functioning democracy, participation by the mass of citizens often needs encouragement from political leaders in order to flourish. But political leaders face an inherent difficulty in drawing the line between potent advocacy and empowering responsiveness. It turns out that advocating on the basis of civic responsibility—encouraging involvement as a generalized social good—is not nearly as persuasive or as effective as exhorting participation in order to achieve a desired value. Thus arises the temptation to accentuate advocacy in order to generate change. This relationship has become even more complex with the rise of social media and the enhanced ability for communities of interest to emerge, form, flower, and recede as new issue constellations arise. An inherent requirement for continual engagement places a special obligation upon leaders to ensure that their support-building activities do not spill over into self-protective efforts designed to insulate them from either citizen demands or effective challenge by other would-be leaders. Most of the American states, for example, have laws that place high barriers on those seeking to register new political parties. Gerrymandering provides a second example. Drawing electoral districts can be undertaken as essentially an effort to insulate the candidates of one party from any effective challenge at the polls. Leaders can encourage citizen empowerment or they can dominate their interactions with citizens in ways that weaken the latter's power. Leaders, by their nature, want to bring about change. They are passionate advocates for their view of how their community should evolve. They must acquire and use power over people to make possible a transition toward their dream. None of these traits lend themselves easily to deference to citizen sovereignty.

3. **Free and Fair Elections.** Elections that can accurately be described as "free and fair" are the essential and fundamental building block of an effective democracy. They are, however, only part of what constitutes a democracy, for alone they do not provide enough protections to ensure a government "of the people, by the people and for the people." After all, numerous totalitarian systems hold regular elections in order to showcase regime support. Instead, elections should matter. To be characterized as fair and free, elections must have the following five characteristics:[18]

- a system by which all adult citizens above a certain age can qualify for voting eligibility, without restrictions based on political beliefs, religious commitments, linguistic preferences or demographic characteristics;
- an established process by which individuals wishing to be elected to public office can qualify to be on the ballot, involving minimal procedural hurdles and no arbitrary or systematic rules for excluding candidates, individually or collectively, based on their age, gender, race, language, religion, or political philosophy. Screening or filtering processes that limit candidacies must be transparent and, at least to some extent, permeable;
- an administrative apparatus devoted to distributing ballots widely so that all eligible citizens have an opportunity to vote and to ensure that only one vote is cast per voter and that all votes are accurately counted and registered in the publicly reported election results;
- minimal and reasonable restrictions on what candidates can say and do in attracting support among the citizens combined with an effective means of reaching potential voters through various available media;
- an absence of governmental support—financial, advocacy, or media access—for one candidate or group of candidates.

It follows that democratic leaders should not endeavor to establish rules or laws that limit the effectiveness of these five properties, even when doing so would increase their own political support and, thus, strengthen the possibilities of achieving their vision for the future. In other words, our argument here is that even though we should not restrict our designation of leadership solely to those with whom we agree in policy preferences, when it comes to *process* questions that determine the successful functioning of the political system, we can be more scrupulous as to whom we accept as true leaders.

4. **Pluralism.** The institutions of politics and government in a democracy should exhibit the quality that political theorists call "pluralism."[19] In simplified terms, pluralism demands that the political system is characterized by dispersed and overlapping structures for acquiring and flexing power. In other words, no single authority, institution, or political group should dominate all channels of political influence within a polity. Instead, citizens and political leaders alike should have available to them multiple channels of effective political influence so that when disappointed or blocked in one institution, they might seek redress through a different channel. As a practical matter, it normally follows that citizens and activists and leaders will gravitate toward one vehicle of influence depending upon the nature of the policy matter of concern. The structure of power influencing education policy, to pick an example, will most likely be quite different from that determining taxation, even though these two policy arenas are interrelated. Moreover, the different political issues will likely engage different actors and groups of citizens.

Dictators hate pluralism. Why? To consolidate their power, they seek to penetrate or undercut all instruments of political influence that might allow challenges to their authority.[20] They wish to enjoy an unchallenged monopoly of power. Their efforts at control and self-protection extend well beyond the formal institutions of government. They seek to control or, at a minimum, to weaken political parties, associations, civil society organizations, universities, religious societies, even cultural groups—anything that might become a basis for political opposition. Their efforts at control easily spill over into the use of coercion and repression, actions that often generate resistance and opposition. A cycle sets in of ever-greater oppression. A degree of paranoia can seize the leader, growing as any spark of resistance becomes perceived as a threat. Tolerating a degree of dissent or disobedience can be perceived by others as a sign of weakness, which can lead to even greater resistance. The regime seeks to extend its power into all walks of life, snuffing out opposition at its first appearance. Thus, dictators avidly work to eviscerate any vestige of pluralism.

Conversely, democratic leaders should seek to expand—not truncate—the institutions through which activists and citizens can address public policy problems, even though doing so may complicate the tasks of their political leadership. By protecting and nurturing multiple channels of citizen influence, democratic leaders maintain institutions that manage the conflicts and contrasting interests in society without resort to violence.

By no means are we proposing an easy undertaking for leaders, for we are asking them to hold themselves accountable to and challengeable by other ambitious thought leaders. But, in the long run, it is the strategy that is most likely to be both successful for society and productive of a lasting legacy. Anyone anxious to take up the burdens of public leadership in a democracy must recognize that adopting this attitude may mean subjecting himself to a great deal of frustration. Pluralism inevitably means challenge, delay, negotiation, compromise, and lots of hard work. While we can sympathize, such is the nature of the job.

The values of pluralism can be secured independent of the precise form taken by the institutions of politics and governance. The ancient Roman Republic, for example, divided governmental powers among two consuls, the Centuriate Assembly and the Senate; and various offices such as the tribunes, praetors, and aedileships.[21] Parliamentary systems—such as developed over time in England and many other countries—allow the executive powers to emerge from legislative power. In contrast, presidential systems separate the executive and legislative powers so as to provide a strong check on abusive control by those exercising the authority of either entity. Due to its unique history reaching right back to its founding, the American Republic further grants significant powers to state governments as a balance to federal authority. Most democracies also provide another check by nurturing an empowered and independent judiciary that adjudicates how broad social policies apply in individual instances. These different and diverse institutional frameworks are designed to divide governmental power and accentuate pluralism. As such, they deserve to be nurtured by competent and professionally ethical political leaders.

5. **Freedom of Discourse.** Dissent and criticism not only emerge from other political managers, it wells up in the thoughts and speech of activists and citizens. Accordingly, a value of democracy is the encouragement—or at least the absence of repression—of political speech. While certainly this is a means for achieving an informed citizenry, it is also a value in itself, for new ideas and undiscovered policy options are more likely to be generated in a society where citizens can speak freely. Ethical political leaders should resist the temptation to repress dissent even when it amounts to condemnation of their plans and goals. Here again, preserving the strengths of a democracy calls for tolerance and forbearance in the face of opposition.

Of particular concern to those in or aspiring to public office is the content of news reporting. Journalists are a threat to political managers largely because they sit athwart many—but not all—of the channels of communication with citizens. Furthermore, while the public may voice some skepticism about journalism, that attitude is likely to be dwarfed by the cynicism they direct toward politicians. As a result, news coverage by reputable journalistic organizations is likely to have greater credibility than the communications emanating directly from political leaders, a fact that makes the latter particularly anxious to influence or control the former. There are certainly legitimate and effective ways of advocacy, persuasion, and even ownership through which those working in public life can seek to shape the content of news coverage. But using the coercive powers of governmental authority to limit the freedom of journalists goes beyond justifiable activity and begins to erode one of the important institutions of politics. Journalists in a democracy, whether they work in print, online, or broadcast media, must be able to report on the activities of those in both politics and in government without undue constraints and without fear of arrest and prosecution.

No political leader ever feels that their actions are always treated fairly by the news media, especially by those journalistic organizations that consider their mission to be holding public officeholders accountable to the public. The best public leaders among us, however, recognize that aggressive criticism from journalists inescapably comes with the job. For them to endeavor to run roughshod over the media—closing some outlets, jailing journalists—inevitably weakens the capacity of the political system to deliver upon the public's will. Much as leaders wish to move forward toward their vision, they need to restrain their instincts for weakening pluralism by attacking those they consider to be enemies in the news media.

6. **Protection of Minority Rights.** Finally, power in a democracy is, by definition, largely determined by majority opinion and action. In the course of political leadership, of all the lines that must be drawn within a given polity, striking an appropriate balance between majority rule and minority rights may well be the most difficult. In nearly all cases, it will be the most controversial and the most subject to perpetual dispute.

The forces arrayed against the rights of minorities are likely to be quite significant, including a numerical majority with its voting power, aggregation of wealth, control of private corporations including news organizations, and so on. Where ethnic loyalties are strong, as in many African countries, for example, democratic elections often mean that one group always wins unless specific steps are taken to protect the voting power of minority groups.[22] The antidote is found in the exercise of judgment by political leaders and, possibly, in constitutional protections, protections that require a supermajority to amend. But, of course, for those who view "democracy" as meaning only majoritarian rule, those protections and the constitution that enshrines them are like to be seen as antidemocratic. Ethical political leaders should not ignore the fact that democracy without these protections can become tyrannous.

David Brooks, the conservative columnist at the *New York Times*, compares the need of nurturing and strengthening democratic institutions to farming.[23] It's not enough merely to plant the seeds. To maintain a democracy, those seeds must be tended, watered, nourished. Brook's lament is that post-World War II—that is, after 75 years—Americans and Western Europeans had come to see democracy as inevitable. Much of the tending of democratic institutions had been neglected. Pointing to a decline in civic education that molded democratic citizenship, he laments, "Democracy is not natural; it is an artificial accomplishment that takes enormous work." Here, I have repeatedly pleaded with political managers that they should not weaken democratic institutions. Brooks implores a higher standard: that they work to strengthen the institutions that make democracy possible.

Leadership versus Strategy

I conclude with two warnings. The first is that sometimes the requirements of strategy and leadership are opposed to each other, and one must decide which skill is more important in a particular situation. The lessons advanced in the first seven chapters need to be balanced by a sense of judgment as to the requirements of public leadership articulated above. For example, strategy counsels that political managers should be unpredictable in order to outdo their opponents and achieve their desired results. But democratic constituencies demand consistency from their leaders. When an officeholder shifts positions on an important issue, for example, his or her opponents are sure to point that out. If a political manager acquires an image of one who "flip-flops" in stated positions, that can be terribly detrimental to a political career. The same is true if the public image becomes that of a "wheeler-dealer." The label "Tricky Dick" haunted President Richard Nixon until his death. Thus, the shapelessness counseled by Sun Tzu, Liddell Hart, and numerous other theorists of strategy should only be carried so far in public life. Maneuvering around opponents behind the scenes, managing associates in an organization, or climbing the career ladder may all require a degree of keeping competitors off balance by surprise. But, when it comes to actions that are likely to be visible to one's constituency, consistency trumps surprise.

Strategy dictates that one needs to be unpredictable, while democratic leadership demands consistency and constancy. Bby no means is this the only contradiction between these two approaches to politics. There are 10 dimensions in which the characteristics demanded of leaders stands at odds with aggressive displays of strategy.

Characteristics Contrasting Strategy versus Leadership

Strategy	Leadership
Unpredictable	Consistency
Flexibility	Steadfast
Deception	Trustworthiness
Manipulative	Forthright
Calculating	Sincere
Amoral	Moral
Controlling	Empowering
Deceitful	Honest
Unscrupulous	Principled
Ruthless	Compassionate

As political managers conduct their professional lives, each of these facets confronts them with difficult balancing tests as to how far they should lean in the direction of leadership versus strategy. It's rather easy for observers to urge young political managers at the threshold of their careers to lean as much as possible toward the dimension of leadership. But such advice ignores their need to accumulate power in the short run. But, if they instead emphasize the characteristics of strategy to the exclusion of leadership, it is likely that their Machiavellian reputation will undermine their capacity to influence others.

There is no better example of achieving an appropriate balance between these two demands of political management than President Abraham Lincoln. He faced two great tasks: preserving the Union and ending slavery. As Frederick Douglass pointed out, to accomplish both tasks, Lincoln needed to maintain the political support essential to accomplishing them.[24] In January 1865, the war had turned into a slow grinding away of the resources of the rebellious states, bringing both sides to the point at which they could consider a peace conference. Lincoln was pressured by the more extreme "radical" Republicans to insist on total surrender and by more moderate northern politicians of both parties to bring the slaughter to a conclusion. Also on Lincoln's table was a draft of the 13th Amendment, which would abolish slavery throughout the entire nation. Successful negotiations with the South would most likely have led to the amendment's defeat. With the amendment nearing a vote, Lincoln—honest Abe—misled his political allies, saying he was not aware of Southern Peace Commissioners being in the city.[25] The amendment was passed and sent to the states for ratification and the peace negotiations failed with each side blaming the other's intransigence. Three months later, General Robert E. Lee surrendered his army at Appomattox and the Confederate government collapsed without a peace agreement. Through adroit political management, balancing the integrity of leadership with the craftiness of strategy, Lincoln had achieved both of his twin goals. Five days later, he was assassinated.

My second warning has been issued repeatedly throughout this book but should be restated here, both for the record and for emphasis: the pursuit of power and the temptations of political leadership are dangerous. The progress of society needs individuals who are strongly committed to a vision of how things ought to be. But even the strongest commitments need to be balanced with responsiveness. The greater the degree of commitment, the more the political leader is likely to see opposition as mere obstructionism or wrongheaded opportunism. Leadership should allow for a two-way street. Power is necessary to achieve purpose and purpose can vindicate the quest for power. Strategy counsels us to view the other party as an enemy to be bested by whatever means as long as we stay both within the law and within the bounds of peaceful conduct of a civil, democratic polity. All is fair in war and politics as long as we avoid damaging the political institutions of a democracy. But do the ends really justify the means? Or is it that some ends can justify some means? Personally, for political leaders, these will be the most difficult internal struggles, the most demanding ethical judgments, and the most challenging pursuit of balance between conflicting values. Political managers will require careful soul-searching and a large dose of strategic judgment to strike the right balance. With all humility, I wish you good fortune in achieving a workable balance in your political career and every success in accomplishing your vision.

Notes

Chapter 1

1. See the full quote from November 11, 1947, advanced by the International Churchill Society, https://winstonchurchill.org/resources/quotes/the-worst-form-of-government/, accessed November 11, 2021.
2. The term "political manager" may be unfamiliar to the reader but constitutes a primary audience for this volume. It refers to individuals who seek to use the instruments of politics broadly defined in order to influence social policy and outcomes. Whether they are elected officials or their staff or private advocates, political managers seek to influence the choices made by government institutions. They may work inside or outside of the formal institutions of democratic politics. They may try to shape legislation, influence policy implementation, or control election outcomes. They may derive their livelihood from politics, or they may be amateur activists. The emergence of a profession of political managers is both dependent upon and measured by the increasing complexity and technical expertise of effective political action.
3. For a discussion of the importance of becoming politically active, see Eitan Hersh, *Politics Is for Power: How to Move Beyond Political Hobbyism, Take Action, and Make Real Change* (New York: Scribner, 2020), 1–20.
4. Numerous scholars have produced an abundant literature on the employment of power in international relations. Here, I will only cite three such volumes: Thomas C. Schelling, *The Strategy of Conflict* (Cambridge, MA: Harvard University Press, 1960, 1980); Joseph S. Nye, Jr., *The Future of Power* (New York: Public Affairs, 2011); and John Lewis Gaddis, *On Grand Strategy* (New York: Penguin Books, 2018).
5. For a discussion of the potent role of nonmilitary means by which nation-states influence each other, see Joseph S. Nye, Jr., *Soft Power: The Means to Success in World Politics* (Cambridge, MA: Public Affairs, 2004).
6. The delineation of the elements of power proposed here closely follows the work of Frederick W. Frey. See "Comment: On Issues and Nonissues

in the Study of Power," *American Political Science Review* 65, no. 4 (1971): 1081–101.
7. Frey (1971) refers to the "scope" of a power relationship to denote the range of behaviors that exhibited the influence in reaction to the power act initiated by the influencer.
8. Max Weber, *The Theory of Social and Economic Organization*, trans. A. M. Henderson and Talcott Parsons (New York: Free Press, 1924/1947), 328, 358ff.
9. Olivia Fox Cabane, *The Charisma Myth: How Anyone Can Master the Art and Science of Personal Magnetism* (New York: Penguin Group, 2012).
10. Among the many versions of Niccolo Machiavelli's, *The Prince*, see the translation by N. H. Thomson (Mineola, NY: Dover Publications, 1992). Also very helpful is the small treatise by Cambridge scholar Quentin Skinner, *Machiavelli: A Very Short Introduction* (Oxford: Oxford University Press, 1981). For a complete rendition of Machiavelli's thinking, turn to Niccolo Machiavelli, *The Prince and The Discourses* (New York: Modern Library, 1950).
11. Sun Tzu, *The Art of War*, trans. Lionel Giles (Blacksburg, VA: Thrifty Books, 2009).
12. Dan Sewell, "'Learning How to Fight': The Art of War" by Sun Tzu contains a Chinese militarist's centuries-old advice that still rings true for personal and global conflicts," *Los Angeles Times*, November 23, 1989, https://www.latimes.com/archives/la-xpm-1989-11-23-vw-403-story.html, accessed April 21, 2020.
13. Karl Van Clausewitz, *On War*, ed. and trans. Michael Howard and Peter Paret (Princeton, NJ: Princeton University Press, 1976). See also Tiha von Ghyczy, Bolko von Oetinger, and Christopher Bassford, *Clausewitz on Strategy* (New York: John Wiley, 2001) or Michael Howard, *Clausewitz: A Very Short Introduction* (New York: Oxford, 2002).
14. Gaddis, *On Grand Strategy*, 115.
15. I am indebted to Carol Darr, my colleague at GW's Graduate School of Political Management, for this analysis. See her forthcoming book *Machiavelli in Plain English: Outrageous, Irreverent, and Very Practical Advice on Life, Leadership & Your Career*.
16. Carol Darr, personal communication. Ms. Darr tells me that her synopsis is derived from a quote by Robert Martin Adams, "Do good when you can, do evil when you must; do both unhesitatingly, and don't lie to yourself about which is which." See Adams, "The Interior Prince, or Machiavelli Mythologized," *The Prince: A Norton Critical Edition*, trans. and ed., Robert M. Adams (New York: Norton, 1977), 243.

17. Bernard Crick, *In Defense of Politics* (Chicago: University of Chicago Press, 1992).
18. Robert A. Dahl, *On Democracy* (New Haven, CT: Yale University Press, 1998) provides some practical guidance for the institutions necessary to a functioning democracy. The second edition of *On Democracy*, published by Yale University Press in 2015, contains a preface and two chapters by Dahl's colleague, Ian Shapiro.
19. Among Robert A. Dahl's many publications, see especially *Democracy and It's Critics* (New Haven: Yale, 1989), and *A Preface to Democratic Theory* (Chicago: University of Chicago Press, 2006).
20. There are, of course, arguments over whether the duty of an elected official is to effectively represent all of the citizens residing in her formal constituency or only those who voted for her. And, what about those outside the defined electorate?
21. Found at https://www.brainyquote.com/quotes/steve_chabot_329192, accessed on April 22, 2010. Of course, we might comment that the comparison of politics to a sport diminishes the former. As argued at the onset, politics is a deadly serious activity through which human beings negotiate their collective future.
22. Winston Churchill was speaking before the UK Parliament on November 11, 1947, see *Churchill by Himself: The Definitive Collection of Quotations*, ed. Richard M. Langworth (New York: PublicAffairs press, 2008), 574.
23. At the conclusion of each chapter, I offer concluding thoughts as to the essence of the chapter's contents. They are not necessarily intended to be comprehensive summaries.

Chapter 2

1. B. H. Liddell Hart, *Strategy* (New York: Meridian, Henry Holt & Co., 1991), 321.
2. See https://en.wikipedia.org/wiki/Strategy or https://www.etymonline.com/word/strategy.
3. Karl Von Clausewitz, *War, Politics and Power: Selections from On War and I Believe and Profess*, trans. Edward M. Collins (Chicago: Gateway, 1962), 81–82.
4. Lawrence Freedman tells me that Michael Foucault, the French social philosopher came to this same conclusion. See Freedman, *Strategy: A History* (London: Oxford University Press, 2013), 426; cited from Julian Reed,

"Life Struggles: War, Discipline, and Biopolitics in the Thought of Michael Foucault," *Social Text* 86, no. 24 (2006).

5. From a conversational exchange with Harold Begbie, as cited in *Master Workers*, Begbie, Methuen & Co. (1906), 177. https://www.brainyquote.com/quotes/winston_churchill_135262, accessed on November 5, 2022.
6. Harold Lasswell, *Politics: Who Gets What, When, How* (Gloucester, MA: Peter Smith pub., 1960), Chapter 1 on elite power.
7. See, for example, George Steiner, *Strategic Planning* (New York: Free Press, 1979), 12–23.
8. As we shall note in Chapter 5, the strategy of tailoring your message to the audience does not mean that one can say different things to different groups. Political leaders lose support when they are "caught" directly contradicting themselves in their appeals to different audiences.
9. Milton Lodge and Ruth Hamill, "A Partisan Schema for Political Information Processing," *American Political Science Review* 80, no. 2 (1986): 505–19. Wendy M. Rahn, "The Role of Partisan Stereotypes in Information Processing about Political Candidates," *American Journal of Political Science* 37, no. 2 (1993): 472–96. Michael F. Meffert, Sungeun Chung, Amber J. Joiner, Leah Waks, and Jennifer Garst, "The Effects of Negativity and Motivated Information Processing During a Political Campaign," *Journal of Communication* 56, no. 1 (2006): 27–51.
10. Martin Reeves and Knut Haanaes, *Your Strategy Needs a Strategy: How to Choose and Execute the Right Approach* (Cambridge, MA: Harvard Business School Press, 2015).

Chapter 3

1. Karl Von Clausewitz, "On War," in *War, Politics, and Power: Selections from On War, and I Believe and Profess*, trans. and ed. Edward M. Collins (Chicago: Henry Regnery Company, 1962), 45, 141, italics in original.
2. Christopher Bassford, "Clausewitz and His Works," in Clausewitz in English: The Reception of Clausewitz in Britain and America (New York: Oxford University Press, 1994), ch. 2. Bassford, a professor at the National War College, maintains a website devoted to the understanding of Clausewitz's work: https://www.clausewitzstudies.org.
3. This definition of politics flows from Harold Lasswell, *Who Gets What, When, How* (Gloucester, MA: Peter Smith Publications, 1990).
4. Hilary Ball, "Security vs. Glory or Security via Glory: Republican Discord and Harmony in Machiavelli's *Discourses on Livy*" (2013),

https://digitalshowcase.lynchburg.edu/agora/vol22/iss2013/9/, accessed September 19, 2022. See also Mauricio Suchowlansky, "Machiavelli's Republicanisms: Society, Discord and the Politics of Equilibrium in the *Florentine Histories* (PhD diss., University of Toronto, 2015).

5. See Stephen Shambuck, ed., *Strategic Leadership Primer*, 3rd ed. (Carlisle, PA: United States Army War College, 2004).
6. Curt B. Southwick, "The Marine Corps Art of War Studies," *Marine Corps Gazette* 75, no. 1 (1991): 47.
7. For a presentation of the core curriculum of the Naval War College, see https://usnwc.edu/college-of-naval-command-and-staff/Core-Curriculum/Strategy-and-Warfare.
8. Francis J. H. Park, "The Strategic Plans and Policy Officer in the Modular Division," *Military Review* 87, no. 6 (2007), https://www.questia.com/library/journal/1G1-172010718/the-strategic-plans-and-policy-officer-in-the-modular.
9. Marine Corps War College, *Command Brief*, July 18, 2012, http://slideplayer.com/slide/5827688/.
10. Herbert F. Barber, "Developing Strategic Leadership: The US Army War College Experience," *Journal of Management Development* 11, no. 6 (1992): 4–12.
11. Steven J. Gerras, ed., *Strategic Leadership: The Competitive Edge*, 3rd ed. (Carlisle Barracks, PA: United States Army War College, 2010), 11–13.
12. The concept of VUCA has readily been adopted by the literature on business management. See Nathan Bennett and G. James Lemoine, "What VUCA Really Means for You," *Harvard Business Review* (January–February 2014).
13. The Wikipedia entry for VUCA presents an extensive definition of each of these components, https://en.wikipedia.org/wiki/Volatility,_uncertainty,_complexity_and_ambiguity, accessed February 13, 2019, and it provides a heavy overload of sociological theory to the concepts.
14. The concept of a fifth generation of warfare posits that human conflict has evolved from cold steal weaponry, through employment of firearms, to mechanized engagements, to conflict employing nuclear weapons, and finally to information-based cyberwarfare. See Terry Daniel Abbott, *Handbook of Fifth-Generation Warfare* (Ann Arbor, MI: Nimble Books, 2010), 15. See also the Wikipedia entry, https://en.wikipedia.org/wiki/Generations_of_warfare#:~:text=Fifth%20generation,-Main%20article%3A%20Fifth&text=Fifth%2Dgeneration%20warfare%20(5GW),intelligence%20and%20fully%20autonomous%20systems, accessed January 6, 2022.

15. Bennett and Lemoine, "What VUCA Really Means for You."
16. See Paul Kingsinger and Karen Walch, "Living and Leading in a VUCA World," Thunderbird School, Arizona State University, July 9, 2012.
17. My teaching colleague William I. Greener, an experienced and successful Republican political consultant, would assure our students that, in normal campaign circumstances, tactical considerations would drive out attention to long-term goals by a factor of four to one and in a crisis by ten to one.
18. Edward M. Collins, trans. and ed., *Karl von Clausewitz: War, Politics and Power* (Chicago: Henry Regnery, 1962), 40.
19. Robert Greene brings together numerous examples from military conflicts reaching back through recorded history to suggest how his readers should conduct their lives. See *The 33 Strategies of War* (New York: Penguin Group, 2006). Greene's synthesis should be classified as "stratagems" rather than as strategies, for they present the reader with practical advice on the level of tactical moves to outdo an opponent. Lawrence Freedman also presents numerous examples throughout the 751 pages of his opus magnus, *Strategy: A History* (London: Oxford University Press, 2013).
20. Sun Tzu, *The Art of War* Ralph D. Sawyer, editor and translator (Boulder, CO: Westview Press, 1994), 231–33.
21. Direct campaign spying does occur every once in a while. See "Campaign Workers Pose as Volunteers for Opponents in Maryland Congressional Race," *NBC Washington*, February 2, 2016, https://www.nbcwashington.com/news/local/campaign-workers-pose-as-volunteers-for-opponents-in-maryland-congressional-race/2074261/, accessed November 30, 2021.
22. See Chapter 7 for a more expansive discussion of the importance and means of predicting the opponent's move.
23. See, for example, one of the numerous psychological profiles of Iraq's Sadam Husain during the 2003 Gulf War. One such was "Saddam Is Iraq; Iraq Is Saddam" by Jerald Post and Amatzia Baram for the United States Air Force Counterproliferation Center (Maxwell Air Force Base, Al, Air University, November 2002), https://apps.dtic.mil/sti/pdfs/ADA424787.pdf, accessed November 18, 2021.
24. B. H. Liddell Hart, *Strategy*, 2d ed. (London: Faber and Faber, 1967).
25. Hart, *Strategy*, 5.
26. Sun Tzu, *The Art of War* (Minneapolis, MN: Filiquarian Publishing, 2006), 7.
27. Hart, *Strategy*, 4. The thought behind Napoleon's remark can be traced back to Xenophon: "Battles are decided more by morale of the troops than by their bodily strength." https://quotes.thefamouspeople.com/xenophon-4212.php, accessed January 18, 2022

28. Jerry Grey, "Rollins Says He Fabricated Payoff Tale to Irk Foes," *New York Times*, November 20, 1993, sec. 1, p. 1, https://www.nytimes.com/1993/11/20/nyregion/rollins-says-he-fabricated-payoff-tale-to-irk-foes.html, accessed November 13, 2021.
29. On Pinkerton's reveal, see https://millercenter.org/the-presidency/presidential-oral-histories/james-p-pinkerton-oral-history. For the "real operation," turn to https://www.nytimes.com/1988/07/28/us/bush-is-lining-up-prospects-for-no-2-spot-on-the-ticket.html, both accessed November 11, 2021.
30. Hart, *Strategy*, 334.
31. Edward N. Luttwak, *Strategy: The Logic of War and Peace* (Cambridge, MA: Belknap Press, 2001), 334.
32. Lyndon Johnson proved to be a master at gaining power over his colleagues, often by his determined manipulation and force of personality in dealings behind the scenes in one-on-one exchanges. See the many instances of this behavior presented throughout by Robert A. Caro, *Master of the Senate: The Years of Lyndon Johnson* (New York: Random House, 2002).
33. Hart, *Strategy*, 334–37.
34. Adam Nagourney, "Hillary Clinton Goes to the Senate; Big Victory for First Lady in Contest with Lazio," *The New York Times*, November 8, 2000, A1, https://www.nytimes.com/2000/11/08/nyregion/hillary-clinton-goes-to-senate-big-victory-for-first-lady-in.html, accessed November 18, 2021.
35. John R. Boyd, *The Essence of Winning and Losing*, document dated June 28, 1995.
36. The Army War College's concept of VUCA (discussed above) serves to deconstruct Clausewitz's fog into four distinct elements, each of which requires political managers to devise a separate approach to mitigate.

Chapter 4

1. B. H. Liddell Hart, *Strategy* (New York: Meridian, Henry Holt & Co., 1991), 319.
2. See Fred Nickols, "Strategy: Definitions and Meaning" for a compilation of many ways in which business authors have defined strategic planning. Written in 2012 and found at http://www.nickols.us/strategy_definition.htm.
3. Lawrence Freedman, *Strategy: A History* (London: Oxford University Press, 2013), 496.

4. Ibid., drawn from Anthony Trythell, *"Boney" Fuller: The Intellectual General* (London: Cassell, 1977).
5. William I. Greener, personal interview, October 2012.
6. Karl von Clausewitz, *War, Politics and Power: Selections from On War, I Believe and Profess*, ed. Edward M. Collins (Chicago: Henry Regnery Co., Gateway, 1962), 70.
7. Sidney Blumenthal, *The Permanent Campaign* (Boston: Beacon, 1980); Norman J. Orenstein and Thomas H. Mann, eds., *The Permanent Campaign and Its Future* (Washington, DC: American Enterprise Institute and The Brookings Institute, 2000); Greg Elmer, Ganaele Langlois, and Fenwick McKelvey, *The Permanent Campaign: New Media, New Politics* (New York: Peter Lang Media, 2012).
8. See, for example, "2020 Post Election Analysis" compiled by three political action committees and published by the *New York Times* in May 2021. https://int.nyt.com/data/documenttools/2020-postelection-analysis/871b6e27d1b7c544/full.pdf, accessed November 28, 2021.
9. One can find several similar variations of this famous quote by Helmuth von Molke, *On Strategy* (Militarische Werke, 1871). https://bootcampmilitaryfitnessinstitute.com/military-and-outdoor-fitness-articles/no-plan-survives-contact-with-the-enemy/, accessed April 12, 2018.
10. President Dwight David Eisenhower, "Remarks at the National Defense Executive Reserve Conference, November 14, 1957." http://www.presidency.ucsb.edu/ws/?pid=10951, accessed April 12, 2018.
11. Julia Galef, *The Scout Mindset: Why Some People See Things Clearly and Others Don't* (New York: Portfolio/Penguin, 2021), 7.
12. Robert Gates is quoted by David E. Sanger in *The Perfect Weapon: War, Sabotage and Fear in the Cyber Age* (New York: Broadway Books, 2019), 54.
13. Those who know Clausewitz's work will certainly recognize the intellectual debt from his description of the "fog of war."
14. David Plouffe, *The Audacity to Win: The Inside Story and Lessons from Barack Obama's Historic Victory* (New York: Viking, 2009).
15. The origins of the SWOT analysis are not entirely clear, but most commentary refers to Albert S. Humphrey, "SWOT Analysis for Management Consulting," Stanford Research Institute, *December 2005 Newsletter* (Menlo Park, CA: SRI, 2005), 7–8, https://web.archive.org/web/20130104102543/http://www.sri.com/sites/default/files/brochures/dec-05.pdf, accessed November 30, 2021.
16. The analysis of scenarios could lead us into a discussion of game theory and its outgrowth, drama theory. See Jim Bryant, *Acting Strategically Using Drama Theory* (Boca Raton, FL: CRC Press, Taylor and Francis Group, 2016).

17. For an excellent and comprehensive examination of political consulting including opposition research, see Dennis W. Johnson, *Democracy For Hire: A History of American Political Consulting* (New York: Oxford University Press, 2017), esp. 143–45.
18. A plethora of research studies documents the importance of economic factors in predicting vote choice. For a summary, see Ray C. Fair, "Econometrics and Presidential Elections," *Journal of Economic Perspectives* 10, no. 3 (1996): 89–192.
19. According to the entry in Wikipedia, https://en.wikipedia.org/wiki/The re_are_known_knowns, Donald Rumsfeld's press conference statement on February 12, 2002, adapted a commonly accepted analytical technique among national security professionals known as the "Johari Window."
20. A description of the Jesse Unruh career can be found at https://www.csmonitor.com/1987/0813/dcurt13.html, accessed on December 2, 2021.
21. Bill Bishop, *The Big Sort: Why the Clustering of Like-Minded America Is Tearing Us Apart* (New York: Mariner Books, 2009).
22. Chapter 9 deals with the intersection of strategy and the ethics of leadership. Here we wish to point out that it is not ethical to endeavor to win by suppressing turnout among your opponent's voters.
23. The fact that election campaigns have an end date serves to differentiate them from, for example, ongoing public relations campaigns. Nonetheless, the latter can draw numerous lessons from the focused planning necessary in election politics.

Chapter 5

1. Robert A. Caro, *Master of the Senate: The Years of Lyndon Johnson* (New York: Alfred A. Knopf, 2002), 315.
2. For more than 15 years, I taught a GSPM seminar on political communications with William I. Greener, Jr., a successful and highly regarded Republican political consultant. Many of the ideas presented in this chapter were developed and explored during those semesters. I fully acknowledge that my colleague Greener initiated our collective thinking as to the elements of an effective message and the evolution of the model of political communications.
3. As we shall see in Chapter 9, autocratic leaders can at times keep their policies and rules cloaked so as to keep their "followers" guessing and insecure. Unpredictable behavior backed up by coercive sanctions can create fear and hyper-vigilant compliance.

4. Change in communications media is an ongoing process to which political managers must adapt. There exist multiple surveys of these changes as new technologies create new channels for reaching citizens and voters. See, for example, "Earned Media Rising," *2018 Global Comms Report: Challenges and Trends* (New York: Cision/PRWeek, 2018), also found at https://www.cision.com/resources/white-papers/2018-global-comms-report/?sf=false.
5. Greener, personal communication.
6. In the chapter on strategic planning, we emphasized the importance of thoroughly debriefing the candidate and conducting a complete "oppo" research profile of your own candidate, just so that you will not be blindsided by attacks of this nature.
7. See news reporting by POLITICO at https://www.politico.com/story/2011/02/abortion-sting-hits-planned-parenthood-048632 and coverage from multiple sources on Wikipedia, https://en.wikipedia.org/wiki/Project_Veritas#Planned_Parenthood_recordings_(2008).
8. See Sasha Issenberg, *The Victory Lab: The Science of Winning Campaigns* (New York: Broadway Books, 2013); Mark Penn and E. Kinney Zalesne, *Microtrends: The Small Forces Behind Tomorrow's Big Changes* (New York: Twelve, Hachette Publications, 2009); and Richard J. Semiatin, *Campaigns on the Cutting Edge*, 2nd ed. (Los Angeles: SAGE Publications, 2008).
9. It should be emphasized here that the author is not aware of any careful, validated studies of the success achieved by campaigns that endeavored to simultaneously communicate numerous messages.
10. Karl Rove, *Courage and Consequence: My Life as a Conservative in the Fight* (New York: Simon and Schuster, Inc., Threshold Editions, 2010), 78.
11. Abraham Harold Maslow, "A Theory of Human Motivation," *Psychological Review* 50, no. 4 (1943): 370–96.
12. Julia Galef, *The Scout Mindset: Why Some People See Things Clearly and Others Don't* (New York: Portfolio/Penguin, 2021).
13. Dr. Frank Luntz, *Words That Work: It's Not What You Say, It's What People Hear* (New York: Hyperion, 2007), 164–66.
14. I am indebted to the presentations of David Payne of Vox Media and a former student and present teaching colleague in developing the acronym PESO to differentiate the evolving structures of media available today to political managers.
15. William A. Dill, "Growth of Newspapers in the United States" (University of Kansas, 1928), found at https://kuscholarworks.ku.edu/bitstream/

handle/1808/21361/dill_1928_3425151.pdf?sequence=1, accessed July 10, 2018.
16. F. Christopher Arterton, *Media Politics: The News Strategies of Presidential Campaigns* (Lexington, MA: Lexington Books, 1984), chs. 2 and 4.
17. Jeffrey B. Abramson, F. Christopher Arterton, and Gary R. Orren, *The Electronic Commonwealth: The Impact of New Media Technologies on Democratic Politics* (New York: Basic Books, 1987).
18. See S. Iyengar and A. Simon, "New Perspectives and Evidence on Political Communication and Campaign Effects," https://stanford.edu/~siyengar/research/papers/effectsreview.html, accessed March 19, 2019.
19. Arterton, *Media Politics*.
20. Given the proprietary nature of this data and its relationship to company valuations, it should be no surprise that a clearly accepted list is impossible to locate. These data came from http://www.statista.com/statistics/265773/market-share-of-the-most-popular-social-media-websites-in-the-us/, accessed October 15, 2014. A different US list can be found at http://www.ebizmba.com/articles/social-networking-websites. China data can be found at https://www.techinasia.com/2013-china-top-10-social-sites-infographic/.
21. I am indebted to several personal conversations and class presentations with William I. Greener, Jr., for the conception and elaboration of this model.
22. Peter W. Singer, a senior fellow in the New America think tank, quoted by Stuart A. Thompson and Davey Alba, "Heroic Tales Spread Fast, and the Facts Trail Behind," *New York Times*, March 4, 2022, B4.
23. See Kevin Granville, "Facebook and Cambridge Analytica: What You Need to Know as Fallout Widens," *New York Times*, March 19, 2018, https://www.nytimes.com/2018/03/19/technology/facebook-cambridge-analytica-explained.html, accessed July 10, 2018.

Chapter 6

1. Tiha von Ghyczy, Bolko von Oetinger, and Christopher Bassford, *Clausewitz on Strategy: Inspiration and Insights from a Master Strategist* (New York: John Wiley and Sons, 2001), 23.
2. I am grateful to Ms. Alexandra P. Dauler, an excellent editor, for suggesting this strategy for avoiding a sidewalk collision.

3. Numerous translations of Sun Tzu's classic *The Art of War* are available. I have found very useful the work of Thomas Cleary, which contains commentary by many disciples of Sun Tzu (Boston: Shambhala Books, 1988).
   "Prospect Theory: An Analysis of Decision under Risk Daniel Kahneman," *Amos Tversky Econometrica* 47, no. 2 (1979): 263–92.
4. Two years into his presidency, Donald J. Trump appears to defy this general rule. He remains completely unpredictable to allies and opponents alike; he frequently changes his position and contradicts himself; and he makes up facts as suits his thinking of the moment. As we shall argue in Chapter 9, on the surface of this behavior he emphasizes strategy over leadership, manipulation over integrity. On the deeper level of policies actually advanced as opposed to the constant rhetoric and comments on his Twitter account, he has been remarkably consistent with the slogan of his presidential campaign, Make America Great Again, which is probably why his support base has remained fairly constant.
5. Given the behavior by President Trump cited in footnote 3 above, it is also remarkable that he has not been branded by a similar label akin to those applied to Nixon and Clinton. In fact, his behavior is so egregious that, unlike his predecessors for whom there was only grain of truth, Trump's strategic machinations so define his character that a label is not needed; it's clearly part of who he is.
6. Sheera Frenkel, Nicholas Confessore, Cecilia Kang, Matthew Rosenberg, and Jack Nicas, "Delay, Deny and Deflect: How Facebook's Leaders Fought Through Crisis," *New York Times*, November 14, 2018; https://www.nytimes.com/2018/11/14/technology/facebook-data-russia-election-racism.html, accessed November 30, 2021.
7. Among the numerous books discussing game theory and its application to public life, the following seem most useful: Bruce Bueno de Mesquita, *The Practitioner's Game: Using the Logic of Brazen Self-Interest to See and Shape the Future* (New York: Random House, 2010); Avinash K. Dixit and Barry J. Nalebuff, *The Art of Strategy: A Game Theorist's Guide to Success in Business and Life* (New York: W. W. Norton, 2010).
8. Aaron Blake, "Trump's Loose Talk on Nuclear Weapons Suddenly Becomes Very Real," *Washington Post*, November 10, 2017; https://www.washingtonpost.com/news/the-fix/wp/2017/10/11/trumps-loose-rhetoric-on-nuclear-weapons-has-become-a-very-real-concern/, accessed September 20, 2022.
9. See Chapter 9 for a contrast between the concepts of strategy versus leadership.

NOTES 231

10. Dixit and Nalebuff also wrote an earlier edition of this discussion of game theory applied mostly to business under the title *Thinking Strategically* (New York: W. W. Norton, 1991).
11. Dixit and Nalebuff, *Art of Strategy*, 60.
12. See Brittany N. Thompson, "Theory of Mind: Understanding Others in a Social World," *Psychology Today*, July 3, 2017; https://www.psychologytoday.com/us/blog/socioemotional-success/201707/theory-mind-understanding-others-in-social-world, accessed July 17, 2018. See also Simon Baron-Cohen, "Precursors to a Theory of Mind: Understanding Attention in Others," in *Natural Theories of Mind: Evolution, Development, and Simulation of Everyday Mindreading*, ed. Andrew Whiten (Oxford, UK, and Cambridge, MA: Blackwell, 1991), 233–51.
13. Wikipedia's entry for Theory of Mind at https://en.wikipedia.org/wiki/Theory_of_mind.
14. At the time of writing, there was some evidence emerging from social psychological studies that people are actually closer to the mark when predicting the possible behavior of others than they are at predicting their own behavior. See Emily Balcetis and David Dunning, "Considering the Situation: Why People Are Better Social Psychologists Than Self-Psychologists," *Self and Identity* 12, no. 1 (2013): 1–15.
15. See the Wikipedia entry for Pattern of Life Analysis at https://en.wikipedia.org/wiki/Pattern-of-life_analysis, accessed January 29, 2022. See also Patrick Biltgen, PhD; Todd S. Bacastow, PhD; Thom Kaye; and Jeffrey M. Young, "Activity-Based Intelligence: Understanding Patterns-of-Life" (United States Geospatial Intelligence Foundation *State & Future of GEOINT Report, 2017*), retrieved from https://medium.com/the-state-and-future-of-geoint-2017-report/activity-based-intelligence-understanding-patterns-of-life-481c78b7d5ae, accessed January 29, 2022.
16. The Clinton example follows closely the analysis of his political advisor Dick Morris. See *Power Plays: Win or Lose—How History's Great Leaders Play the Game* (New York: Harper Collins, 2002), 90–91, 111–19.
17. Ibid., 111–13.
18. Marjorie Randon Hershey, *The Making of Campaign Strategy* (Lexington, MA: Lexington Books, 1974).
19. James David Barber, *Presidential Character: Predicting Performance in the White House*, 2nd ed. (New York: Prentice Hall, 1977).
20. https://en.wikipedia.org/wiki/Al_Gore#House_and_Senate and https://en.wikipedia.org/wiki/Al_Gore#Second_presidential_run_(2000).
21. See Donald J. Trump and Tony Schwartz, *The Art of the Deal* (New York: Balentine Books, 2009).

22. Douglas Bailey, personal conversation, circa 2000. For five years, Bailey and I taught a class on political communications at the Graduate School of Political Management. For a profile of Doug Bailey, see Dennis W. Johnson, *Democracy for Hire: A History of American Political Consulting* (New York: Oxford University Press, 2017), 96–98.
23. Bradley Tusk, *The Fixer: My Adventures Saving Startups from Death by Politics* (New York: Portfolio|Penguin, 2018), 118–129.
24. Ibid., 121.
25. Ibid., 122.
26. Edward N. Luttwak, *Strategy: The Logic of War and Peace*, rev. and enlarged ed. (Cambridge, MA: Belknap Press, 2002).
27. Dixit and Nalebuff, *Art of Strategy*, ch. 7.

Chapter 7

1. Robert Greene has produced two volumes that, on the surface, purport to define a set of laws that determine the pursuit of power: *The 48 Laws of Power* (New York: Viking Books, 1998) and *The 23 Strategies of War* (New York: Penguin Books, 2006). Reading through these "laws," however, one discovers that they are riddled with internal contradictions that complicate their applicability to any particular situation.
2. The dictum that there are no firm rules that govern the formulation of political strategy is analogous to Clausewitz's exhortations to the Prussian generals that they should not follow formulaic prescriptions for the employment of armed forces. Rules dictate predictability.
3. On the nature of "grit" as a necessary characteristic for success, see Angela Duckworth, *Grit: The Power of Passion and Perseverance* (New York: Simon and Schuster, 2016).
4. See the documentary film "The War Room," directed by D. A. Pennnebaker and Chris Hegedus (1994) and Dennis W. Johnson, *Democracy for Hire: A History of American Political Consulting* (New York: Oxford University Press, 2017), 315.
5. Mead's quote has circulated widely but was first attributed to her in Frank G. Sommers and Tana Dineen, *Curing Nuclear Madness* (London: Methuen, 1984), 158.
6. The phrase is often attributed to Sam Rayburn, the longest serving Speaker of the US House of Representatives, but I have been unable to find definitive documentation.

7. Jake Sherman and Anna Palmer, "Trump Got Nothing," *POLITICO Playbook*, December 28, 2020, https://www.politico.com/newsletters/playbook/2020/12/28/trump-got-nothing-491250, accessed December 28, 2020 Emily Cochrane, Nelson D. Schwartz, and Gillian Friedman, "Trump Signs Pandemic Relief Bill After Unemployment Aid Lapses," *New York Times*, December 28, 2020, A1.
8. One of these instances was told to me by Douglas Bailey, one of the most senior and successful political consultants in the early years of the development of that profession.
9. Lawrence Freedman, *Strategy: A History* (New York: Oxford University Press, 2013).
10. See Karl Marx and Friedrich Engels, *The Communist Manifesto* (Seattle, WA: CreateSpace Independent Publishing Platform, 2018) and Karl Marx, *Das Kapital* (Seattle, WA: CreateSpace Independent Publishing Platform, 2011).
11. Silvio Pons, *The Cambridge History of Communism*, Vol. 1 (Cambridge: Cambridge University Press, 2017).
12. Freedman, *Strategy*, 581–84.
13. For one example of reputational campaigns, pro and con, see the article on Facebook's efforts to tarnish TikTok's reputation in https://www.washingtonpost.com/technology/2022/03/30/facebook-tiktok-targeted-victory/, accessed September 22, 2022.
14. For similar ideas about power, hard, and soft, see Joseph S. Nye, Jr., *Soft Power: The Means to Success in World Politics* (New York: Public Affairs, 2004), 1–11.

Chapter 8

1. James Freund, *Smart Negotiating: How to Make Good Deals in the Real World* (New York: Simon and Schuster, 1993).
2. A popular book on negotiations suggests this approach in the title, although the text suggests more of a compromising approach. See Herb Cohen, *You Can Negotiate Anything: The World's Best Negotiator Tells You How to Get What You Want* (New York: Bantam Books, 1982).
3. One reason why a negotiator may lose sight of his/her MAD during the course of negotiations is due to increasing "opportunity costs." The here-and-now deal may grow in attractiveness as the buyer contemplates locating another suitable car, and the seller wonders if another buyer will surface.

4. See Roy J. Lewicki, John Minton, and David Saunders, *Negotiation*, 3rd ed. (Burr Ridge, IL: Irwin-McGraw Hill, 1999), 51.
5. See Roger Fisher, William Ury, and Bruce Patton, *Getting to Yes: Negotiating Agreement without Giving In*, 2nd ed. (New York: Penguin Books, 1991), 97–106; and Roger Fisher and Danny Ertel, *Getting Ready to Negotiate: The Getting to Yes Workbook* (New York: Penguin Books, 1995), ch. 5, pp. 45–60.
6. Matt Reese, one of the founders of the political management profession, told me that when he made a pitch to consult for a campaign, he would name a high salary figure as his "usual fee" and carefully study the candidate's reaction. If, on the one hand, he saw surprise and displeasure, he would quickly add, "But, because I'm committed to your cause, I could do this for a lower price." If, on the other hand, he observed no adverse reaction, he would continue, ". . . plus the normal telephone and travel expenses, and . . ." For a profile of Matthew Reese, see Dennis W. Johnson, *Democracy for Hire* (New York: Oxford University Press, 2017), 103–4.
7. Lawrence Freedman, *Strategy: A History* (New York: Oxford University Press, 2013), 581–84.
8. For a discussion of "principled negotiations," see Fisher, Ury, and Patton, *Getting to Yes*, ch. 2.
9. In democratic politics, there are formal constituencies defined as the set of all citizens who reside within defined geographical boundaries. But there are also informal definitions that may be employed by individual elected officials to describe the group to which they feel primarily responsible, whether that is the set of all voters or only those that actually voted for him or her. Moreover, public officials may adopt a broader definition that transcends the geography of a formal constituency and includes loyalists based on personal charisma or supporters of particular policy positions.
10. David R. Mayhew argues that re-election is the prime incentive for public officeholders. See his book, *Congress: The Electoral Connection* (New Haven, CT: Yale University Press), 1975
11. The author served as a delegate from Massachusetts to the 1972 Democratic National Committee and was elected by the Massachusetts delegation to the platform committee and ultimately to the drafting subcommittee. The comments that follow reflect his personal observations during negotiations over the party's national platform.
12. The discussion of leverage follows closely the thinking of James C. Freund who has written a superb book on the process and strategy of negotiations. See *Smart Negotiating*, 42–54.
13. Freund, *Smart Negotiating*, 42–45.

14. Adam M. Brandenburger and Barry J. Nalebuff, *Co-opetition* (New York: Doubleday, 1996), ch. 4.
15. Freund, *Smart Negotiating*, 43.
16. Walter Mondale and David Hage, *The Good Fight: A Life in Liberal Politics* (New York: Scribner, 2010).
17. Fisher, Ury, and Patton, *Getting to Yes* (1991), 17–39.

Chapter 9

1. The students' comments and papers that have informed my understanding of leadership include those of Edward Gilman, Emily MacGillivray, Julie Barko, Jeffrey Klinger, Hannah Lambiotte, and Kyle Reliford.
2. I could have used the term "comrade," but it is too closely associated with 20th-century communism. Nevertheless, the essence of leadership is, in fact, an effort to create a communal bond of reciprocal support and loyalty. In Chapter 5, we noted how the evolution of communications media is pushing leaders toward creating communities with enhanced reciprocal influence directed by followers or supporters toward influencing the behavior of their leaders. In this context, "constituent" seems too hierarchical and "comrade" too companionable.
3. Responding to a reporter's question, President George H. W. Bush referred to "the vision thing," a remark that dogged him throughout his presidency. See Damon Wilson, "President George H.W. Bush Had the Vison Thing in Spades" (Washington, DC: The Atlantic Council, December 3, 2018), https://www.atlanticcouncil.org/blogs/new-atlanticist/president-george-h-w-bush-had-the-vision-thing-in-spades/.
4. Over the years 1995–2013, Carol C. Darr served as a regular lecturer on Machiavelli to my class on strategy in politics during which she presented her analysis that Machiavelli recommended three techniques for dealing with others: force, trickery, and agreement.
5. John W. Gardner, *On Leadership* (New York: The Free Press, 1990), 4.
6. On a hierarchy of human needs and wants, see Abraham Harold Maslow, "A Theory of Human Motivation," *Psychological Review* 50, no. 4 (1943): 370–96.
7. James MacGregor Burns, *Leadership* (New York: Harper Torchbooks, 1978), 43.
8. Burns, *Leadership*, 43. See also, Ronald A. Heifetz, Leadership Without Easy Answers (Cambridge MA: Belknap Press of Harvard University, 1994).

9. William A. Cohen, *The New Art of the Leader* (Paramus, NJ: Prentice Hall, 2000).
10. Xenophon quote found at https://www.goldstandardmanagement.org/SupportResources/Articles/LeadQuotes.html , ccessed January 11, 2022. A different phrasing of the quote reads "Obedience should not be the result of compulsion."
11. Headquarters, Department of the Army, *Army Leadership: Be, Know, Do* (Army Field Manual 22-100, Paragraph 1-7, August 1999), 18; https://www.armyheritage.org/wp-content/uploads/2020/08/FM-22-100-Aug99.pdf, accessed January 1, 2022
12. Robert E. Kelley, *The Power of Followership* (New York: Doubleday, 1992).
13. Robert A. Dahl, *A Preface to Democratic Theory* (Chicago: University of Chicago Press, 2006); and *How Democratic Is the American Constitution?* (New Haven, CT: Yale University Press, 2003).
14. For a discussion of the evolution of the US Senate as an example of how political institutions adapt over time, see Robert A. Caro, *Master of the Senate: The Years of Lyndon Johnson* (New York: Vintage Books, 2002), 3–105.
15. Elaine C. Kamarck has provided a detailed history of how the Democratic Party employed a series of commissions to craft their rules governing delegate selection and convention business. See *Primary Politics: How Presidential Candidates Have Shaped the Modern Nominating System* (Washington, DC: Brookings Institution, 2009).
16. There are, of course, many values that democratic systems endeavor to achieve for the societies that are lucky enough to enjoy them and much discussion of those in the democracy literature, but the following seem fundamental to me. I advance them here with the acknowledgment that these all involve tough questions of line drawing where there are important values to be achieved on either side, values that are to some extent competing, and therefore require normative choice as to where the appropriate boundaries fall.
17. At the time of writing, US President Donald J. Trump is engaged repeatedly in rhetoric that is demonstrably false and deliberately misleading. The American public will not deliver a verdict on this behavior until the campaign of 2020.
18. The list that follows is my own creation, but there are numerous value statements of what constitutes free and fair elections, in many cases drafted by branches of the US government dedicated to advancing democracy worldwide. For its bold and simple advocacy, I recommend the "Explainer: Free and Fair Elections," produced by Facing History and

Ourselves (Brookline, MA, 2019), https://www.facinghistory.org/sites/default/files/Explainer_Free_and_Fair_Elections.pdf, accessed January 27, 2020.

19. For a detailed discussion of the importance of pluralism in democratic systems, see Robert A. Dahl, *Democracy and Its Critics* (New Haven, CT: Yale University Press, 1989); and Robert A. Dahl and Ian Shapiro, *On Democracy* (New Haven, CT: Yale University Press, 2015).

20. See Bruce Bueno de Mesquita and Alastair Smith, *The Dictator's Handbook: Why Bad Behavior Is Almost Always Good Politics* (New York: Public Affairs, 2011).

21. For a description of the evolution of governmental institutions during 500 years of the Roman Republic, see https://en.wikipedia.org/wiki/Centuriate_Assembly.

22. Jeremie Gilbert, "Constitutionalism, Ethnicity and Minority Rights in Africa: A Legal Appraisal from the Great Lakes Region," *International Journal of Constitutional Law* 11, no. 2 (2013): 414–47, found at http://icon.oxfordjournals.org/content/11/2/414.full#content-block.

23. David Brooks, "The Century of the Strongman Begins," *The New York Times*, February 18, 2022, A23).

24. Frederick Douglass speech upon the unveiling of the Emancipation Monument in Lincoln Park in Washington on April 14, 1876: "Viewed from the genuine abolition ground, Mr. Lincoln seemed tardy, cold, dull, and indifferent; but measuring him by the sentiment of his country, a sentiment he was bound as a statesman to consult, he was swift, zealous, radical, and determined." https://www.goodreads.com/quotes/7585359-abraham-lincoln-was-not-in-the-fullest-sense-of-the, accessed January 11, 2022.

25. Doris Kearns Goodwin, *Team of Rivals: The Political Genius of Abraham Lincoln* (New York: Simon and Schuster, 2005), ch. 25, pp. 667–700.

Index

For the benefit of digital users, indexed terms that span two pages (e.g., 52–53) may, on occasion, appear on only one of those pages.
Note: Tables and figures are indicated by *t* and *f* following the page number

abortion rights, 56, 152
abuse of power, 12–13
action. *See also* strategic interaction management
collective action, 7, 9–10, 173, 197, 208–9
influential action, 8
by political managers, 31, 34, 45–46
predicting opponent' actions, 134–41, 136*t*, 138*t*, 154–56
activists, 3, 4–5, 6–7, 20, 79, 153, 207, 211, 212, 213
advocacy in political leadership, 208–10
aerial combat, 57–58
agreement in engagement, 18–19
Air War College, 43
ambiguity in VUCA, 44
American Revolution, 108
American Society for Control of Cancer (American Cancer Society), 4–5
anarchy, 17–18, 42
Arab-Israel War (1948-49), 51–52
Army War College, 43, 44
The Art of Strategy (Dixit, Nalebuff), 133
The Art of War (Sun Tzu), 51–52, 120–26
assumptions in SOAR, 74–77
Atwater, Lee, 120
Audacity to Win (Plouffe), 68
audience delineation in strategic political communications, 92–98
authoritarian dictatorship, 21
authority, defined, 8, 12–13

backward reasoning, 133–34

Barber, James David, 139
bargaining leverage, 185–89
Bassford, Christopher, 41
BATNA (Best Alternative to a Negotiated Agreement), 179–81, 182, 186
battlefield strategy. *See also* warfare
deception in, 123–25
democratic conflict and, 46, 48–49, 54–55
intelligence in, 126
military leadership, 44–45, 60
negotiations in, 174
outhinking rival in, 121–23
preparedness in, 120–21
Begala, Paul, 147
Bentsen, Lloyd, 47
Berra, Yogi, 73
Biden, Joe, 169
Bishop, Bill, 78
Bonaparte, Napoleon, 52–53, 153–54
Boston Children's Hospital, 4–5
Boyd, John, 57–58
Brooks, David, 214–15
budgets/budgeting in election campaigns, 86–87
Burns, James McGregor, 201–3
Bush, George H. W., 53
Bush, George W., 100–2, 122
business strategy, 36–37

cable television, 108
Cambridge Analytica, 83
Caro, Robert A., 91
Carville, James, 147

Central Intelligence Agency, 134–35
Chabot, Steve, 26
Chandler, Arthur, Jr., 61–62
charisma, 14, 23–24
charter schools, 103–4
chemical weapons, 158
Churchill, Winston, 19, 32
citizenry and political leadership, 206–8
Citizens Committee for the Conquest of Cancer, 4–5
civil politics, 60
civil wars, 11–12
Clausewitz, Karl von
  fog of war, 58–59, 164–65
  friction in warfare, 58–59, 60, 164–65
  military strategy, 32, 41, 42, 58–60, 119
  politics and warfare, 41, 42
  strategic planning, 61, 63
  uncertainty strategy, 146, 156
Clinton, Bill, 125, 137, 139, 147, 169
Clinton, Hillary, 56
closed-door negotiations, 55
CNN, 108
coalition strategy, 163–64
coercive power, 3–4, 15–16, 203
cognitive processes, 15
Cohen, William A., 203–4
Cold War, 56–57, 161–62
collective action, 7, 9–10, 173, 197, 208–9
Collins, Edward M., 47–48
commercial communications, 98–99
communication. *See also* strategic political communications
  commercial communications, 98–99
  dynamics of leverage, 190
  in election campaigns, 80, 88
  in leadership, 198
  in political leadership, 149–50
  strategic communication, 35, 95–96, 119
communism, 164
comparative advantages, 53–54
competition in bargaining leverage, 187
complexity in VUCA, 44
conflict
  democratic conflict and battlefield strategy, 46, 48–49, 54–55
  engagement in by political managers, 48
  military strategy and, 30, 31–33
  peaceful conflict, 32
  political disagreements/disputes, 12–13, 29, 42, 146, 151–52, 153, 166, 207
  pre-conflict situations, 18–19
  psychological dimension of, 52–53
  social conflict, 32, 33, 41
  VUCA curriculum on, 44
  warfare and politics, 31–33, 41–60
congressional power, 10–11
constituencies, 23–24, 184–85, 234n.8
Constitutional Convention, 18
contract law, 11
controllable factors, 148–50
COVID-19 pandemic, 105, 160–61
credibility in power, 9–12
Crick, Bernard, 21
crimes against humanity, 19

Dahl, Robert A., 22, 205
Dalberg-Acton, John Emerich Edward, 25–26
D'Albret, Charles, 122–23
Darr, Carol, 18–19
death tax, 105
de Blasio, Bill, 141–42
deception in warfare, 51–52, 123–25
defiance, 8–9
democratic politics
  constituencies and, 234n.8
  contests for political influence, 23
  introduction to, 5–6
  managing expectation of others, 154–55
  nature of, 21
  pluralism and, 23, 27, 211–13
  political leadership in, 205–15
  power in, 3, 20–25, 27
  reciprocal power and, 16–17
  social conflict and, 33
  warfare and, 31–33, 41–60
desire in bargaining leverage, 186–87
dictatorial governments, 15–16, 211–12
direct communication, 106–7, 109f, 111f
Discourses (Machiavelli), 3–4
Dixit, Avinash, 133–35, 142

domain of civility, 60
domain of violence, 60
dominant strategy, 135
Douglass, Frederick, 216–17
dynamic interaction, 119

earned media, 108–10
effective strategy guidelines
  controllable factors, 148–50
  for engagement, 159–62
  essence of, 170
  introduction to, 145–47
  against loss of power, 168–69
  predicting opponent' actions, 134–41, 136t, 138t, 154–56
  rational decision-making, 157–58
  tactics of, 163–65
  timing factor in, 165–66
  uncontrollable factors, 150–54
  winning from a weak position, 166–68
Eisenhower, Dwight, 65
election campaigns
  budgets/budgeting in, 86–87
  communication in, 80, 88
  constituencies, 23–24, 184–85
  deception in, 124, 125
  fluidity of power within, 147
  free and fair elections, 210–11
  fundraising plans, 85–86
  get-out-the-vote (GOTV) effort, 81, 96
  media in, 88
  messages and themes, 80, 84
  personnel, 79–80
  policy research, 84
  politics of, 47, 53
  rapid response units in, 84
  scheduling consideration, 87–88
  strategic interaction management, 139
  strategic planning in, 63–64, 69–81
  strategic political communications, 96–98
  tactics and strategy, 72–73, 77–79, 81–88, 82t
  votes/voting in, 74, 80
election politics, 6–7, 21
engagement strategy, 23–24, 159–62
estate tax, 105
evil leadership, 201

executive training, 128

fallback plan, 180–81
Farber, Sidney, 4–5
fast track authority, 152–53
Federal Reserve, 77
Fisher, Roger, 195
fog of war, 58–59, 164–65
force in engagement, 18–19
Foreign Intelligence Surveillance Act (FISA), 112–13
formlessness argument, 146
Franklin, Benjamin, 61
free and fair elections, 210–11
Freedman, Lawrence, 163–64, 167–68
freedom of discourse, 213–14
free media, 78
Freund, James, 173–74, 188–89
Frey, Frederick W., 7–8
friction in warfare, 58–59, 60, 164–65
fundraising strategy, 30, 85–86

Galef, Julia, 66, 105
gamesmanship, 122
game theory, 127–29
Gandhi, Mahatma (Mohandas Karamchand Gandhi), 20–21, 203
Gardner, John W., 201, 203
geography in campaigns, 78
gerrymandering, 209–10
get-out-the-vote (GOTV) effort, 81, 96
Getting to Yes (Fisher, Ury), 195
Giuliani, Rudy, 56
Gore, Al, 139
grand strategy, 30
grassroots lobbying, 57
Greener, Bill, 62–63

Haanaes, Knut, 37
Henry V, King, 122–23
Hershey, Marjorie Randon, 139
Hitler, Adolf, 199–201
human interaction, 15, 36
Hussein, Saddam, 122, 158

In Defense of Politics (Crick), 21
indirect approach to success, 51–52
individual power, 6, 7

influential action, 8
information power, 13, 193–95
inheritance tax, 105
institutionalization of political parties, 21
integrity, 11
intelligence gathering, 49–51
intelligence in battlefield strategy, 126
international power, 6
interpersonal relationships, 16
Iraq invasion, 122

Kalanick, Travis, 141–42
Kelly, Robert, 204
Kennedy, John F., 118–19, 161
Kerry, John, 100–3
Khrushchev, Nikita, 118–19, 161–62
Kimmit, Robert, 53
King, Martin Luther, Jr., 20–21, 203

Lasker, Mary Woodward, 4–5
Lasswell, Harold, 32–33
Lazio, Rick, 56
leadership. *See also* political leadership
 communication in, 198
 evil leadership, 201
 military strategy, 44–45, 60
 moral leadership, 201–2
 transactional leadership, 202–3
 transformational leadership, 202–3
Lee, Robert E., 48–49, 216–17
Leesburg Grid, 99–104, 101t, 103t
legislative politics, 6–7, 42, 64–65, 166
Lenin, Vladimir, 164
leverage dynamics, 185–93
Liddell Hart, B. H., 30–31, 51–52, 53–54, 55–56, 57
limitations on political communications, 98–99
Lincoln, Abraham, 216–17
Luntz, Frank, 105
Luttwak, Edward, 54–55, 142

Machiavelli, Niccolo, 3–4, 6, 17–19, 26, 41–42, 199, 203
MAD (minimally acceptable deal), 178–79, 180–82, 186, 233n.3
majoritarian rule, 21

The Making of Campaign Strategy (Hershey), 139
Mandela, Nelson, 199–200
manipulation and power, 124–25, 127, 195, 197–98, 225n.32
Marine Corps War College, 43
Marine War College, 43
market share, 36–37
Maslow's hierarchy of needs, 104–5
mass voting, 21
material resources influence, 13
maxi-min strategy, 138–39
McGovern, George, 185
Mead, Margaret, 4–5, 153
media
 channels in political communications, 106–15, 109f, 111f, 228n.4
 earned media, 108–10
 in election campaigns, 88
 free media, 78
 networked connections in, 113
 paid media, 88, 107–8, 116
 shared information media, 113
 social media, 51, 110–15, 116, 209–10
Medici, Lorenzo de', 6
message delineation in strategic political communications, 98–105
Middle Ages, 16
military intelligence, 48–49
military leadership, 44–45, 60
military strategy
 aerial combat, 57–58
 battlefield strategy, 46, 48–49, 54–55
 Clausewitz on, 41, 42, 58–60, 119
 conflict and, 30, 31–33
 deception in warfare, 51–52
 direct advice in, 55–56
 essence of, 60
 fog of war, 58–59
 friction in warfare, 58–59, 60
 intelligence gathering, 49–51
 spies/spying, 49–50
 strategic planning, 65
 VUCA analysis, 44–46, 59
minority rights protections, 214–15
mission creep, 33–34
Moltke, Helmuth Karl Bernhard Graf von, 65

INDEX 243

Mondale, Walter, 191–92
money influence, 13, 78
moral leadership, 201–2
moral responsibility, 17–19
Morris, Dick, 137
multiparty systems, 64

Nalebuff, Barry, 133–35, 142
National Cancer Act (1971), 4–5
National Cancer Institute, 4–5
National Defense University, 43
nation-states, 11–12
Naval War College, 43
need in bargaining leverage, 186–87
negotiations in public life
   BATNA and, 179–81, 182, 186
   buyer/seller dynamics, 177–82
   constituency impacts, 184–85
   essence of, 196
   information power, 193–95
   introduction to, 173–77
   leverage dynamics, 185–93
   MAD and, 178–79, 180–82, 186, 233n.3
   one off vs. enduring relationships, 182–84
   peace negotiations, 162, 174, 175–76
   ZOPA and, 179, 180–81
networked connections in media, 113
networks of connections, 14
New Deal, 153
Newton, Isaac, 36
New York Times, 4–5, 125, 126
Nickols, Fred, 61–62
Nixon, Richard, 4–5, 56–57, 125, 215
nongovernmental organization (NGO), 7
North Korea, 11–12

Obama, Barack, 11–12, 68, 83, 87, 112–13, 114, 161
objectives in SOAR, 73–74
one off vs. enduring relationships, 182–84, 192–93
OODA (observe, orient, decide, act) loop, 57–58, 159–60
opportunity costs, 233n.3
opposition research, 51, 71–72

outthinking rival in battlefield strategy, 121–23

paid media, 88, 107–8, 116
partisanship, 42
past performance targeting, 81
pattern of life circumstances, 134–35
payoff matrix, 134–40, 138*t*
peaceful conflict, 32
peace negotiations, 162, 174, 175–76
personal freedom, 105
personal wealth tax, 105
PESO (paid, earned, social, and owned), 106–15
Philosophiae Naturalis Principia Mathematica (Newton), 36
Pinkerton, Jim, 53
Planned Parenthood, 95–96
planning in strategy, 33–34
Plouffe, David, 68, 87
pluralism, 23, 27, 211–13
policymaking process, 174–76, 183
political combat, 16–17, 23, 49–50, 52, 66–67, 91–92, 170
political communications. *See* strategic political communications
political disagreements/disputes, 12–13, 29, 42, 146, 151–52, 153, 166, 207
political engagement, 3, 21, 26, 58, 119, 145, 146, 151–52, 165
political influence, 3–4, 23, 211–12
political leadership
   advocacy and responsiveness, 208–10
   assessment of, 199–205
   citizenry and, 206–8
   communication in, 149–50
   in democratic politics, 205–15
   denotation vs. connotation, 200–1
   evil leadership, 201
   free and fair elections, 210–11
   freedom of discourse, 213–14
   introduction to, 197–99
   loss of support, 222n.8
   minority rights protections, 214–15
   pluralism and, 211–13
   strategy vs., 215, 216*t*–17
political managers/management
   access to resources, 13

political managers/management (cont.)
   action by, 31, 34, 45–46
   defined, 219n.2
   in democratic politics, 4, 9, 16–17, 20
   effectiveness of, 26
   engaging in conflict, 48
   fundraising plans in election campaigns, 85–86
   generalized habits of, 145–47
   hazards in combat planning, 66–67
   negotiations in public life, 175–76
   networks of connections, 14
   opposition research by, 51, 71–72
   power of, 14, 22–23, 26
   reputation of reliability, 9–10
   trust in reliability of, 9–10
political power
   constituencies and, 23–24
   effective strategy against loss of, 168–69
   management of, 17–18
   nuances of, 15
   presidential power, 10–11
   sources of, 14
political science, 32–33
political strategy, 29–30, 36, 37–38, 49–50, 145
political support, 14, 24, 28, 45–46, 52, 106–7, 108–11, 112–13, 115–16, 193–94, 199, 202, 216–17
politics. *See also* strategic political communications
   coercive nature of, 3–4
   legislative politics, 6–7, 42, 64–65, 166
   strategic planning in, 62–69
   strategy and, 36
   warfare and, 31–33, 41–60
popular sovereignty, 199
power. *See also* political power
   abuse of, 12–13
   coercive power, 3–4, 15–16, 203
   congressional power, 10–11
   credibility in, 9–12
   defined, 3, 20
   in democratic politics, 3, 20–25, 27
   elements of, 7–8, 7*f*
   establishing credibility, 9–12
   exercising within democratic politics, 20–25
   fluidity within election campaigns, 147
   individual power, 6, 7
   information power, 13, 193–95
   international power, 6
   limiting pursuit of, 25–26
   manipulation and, 124–25, 127, 195, 197–98, 225n.32
   moral responsibility and, 17–19
   negotiations in public life, 193–95
   of political managers, 14, 22–23, 26
   quest for, 3–6
   reciprocal power, 16–17
   sanction power, 8, 9–10, 24, 149–50
   social power, 6
   sources of, 12–14, 12*t*
   stakeholder power, 11
   strategy against loss of, 168–69
   strategy and, 5–6
   subtleties of, 15–17
   ways of, 6–9
The Power of Followership (Kelly), 204
pre-conflict situations, 18–19
predicting opponent' actions, 134–41, 136*t*, 138*t*, 154–56
preparedness in battle strategy, 120–21
Presidential Character (Barber), 139
presidential power, 10–11
The Prince (Machiavelli), 3–4, 6
Prisoner's Dilemma, 129–34, 130*t*
Project Veritas, 95–96
psychological dimension of conflict, 52–53
public policy in political communications, 104–5

rapid response units in campaigns, 84
rational decision-making, 157–58
reciprocal power, 16–17
Reeves, Martin, 37
repetition in political communications, 99
reputation of reliability, 9–10
responsiveness in political leadership, 208–10
Robocalls, 115
Rollins, Ed, 53

INDEX

Roman republic, 41–42
Rove, Karl, 102
Rumsfeld, Donald, 75–76

sanction power, 8, 9–10, 24, 149–50
self-aggrandizement, 15–16
self-confidence, 23–24, 197
shared information media, 113
Sima Qian, 121
simplicity in political communications, 99
Situation, Objectives, Assumptions, and Resources (SOAR), 69–81, 70*t*, 89
  situation in SOAR, 69–73
social conflict, 32, 33, 41
social identity, 32
social media, 51, 110–15, 116, 209–10
social policies, 29–30, 169, 212–13
social power, 6
social values, 14, 104
Soros, George, 125
sovereign entities, 17–18
Soviet Union, 118–19, 140
spies/spying, 49–50
stakeholder power, 11
Stephanopoulos, George, 147
strategic communication, 35, 95–96, 119. *See also* strategic political communications
strategic interaction management
  essence of, 143
  game theory and, 127–29
  introduction to, 117–19
  payoff matrix, 134–40, 138*t*
  predicting others' actions, 134–41, 136*t*, 138*t*
  Prisoner's Dilemma, 129–34, 130*t*
  Sun Tzu on, 120–26, 142
  uncontrolled interaction, 117–18
  unpredictable behavior, 141–42
strategic planning in politics
  elements in, 69–81
  essence of, 89–90
  introduction to, 61–62
  in political settings, 33–34, 62–69
  summary of, 88–89
  tactical elements in election campaigns, 72–73, 77–79, 81–88, 82*t*

strategic political communications
  audience delineation, 92–98
  essence of, 116
  introduction to, 21, 91–92
  Leesburg Grid, 99–104, 101*t*, 103*t*
  limitations on, 98–99
  media channels and, 106–15, 109*f*, 111*f*
  message delineation, 98–105
  policy *vs.* values, 104–5
  simplicity and repetition in, 99
  summary of, 115–16
  targeting of, 96–98
strategic thinking, 29, 38, 42–43, 47, 54–55, 60, 69, 93, 148, 164, 173, 199
strategy. *See also* battlefield strategy; effective strategy guidelines; military strategy; tactics and strategy
  in business, 36–37
  coalition strategy, 163–64
  communication and, 35
  defined, 29–30, 31
  dominant strategy, 135
  engagement strategy, 23–24, 159–62
  fundraising strategy, 30, 85–86
  grand strategy, 30
  human interaction and, 36
  introduction to, 28–31
  maxi-min strategy, 138–39
  military strategy, 30, 31–33
  planning and, 33–34
  political leadership *vs.*, 215, 216*t*–17
  political strategy, 29–30, 36, 37–38, 49–50, 145
  politics and, 36
  power and, 5–6, 168–69
  timing factor in guidelines for, 165–66
  uncertainty strategy, 44, 146
strength assessment, 53–54
strength of conviction, 14
Stuart, Jeb, 48–49
sunk costs in bargaining leverage, 188–89
Sun Tzu, 17–18, 28, 49, 120–26, 142, 146, 148
Swift Boat Veterans for Truth, 102
SWOT analysis, 70–71, 150

tactics and strategy
  distinction between, 30–31

tactics and strategy (*cont.*)
   effective guidelines, 163–65
   election campaigns, 72–73, 77–79, 81–88, 82*t*
   elements of planning in politics, 81–88, 82*t*
   in political communications, 91–92
   in political leadership, 198
   television broadcasting, 108
Temple, Henry John, 168
thinking outside the box, 127, 132–33
three C's (content, channels, and communities) in social media, 111–12, 114–15
time deadlines in bargaining leverage, 187–88
time in campaigns, 79
timing factor in strategy guidelines, 165–66
totalitarian systems, 210
transactional leadership, 202–3
transformational leadership, 202–3
triage system in campaigns, 78–79
trickery in engagement, 18–19
Trump, Donald, 114–15, 125, 132–33, 139, 160–61
trust in reliability, 9–10
Tusk, Bradley, 141–42

Uber, 141–42
uncertainty strategy, 44, 146
uncontrollable factors, 150–54
uncontrolled interaction, 117–18
United Nations, 7
unpredictable behavior, 141–42, 230n.4
Unruh, Jesse, 78
Ury, William, 195
US Air Force, 57–58
US Congress, 4–5
US Constitution, 12–13, 206

Valenti, Jack, 44–45

values in political communications, 104–5
veto threats, 10
Vietnam Veterans Against the War, 102
volatility in VUCA, 44
votes/voting
   direct communication, 106–7, 109*f*, 111*f*
   in election campaigns, 74, 80
   get-out-the-vote (GOTV) effort, 81, 96
   mass voting, 21
   tactical analysis of, 81
VUCA Prime, 45
VUCA (volatility, uncertainty, complexity, and ambiguity) analysis, 44–46, 59

walk-away point, 178
Wallace, George C., 185
warfare. *See also* battlefield strategy
   aerial combat, 57–58
   chemical weapons, 158
   civil wars, 11–12
   deception in, 51–52, 123–25
   friction in, 58–59, 60, 164–65
   military strategy and, 30, 31–33
   politics and, 31–33, 41–60
   weapons of mass destruction, 158
Washington Post, 4–5, 126
weapons of mass destruction, 158
Weber, Max, 14
winner-take-all mentality, 36–37
winning from a weak position, 166–68
World Trade Center, 112–13
World War I, 157

Xenophon, 203–4

zero-sum game, 127
ZOPA (zone of possible agreement), 179, 180–81